Xenophon's Socratic Education

XENOPHON'S SOCRATIC EDUCATION

Reason, Religion,
and the Limits of Politics

Dustin Sebell

PENN

UNIVERSITY OF PENNSYLVANIA PRESS

PHILADELPHIA

Published by
University of Pennsylvania Press
Philadelphia, Pennsylvania 19104-4112
www.upenn.edu/pennpress

Printed in the United States of America on acid-free paper
10 9 8 7 6 5 4 3 2 1

Library of Congress Cataloging-in-Publication Data
Names: Sebell, Dustin, author.
Title: Xenophon's Socratic education : reason, religion, and the limits of politics / Dustin Sebell.
Description: 1st edition. | Philadelphia : University of Pennsylvania Press, [2021] | Includes index.
Identifiers: LCCN 2020022844 | ISBN 9780812252859 (hardcover)
Subjects: LCSH: Xenophon. Memorabilia. | Socrates. | Philosophy, Ancient.
Classification: LCC PA4494.M6 S43 2021 | DDC 183/.2—dc23
LC record available at https://lccn.loc.gov/2020022844

To my parents

CONTENTS

ACKNOWLEDGMENTS

To David Bolotin, who read and made detailed comments on the whole manuscript, I am particularly grateful. But I am also extremely grateful to Christopher Bruell, Eric Buzzetti, David Levy, and the anonymous readers for the University of Pennsylvania Press for their feedback. I am deeply indebted to Damon Linker, my editor, for his guidance and support and to Richard Zinman and Arthur Melzer, my friends and colleagues, for theirs. I want to thank Chuck Ostrom who, as department chair, generously offered me time off to write. And special thanks are due to Bradley Jackson as well. Above all, though, I am grateful to Lauren, my wife, for her help translating French, for all the proofreading that she did, and for the many other ways—too many to count—in which she made this book possible.

Introduction

I

According to the first sentence of the First Amendment to the Constitution, "Congress shall make no law respecting an establishment of religion, or prohibiting the free exercise thereof." But are there not religions that demand, to varying degrees, to be established by law? And what happens, then, when there is a religion whose free exercise is prohibited if it is not established, to one degree or another, by law? There are two, and only two, options: either prohibit the free exercise of the religion (and do not establish it by law) or establish the religion by law (and do not prohibit its free exercise). In such cases, when the supreme law of the land appears to come into contradiction with itself, what are we to do?

If we have to ask, if we have to answer the question only by reasoning from premises shared by all parties to the controversy, we have no choice but to turn to a philosopher for guidance. And no one in living memory is more famous for philosophy than John Rawls. To Rawls, moreover, this very question was a "torturing" one.[1] As he put it, "how is it possible—or is it—for those of faith to endorse a constitutional regime even when their comprehensive doctrines may not prosper under it, and indeed may decline?"[2] And his answer, at least where those who affirm "fundamentalist religious doctrines" are concerned, was clear enough: it is *not* possible. Such people are, he said, "a threat to democratic institutions, since it is impossible for them to abide by a constitutional regime except as a *modus vivendi*."[3] "For them the social world envisaged by political liberalism is a nightmare of social fragmentation and false doctrines, if not positively evil."[4] Still, while Rawls was clear enough about the fact that liberal or constitutional democracies prohibit the free exercise of "fundamentalist religious doctrines," he was loath to let them exclude anyone without reason. There is perhaps no better indication of Rawls's highest aspiration than the fact that he spoke of those who affirm "fundamentalist religious doctrines" as "unreasonable," and indeed, "mad."[5] Rawls believed that "a liberal constitutional democracy is, in fact, superior to other forms of society."[6] And he aspired, at least, to make the case that it is "unreasonable" or "mad" to believe otherwise.[7]

Those who affirm "fundamentalist religious doctrines" are "mad," however, only if they are grievously mistaken about "the highest things," not least, "salvation and eternal life."[8] If they are not at all mistaken about such things, *they* are not "mad," *we* are. And there was, then, "no way [for Rawls] to avoid implying [religious fundamentalism's] lack of truth."[9] The only reasonable thing for him to do, in this situation, was to try to reason with those who affirm "fundamentalist religious doctrines"—that is, to try to teach those who do not feel any "allegiance to a democratic society's political (moral) ideals and values" the truth, as he saw it, that their allegiance should lie with "a democratic society's political (moral) ideals and values."[10] By his own admission, however, "Political liberalism does not engage those who think this way."[11] Without making a serious effort to find an answer to the question on the plane of reason—an answer that would perhaps have given him some assurance that he himself knew, and was not grievously mistaken about, where his own allegiance should lie—he was forced, by that very fact, to find a merely practical solution. "Allegiance to a democratic society's political (moral) ideals and values," while not reasonable or teachable in the precise sense of the term, can no doubt be produced in those of us who grow up in one by a process of habituation, or "cultural conditioning," not a little reminiscent of dog training.[12] And Rawls expected that it would, in fact, be produced in this way. At the same time, looking forward to a time when his foes would "cease to exist," "die out," or else "survive only barely," owing to the coming of the "well-ordered society"[13] or the "kingdom," if we can call it that,[14] Rawls exhorted his friends to take up, in the meantime, "the practical task of containing them—*like war and disease*."[15] To his credit, it is true, Rawls never could bring himself to face the fact that, having bid farewell to reason, he was left seeking to get the better of those who affirm "fundamentalist religious doctrines" on the field of battle—or, at any rate, politically, not philosophically.[16] Nevertheless, although he never could bring himself to acknowledge frankly "the priority," as Richard Rorty put it, of democracy to philosophy, he was not willing or able to lay philosophic foundations for democracy either.[17] And, like it or not, there is no tertium quid. Divine laws, Rawls was forced to admit, "have not been excluded by deductive argument. . . . Instead, they are ruled out by the historical conditions and the public culture of democracy."[18] Thus, without realizing it, Rawls stopped just barely short of the view, best expressed by Alexandre Kojève, according to which, "at the opportune moment, History itself will take care to put an end to the endlessly ongoing 'philosophical discussion' of a problem it has virtually 'resolved.'"[19]

And yet, to counter, in this way, "religious fundamentalism" with irreligious fundamentalism is to teeter on the brink of madness, if not to descend into it. For to Rawls the reply will be made by those who affirm "fundamentalist religious doctrines" that it is he, and not they, who should be treated "like war and disease." Indeed, as Rawls well knew, Thomas Aquinas had made this reply in advance (*Summa Theologica* II-II, q.11a.3). And even, or precisely, if Rawls was right to say that "the premises on which Aquinas relies cannot be established by modes of reasoning commonly recognized," nothing prevents Aquinas from turning the tables on him. After all, "the premises on which [*Rawls*] relies," first and foremost, that the world is eternal, "cannot be established by modes of reasoning commonly recognized" either.[20] But then, Rawls would have to admit, maybe the world was created in time, in which case, surely, "It is better to trust in the Lord than to put confidence in man. It is better to trust in the Lord than to put confidence in princes" (Psalms 118:8–12, see also 146:3–5). And to trust in our "knowledge" without knowing that we are better off doing so—to trust in our "knowledge," that is, without knowing that we are better off *not* trusting in God—is not to trust in our "knowledge" at all. That is, on the contrary, a leap of faith, an act of will. And if, for an act to be permitted, it is enough to will the act, what acts will not be permitted? Rawls was unwittingly carrying on a tradition of reflection, going back a century or more, according to which the political is really only a clash of wills, none of which is more or less reasonable, or "worthy," than any other.[21] As he himself put it, "it is often thought that the task of philosophy is to uncover a form of argument that will always prove convincing against all other arguments. There is, however, no such argument. Peoples may often have final ends that require them to oppose one another without compromise. And if these ends are fundamental enough . . . an impasse may arise between them, and war comes."[22] Peoples are going to keep on opposing one another without compromise—"their differences are profound," after all, "*and no one knows how to reconcile them by reason*"[23]—until such time as war concludes, "someday, somewhere," with the triumph of the will. Whose is anyone's guess, though, and no one's to judge.

According to Jürgen Habermas, Rawls's tougher or even more complacent, "German counterpart,"[24] "two countervailing trends mark the intellectual tenor of the age—the spread of naturalistic worldviews and the growing political influence of religious orthodoxies."[25] Now this did not stop Habermas from saying, in almost the same breath, "the aggressive conflict between anthropocentric and theocentric understandings of self and world is yesterday's battle."[26] And yet, if the spread of naturalistic worldviews and the growing political influence of religious orthodoxies are *the* two countervailing trends marking the intellectual tenor of the age, how can the conflict between anthropocentric and theocentric understandings of self and world be "yesterday's battle"? In all times and places, there is a powerful temptation not to engage those whose understanding of self and world conflicts with our own for the simple reason that to do so is to open ourselves and our world up to attack. And Rawls, for one, owes his fame as a philosopher here and now in no small part to the fact that he gave in to this temptation, even as he aspired to be reasonable.[27] But the other predictable result of not engaging those whose understanding of self and world conflicts with our own, aside from flattering "us," is that we make "them" out to be foes, as Rawls would say, with whom all communication is cut off. Doing so not only brutalizes us, but also pulls the rug out from under us. Reason, unable to defend itself, self-destructs.[28] If, then, we cannot bring ourselves to bid farewell to reason, there is nothing for us to do but look elsewhere for guidance. Rawls can, however, point us in the right direction. And he can do so not only, as we saw, by impressing upon us the importance of engaging those whose understanding of self and world conflicts with our own, but also by giving us a clue as to how to do this without begging the question, on the basis of some common ground.

After Rawls passed away, there was found among his papers a brief account of how he lost his faith as a young man, to which he had given the title, "On My Religion." And while Rawls begins by saying that the account is "not unusual or especially instructive," that is not entirely true. The account is instructive precisely because it is not unusual. Now, by this account, Rawls never understood (although he often wondered) why he lost his faith.[29] But this much, at least, he did understand: "[His] difficulties were always moral ones." During the war, his doubts about divine providence mounted on the battlefield, particularly when "a splendid man," tentmate, and friend of his died in his place by a remarkable coincidence; and they only mounted further when news of the Holocaust reached him. God's will, or general providence, no longer appeared to "accord with the most basic ideas of justice," as he knew them. Over the course of the following months and years, the "ideas of right and justice expressed in Christian doctrine" increasingly appeared to be, to him, "morally wrong."[30] The account points therefore to a connection, which is not unusual, between morality or politics and religion. Does the one somehow depend on the other? Abraham debated with God about the justice of destroying Sodom, as if he knew of God that He would not do anything unjust (Genesis 18:16ff.). Of course, Abraham's faith was no simple matter (Genesis 22:1–10). And perhaps, when all is said and done, there is no discernable connection between morality or politics and religion, much less any dependence of the one upon the other. Still, if we have to answer the question on which our law appears to be divided against itself only by reasoning from premises shared by all parties to the controversy, there is perhaps no better guide than Socrates. For Socrates was the philosopher who *did*, famously, engage those whose understanding of self and world conflicted with his own. And he did so, what is more, by going out into the marketplace and engaging them in conversation, first and foremost, about morality or politics.

II

Now, aside from Aristophanes, the writers on whom we depend for whatever knowledge we have of the thought of Socrates are Xenophon, Plato, and Aristotle. But neither Aristotle nor even Plato is more important for our purposes than Xenophon. According to Aristophanes, Socrates did not believe in the gods in whom the city believed, on one hand, and he made the unjust speech stronger than the just speech, on the other (*Clouds* 94–99, 366–407, 1148–54; Plato, *Apology* 18b4–d2, 19b4–c3, 23d2–7). And Xenophon, no less than Plato (*Phaedo* 96a6–100a8), suggests that Aristophanes was not entirely wrong: Socrates *was* that way, at least in his youth. For there was a time, according to Xenophon's indications, when Socrates was infamous as a "pre-Socratic" natural philosopher, on one hand, and as a rhetorician or sophist, on the other (*Oeconomicus* 11.3). At that time, he did not take seriously the practice of (moral or political) virtue for the simple reason that he—and, it would only be slightly misleading to say, he alone—did not even believe he knew what that was (11.6–7, 6.12–17). But eventually, to paraphrase Cicero,[31] Socrates turned philosophy's attention away somewhat from the whole of nature, toward morality or politics, which is as much as to say, toward moral or political opinions (6.12–17). And he was enabled or compelled to do so, if the defining moment of Xenophon's *Oeconomicus* is any indication, only after coming to understand that, owing to the limits of human knowledge, "the premises on which [the philosopher] relies cannot be established by modes of reasoning commonly recognized" (compare

5.18–20, 6.1, 6.11, and 3.5–6 with 6.12, on one hand, and contrast 1.16ff., on the other). Plato, in the intellectual autobiography of Socrates in the *Phaedo*, and even Aristotle, in *Parts of Animals* A1, *Metaphysics* A4, and M6, confirm as much: the Socratic turn toward moral or political opinion was made possible, if not necessary, by the failure of "pre-Socratic" natural philosophy to establish the premises on which the philosopher relies.[32] Thus, faced with others who laid claim to a wisdom far superior to his own, merely human wisdom, did Socrates go out into the marketplace and engage them in conversation about morality or politics in hopes of learning from them the truth about their purportedly superhuman wisdom?

Plato's *Apology*, in which Socrates gives an account of his "Delphic mission," deals with precisely this. And readers of my first book, *The Socratic Turn*, will be surprised to hear me say here, in the sequel, that Xenophon is more important for our purposes than Plato. But perhaps there is no better place to start looking into the possibility that Socrates was teaching others something about morality or politics—or trying and failing to do so—in hopes of learning something from them about religion, than the fourth and final book of Xenophon's *Memorabilia*. Alfarabi, the Islamic philosopher of the Middle Ages, wrote a book titled *The Philosophy of Plato, Its Parts, the Rank of Order of Its Parts, from Beginning to End*, and Leo Strauss once said, with that in mind, that Book IV of Xenophon's *Memorabilia* presents "the core of Socrates' teaching according to its intrinsic order from its beginning to its end."[33] And so it does. Here we have, in Book IV, the whole course of a Socratic education, touching on everything relevant to the purpose, in order, from start to finish. It is as if Xenophon wrote a book titled *The Philosophy of Socrates, Its Parts, the Rank of Order of Its Parts, from Beginning to End*. Nowhere else—not in Aristotle, nor even in Plato—do we find such a thing.[34] Xenophon alone sets forth the Socratic teaching in systematic order. And the following study is devoted, therefore, to Book IV of his *Memorabilia*.

III

That said, no study of Xenophon's Socratic writings can safely avoid the subject of the dim view taken of him in recent times. The view in question is best captured by the following, oft-quoted remark of Bertrand Russell. "Xenophon," he said, "[was] a military man, not very liberally endowed with brains, and on the whole conventional in his outlook. . . . There has been a tendency to think that everything Xenophon says [of Socrates] must be true, because he had not the wits to think of anything untrue. This is a very invalid line of argument. A stupid man's report of what a clever man says is never accurate, because he unconsciously translates what he hears into something that he can understand. I would rather be reported by my bitterest enemies among philosophers than by a friend innocent of philosophy."[35] Now, by the time Russell made this remark in the middle of the twentieth century, he was not saying anything new. Xenophon's fall from grace first began, on the authority of the theologian Friedrich Schleiermacher, in the early nineteenth century. According to Schleiermacher, "Xenophon was a statesman, but no philosopher, and beside the purity of his character . . . which Xenophon loved and respected in Socrates, the latter may have possessed some really philosophical elements which Xenophon was unable to appropriate to himself, and which he suffered to pass unnoticed; which, indeed, he can have felt no temptation to exhibit, for fear of betraying defects such as those which his Socrates was want to expose."[36] A century later and Schleiermacher's view had become so influential that it was widely believed that Xenophon was so "incapable of appreciating the real message of Socrates . . . that we have [in his Socratic writings] work not only of no historical value but full of commonplace and triviality . . . showing us a Socrates who is merely a tiresome pedant and moralizer and paragon of virtue."[37] Half a century after that, Terence Irwin casually remarked that "Xenophon quite closely resembles a familiar British figure—the retired general, staunch Tory and Anglican, firm defender of the Establishment in Church and State, and at the same time a reflective man with ambitions to write edifying literature. . . . Xenophon's Socrates discusses some questions of interest to Xenophon himself and offers edifying but philosophically unexciting remarks."[38] And now, in the twenty-first century, classicists will still tell you that "Xenophon was *not* a philosopher. . . . [Socrates] was greatly admired by a host of young men, including Xenophon, for his unshakable commitment to moral virtue. But it is impossible to see how the person Xenophon describes . . . would have won the devotion of so many philosophers."[39]

Until the beginning of the nineteenth century, however, this view of Xenophon was practically unheard-of. According to Hegel, Schleiermacher's most illustrious contemporary, "in regard to the content of [Socrates's] teaching and the point reached by him in the development of thought, we have in the main to look to Xenophon."[40] Before that, there was Montaigne—a man not the least bit innocent of philosophy, and thus in a position to know a philosopher when he saw one—according to whom Xenophon was "an author of marvelous weight... a philosopher among the first disciples of Socrates."[41] And Montaigne was not alone. Arrayed against the classicists who, in recent memory, have dragged Xenophon's name through the mud are the giants of the past. In antiquity, Xenophon was regarded as a philosopher of the rank of Plato by the likes of Polybius, Cicero, Tacitus, and Quintilian.[42] And the moderns—from Machiavelli to Bacon, Montesquieu, Rousseau, and Nietzsche—were in broad agreement with the ancients. As Nietzsche put it, even after the tide had already turned against Xenophon, "the *Memorabilia* of Xenophon give a really true picture, that is just as spiritually rich as was the model for the picture; one must, however, understand how to read this book. The classicists believe at bottom that Socrates has nothing to say to them, and therefore are bored by it. Others feel that this book points you to, and at the same time gives you, happiness."[43] The *Memorabilia*, Nietzsche thus gives us to understand, is one of those books written by the wise men of old and filled with their treasures to which the *Memorabilia* itself, in Book I, Chapter 6, points. But again, by then, Nietzsche was already swimming against the tide.

Xenophon deserved every bit of the reputation he once enjoyed, and more. Even if he falls a whit short of Plato, only someone of their stature would be in a position to know. But how, then, did the classicists of the nineteenth and twentieth centuries find themselves—all at once, to exaggerate somewhat for the sake of clarity, and all of a sudden—completely at variance with the giants of the past two millennia? How did they unconsciously translate one of the greatest philosophers who ever lived into a statesman at best, a fool at worst?[44]

There is a famous story told by Diogenes Laertius about how Xenophon first came under Socrates's influence (II.48). Socrates stopped Xenophon in an alley and asked the youth where he might be able to buy all kinds of food. Again and again, Xenophon told him what he wanted to know. Finally, Socrates asked, "And where do men become noble and good?" The youth was at a loss. "Then follow me," said Socrates, "and learn." Now, readers used to turn to Xenophon for at least somewhat the same reason that Xenophon, according to Diogenes Laertius, turned to Socrates. "The other night," a young John Adams wrote in his diary, "[Xenophon's] Choice of Hercules came into my mind, and left Impressions there which I hope will never be effaced nor long unheeded." "Let Virtue address me," he wrote, "Which, dear Youth, will you prefer? a Life of Effeminacy, Indolence and obscurity, or a Life of Industry, Temperance, and Honour?"[45] In his "favorite author, that ancient and immortal husbandman, philosopher, politician, and general, Xenophon,"[46] Adams sought and found the inspiration to choose a life of virtue. No longer, though, do we read the great books of the past in order to learn or to be urged on toward the right or best way of life and all that it entails. Introducing an old poem much in keeping with the real and apparent taste of Xenophon, someone once said, "educated men of [the past]," unlike those of modern times, "were apt to read [books] for what they could get out of them . . . of instruction for themselves, and their times."[47] Books written for such readers—and Xenophon, more than any other philosopher, wrote his books for such readers—would seem, therefore, to have outlived their usefulness. Consider, again, the recent reports of Xenophon quoted earlier. In each and every case, there was a distinction drawn, more or less clearly, between morality or politics, on one hand, and philosophy, on the other. And it was implied, more or less clearly, that even the inspiration that Adams sought and found in Xenophon—to say nothing of the many, supposedly "simple and even embarrassingly obvious pointers on how to make friends, how to prosper, how to treat friends and enemies, how to become a good general,"[48] and so on—is somehow beneath the dignity of philosophy. This is one reason for the dim view taken of Xenophon in recent times: modern readers are too sophisticated for such edifying, "but philosophically unexciting," literature.[49]

But there is another reason for this, too, one with which our sophistication uneasily, albeit necessarily, coexists. Benjamin Franklin also read Xenophon's *Memorabilia* as a young man. And he was so taken with it that he adopted "the Socratic method," for some years himself. By that time in his life, he had "become a real Doubter in many Points of our Religious Doctrine." Accordingly, he says, "I found this Method safest for my self & very embarrassing to those against whom I used it, therefore I . . . grew very skilled & expert in drawing People even of superior Knowledge into Concessions the Consequences of which they did not foresee, entangling them in Difficulties . . . and so obtaining Victories that neither my self nor my Cause always deserved."[50] Franklin thus came away from his reading of Xenophon with the view that Socrates did at least somewhat the same thing that Hippias, in Book IV, Chapter 4, accused him of doing: ridiculing others by questioning and refuting them, while never revealing his own thought about anything to anyone. Much to his delight, Franklin found in Xenophon a Socrates whose method called for something like "irony," as Thrasymachus put it in Plato's *Republic* (337a3-7), as well as "sophistry." But how does this Socrates, Franklin's Socrates, square with the Socrates whose account of the choice of Hercules inspired Adams? Even today, with a rehabilitation of Xenophon underway thanks in no small part to a new generation of classicists who are returning to his writings a measure of their former glory, Franklin's Socrates remains largely unknown. To Franklin, it will be hastily replied that Hippias's accusation of Socrates is Xenophon's tribute, "doubtless inadvertent, to the truth suppressed throughout [the *Memorabilia*]," and found only in Plato, that Socrates, so far from teaching morality or politics, was always refuting others about such things.[51] But what if Xenophon did not suppress the truth so well throughout the *Memorabilia* that a youth as perceptive as Franklin could not catch a glimpse of it? And what if, insofar as Xenophon did suppress the truth throughout the *Memorabilia*, he did not do so inadvertently? According to W. K. C. Guthrie, to put this differently, "there is indeed something to the claim that, in accordance with his avowed purpose of winning over the ordinary Athenian, we must be prepared to find [Xenophon] putting a somewhat one-sided emphasis on the conventionally virtuous side of Socrates rather than on his uniqueness and eccentricity. Yet even this," he says, "did not prevent him from letting Socrates argue for his disturbing paradox."[52] To distinguish himself from A. E. Taylor, however, according to whom, "[Xenophon] carefully suppresses, as far as he can, all mention of the personal peculiarities which distinguish Socrates from the average decent Athenian,"[53] Guthrie adds straightaway that, "since Xenophon was something of an 'average decent Athenian' himself, perhaps 'was less aware of' would be truer than 'carefully suppresses.'"[54] Perhaps. Then again, perhaps not. For persecution for "dissenting views," to say nothing of other, more important considerations, was a fact of life in those days.[55] And Xenophon was perhaps nothing like the average Athenian.

It is no accident that Schleiermacher, the man who bears much of the responsibility for Xenophon's fall from grace, also bears much of the responsibility for banishing all talk of the exotericism of the ancient philosophers from polite conversation. Early in the nineteenth century, Goethe wrote, "I have always considered it an evil, indeed a disaster which, in the second half of the previous century, gained more and more ground that one no longer drew a distinction between the exoteric and the esoteric."[56] And had it not been for Leo Strauss, who was not by accident more responsible than anyone else for the rehabilitation of Xenophon too,[57] the distinction between the exoteric and the esoteric would in all likelihood still be lost in the mists of time. Now, it would be the height of absurdity to say that the distinction between the exoteric and the esoteric is "Straussian." For in that case Montaigne, Bacon, Leibniz, Bayle, Rousseau, Diderot, Lessing, Goethe, and Nietzsche, to name but a few, would all be "Straussians."[58] Diderot, to give just one example of this sort of thing, devoted an entry of his *Encyclopédie* to the distinction, in which Samuel Formey wrote, "The ancient philosophers had a double doctrine; the one external, public, or *exoteric*; the other internal, secret or *esoteric*." But the suggestion that "the ancients distinguished the 'exoteric' or popular mode of exposition from the 'esoteric' one which is suitable for those who are seriously concerned to discover the truth," although made in this case by Leibniz,[59] is nowadays said to be "Straussian," all the same. For so much indignation is kindled against the "perverse," "twisted" suggestion that the ancient philosophers deceived the reading public—that they intentionally suppressed the truth throughout their writings—that "Straussian" has become, in some circles, little or nothing more than a term of abuse heaped upon anyone who makes it.[60] Even direct evidence, meanwhile, gets swept under the rug.[61] And this is all very telling. Another reason for the dim view taken of Xenophon in recent times is that modern readers are too naïve for such "philosophically exciting," but shocking, literature.

Xenophon's fall from grace was, then, the result of a strange brew—about which we will have a bit more to say later—of sophistication and naivete, "realism" and "idealism." Even today, with a rehabilitation of Xenophon underway, readers look down upon Xenophon's exoteric teaching, which elicits nothing but "a sneer . . . and a yawn," and overlook his esoteric one, the mere suggestion of which shocks them. Looking down upon Xenophon's exoteric teaching and overlooking his esoteric one, they cannot help but judge Xenophon harshly—as if *he* were not a philosopher. But perhaps, since Bertrand Russell was right about one thing, at least, they merely betray their own innocence of philosophy when they say that Xenophon was not a philosopher? Originally, at any rate, philosophy meant ascending from the cave to the sunlight, or ascending from moral or political opinion to knowledge of the truth about morality or politics, to say nothing of religion.[62] Although the gulf between the exoteric and the esoteric teaching is so much wider in Xenophon's writings than in any other philosopher's, nevertheless Xenophon gives readers the opportunity to make the ascent from the one to the other. In this, Xenophon's art of writing imitates reality, as he saw it. For the difference between Xenophon's exoteric and his esoteric teaching is not based on the difference between what is written and what is not written yet somehow divined by the "initiated" reader.[63] The difference is based, rather, on the difference between what is not written, but seems to be, and what is written, but does not seem to be. That is, whereas Xenophon's exoteric teaching is based on a figment of the cursory reader's imagination, his esoteric teaching is based on his words exactly as written. Only Xenophon's exact words, when thought through, yield his esoteric teaching. And much the same can be said for reality itself, as he saw it. Since moral or political opinion is not entirely clear, according to him, only moral or political opinion taken exactly, and then thought through, yields knowledge. In conclusion, the classicists of the nineteenth and twentieth centuries were too quick to forget that Xenophon did not write for them. Xenophon wrote, above all, for readers who desire to learn from him the very same thing that the youths whom Socrates taught desired to learn from Socrates: namely, how to become noble and good. And even today his Socratic writings give such readers the opportunity to come to grips with the original, and perhaps only, meaning of philosophy.

PART ONE

CHAPTER 1

Socratic Rhetoric

I

Xenophon's writings can be divided into Socratic and non-Socratic writings. There are four Socratic writings: the *Memorabilia*, the *Symposium*, the *Oeconomicus*, and the *Apology*. Xenophon's Socrates drew a distinction between a man's deeds, his speeches, and his thoughts (*Memorabilia* I.1.19; compare IV.3.1 with IV.5.1, IV.6.1, and IV.7.1).[1] And thus, if the opening remarks of Xenophon's Socratic works are any indication, the *Symposium* would seem to be devoted Socrates's (playful) deeds (*Symposium* 1.1), the *Oeconomicus* to his speeches (*Oeconomicus* 1.1), and the *Apology* to his thoughts (*Apology* 1). But what, then, are we to make of the *Memorabilia*?

The *Memorabilia*, by far the longest of Xenophon's Socratic writings, opens with the question of how, by what speeches, the Athenians were persuaded to put Socrates to death for not believing in the gods in whom the city believed, introducing new *daimonia*, and corrupting the youth (I.1.1). There follows a defense of Socrates—first and foremost, against the charge that he did not believe in the gods of the city (I.1) and, second, against the charge that he corrupted the youth (I.2)—after which, with the legal case against him settled one way or another, Xenophon goes on to write as much as he can recall about how Socrates benefited his companions by his deeds and by his speeches (I.3.1ff.). Thus, after concluding his legal defense of Socrates, Xenophon would seem to devote the rest of the *Memorabilia* to an extralegal defense of Socrates. Since not only lawfulness (IV.4, IV.6.5–6) but also, or instead, benefiting others can be called justice (IV.8.11), it would seem that the *Memorabilia* as a whole is devoted to Socrates's justice: first, but very briefly, to his innocence of the charges brought against him and second, but at great length, to his beneficial deeds and speeches.[2]

So far, this is well-trodden ground.[3] Just beyond it, however, there lies some untrodden ground to which we can now make our way.

To begin with, precisely if the *Memorabilia* is the most defensive or apologetic of Xenophon's four Socratic writings,[4] would it not make sense for it to be also, in places, his most daring? One indication of this is that only in the *Memorabilia*—in the safety afforded Xenophon, not least of all, by his defense of Socrates against the charge of unbelief, a defense in which he differentiates Socrates from the other, "pre-Socratic" philosophers (I.1.11–16)—does Xenophon feel free to report not one but two Socratic conversations about the nature of all things (I.4, IV.3; consider I.1.16).[5] For another, better indication of this, however, take another look at the *Memorabilia* as a whole. One or two things seem to be missing from Xenophon's legal defense of Socrates. In the first place, in the course of defending Socrates against the charge that he did not believe in the gods of the city, Xenophon says that Socrates spoke about the nature of all things differently than the other, "pre-Socratic" philosophers did (I.1.11). By asking "what is" questions, Socrates was always speaking about the human things and about the other (nonhuman) things (*kai peri tōn allōn*), knowledge of which, he believed, makes one a gentleman in the strict sense. For example, he was always speaking in this way about the pious and the just (I.1.16). Now, according to Xenophon, how Socrates thought about such things was by no means evident to all (I.1.17). "'What all know' is precisely not what is going on in the mind of the doer. . . . It is what he does or says but not what he silently deliberates."[6] And yet, in the course of defending Socrates against the thoughtcrimes with which he was charged, Xenophon himself avoids the subject of his thought. Casting only sideways glances at how Socrates thought, for example, about the gods, he finally rests his case on the man's deeds and his speeches alone (consider I.1.20).[7] In the second place, in the course of defending Socrates against the charge that he corrupted the youth, Xenophon lets it be known that Socrates did teach the youth (consider I.2.8, I.2.52). Socrates taught "the political things" (I.2.17) and "an art of speeches" (I.2.31–38; consider I.2.21). And he taught the latter, according to Xenophon's indications, if not also the former, by asking the youth questions to which he himself already knew the answers—for example, about the just and the holy as compared, or contrasted, with the arts (I.2.35–37; consider I.2.32, I.2.38).[8] The two charges brought against Socrates are linked by the fact that Socrates taught the youth to think like him (consider I.2.8, I.2.52). But then, assuming that Xenophon makes his case that Socrates *did not* think unlawful thoughts or teach the youth to think such thoughts either, what is missing from the first part of the

Memorabilia is any perfectly obvious treatment of what it was that Socrates *did* think or teach the youth to think. Or what is missing, to be more precise, is any perfectly obvious treatment of what it was that Socrates thought or taught the youth to think about the "what is" questions—for example, "What is impiety?" or "What is lawbreaking?" (consider I.2.2)—knowledge of the true answers to which, he believed, makes one a gentleman in the strict sense. And Xenophon does not appear to be in any rush to fill the gap. As we make our way through second part of the *Memorabilia*, it quickly becomes obvious that Socrates was a benefactor to his companions, both by his deeds and by his speeches, in great and small matters alike. Much less obvious, however, is the fact that he was a teacher. Or much less obvious is the fact that he was a benefactor to his companions, in particular, by teaching them to think like him about the "what is" questions on which his new and different way of philosophizing came to depend.[9] And that means, since education is the greatest good for a human being (*Apology* 21), it is not so obvious from the *Memorabilia* that Socrates was the benefactor par excellence, a benefactor when it comes to the greatest good—not until Book IV, at least.

The second part of the *Memorabilia* has two parts of its own. According to the opening remarks of Book IV, *Memorabilia* I.3–III.14 confirmed that Socrates benefited his companions by treating different matters in different places, whereas the rest of the *Memorabilia* confirms that Socrates benefited his companions by treating one and the same matter in different ways. And Xenophon all but concludes Book IV with the remark, which has to be considered together with this, that Book IV confirms that Socrates revealed his thought in some way. About the opening and concluding remarks of Book IV, we will have more to say soon enough. For now, whatever else they may mean, we can say this much: *Memorabilia* I.3–III.14 confirms that Socrates benefited his companions, in deed and in speech, by treating different matters in different places, whereas *Memorabilia* IV confirms that Socrates benefited his companions, in deed and in speech, by revealing his thought—not least of all, if we follow Xenophon's indications, his thought about the pious and the just—in some way.[10] Book IV, coming full circle, thus returns to the matters treated in the first part of the *Memorabilia*: what did Socrates think or teach the youth to think? But Xenophon himself treats such matters, in Book IV, in a different way. No longer treating what Socrates thought or taught the youth to think with a view to making the case that there was nothing illegal going on, Xenophon does so, instead, with a view to proving how beneficial Socrates was. Socrates at his most beneficial,

Socrates as teacher—that is the most Xenophon ever lets us see, in any of his writings, of the philosopher himself.[11]

II

According to Xenophon's opening remarks, Socrates was beneficial "in every matter" and "in every way." But to prove just how beneficial Socrates was in these regards Xenophon goes on to mention that, according to someone less perceptive than himself,[12] nothing was more beneficial than being together with Socrates "in any place" and "in any matter" (IV.1.1). Socrates could be beneficial (in every matter) in any number of different *ways* according to Xenophon, whereas he could be supremely beneficial (in every matter) in any number of different *places* according to someone less perceptive than Xenophon. So far, most of Xenophon's memorabilia or recollections of Socrates have tended to shed more light on the different places in which Socrates treated matters than on the different ways in which he did so. And yet the places, which were clear even to the less perceptive, stand in much less need of illumination than the ways. In other words, the *Memorabilia* itself has so far tended to confirm the rather obvious fact that Socrates could benefit others by treating different matters in different places (consider I.1.10). But we still await confirmation of the much less obvious fact, which was clear to Xenophon, if not to the less perceptive, that Socrates could benefit others by treating different matters—or indeed, one and the same matter—in different ways (compare I.3.1 with IV.1.1). Accordingly, after confirming on the basis of *Memorabilia* I.3–III.14 that Socrates was beneficial "in any place," Xenophon sets out in Book IV to confirm that Socrates was beneficial "in every way." For he shifts from the benefits connected with remembering Socrates, even when Socrates was not present, to the benefits connected with accompanying or remembering Socrates, even when Socrates was not being entirely serious or straightforward. Socrates, Xenophon contends, was no less beneficial when treating a matter in a joking way than he was when treating the matter in a serious way (IV.1.1; consider I.3.7–8). And if Xenophon were to prove this particular contention in the course of his subsequent recollections, would he not thereby confirm the more general contention that the many ways of Socrates were beneficial?

Although Socrates would frequently say that he was in love with someone, it was clear to Xenophon at least that he did not desire those whose bodies were beautiful, but those whose natures were fit for virtue of the soul (consider I.3.8–14).

These "good natures" were distinguished in Socrates's eyes by qualities of heart, not least, and mind. They learned quickly what they applied themselves to, they remembered what they learned, and they desired all subjects of learning on account of which it is possible to manage a household and a city nobly (IV.1.2; contrast *Oeconomicus* 13.9). Because good natures were liable to learn these subjects quickly—after all, they desired to do so—and to remember what they learned of them, they were distinguished by their self-sufficiency when it came to education. But they were not altogether self-sufficient. At any rate, Socrates desired them because he thought that, after having been educated, they would not only be happy themselves and manage their own households nobly but also be capable of making other human beings and cities happy (IV.1.2). He saw fit, that is, to help them reach their potential. As for those who reached their potential, it is not certain whether Socrates thought that, in addition to being happy themselves, they would go on in the next place to use their capacity to make other human beings, much less cities, happy (consider I.6.15).[13] Either way, they do not get exactly what they bargained for: the state reached by good natures who receive an education is not exactly the state good natures desire to reach prior to receiving an education. An education changes for the better even, or precisely, their expectations of what an education is or does. Exactly what an education is or does remains uncertain for now. But Xenophon leaves no doubt about the fact that, although Socrates approached good natures as a lover, he was only joking; his serious desire was for their education. Were Xenophon to prove that Socrates, by joking in this way, was most beneficial and, in particular, able to satisfy his serious desire for the education of good natures, then Xenophon would confirm his original contention about the many ways of Socrates more generally. Presumably, then, he will prove as much next.

In fact, however, he does not even try to do so. Instead, he says that Socrates did not approach all natures in the same "way" (IV.1.3).[14] And then he abruptly descends from good natures and Socrates's way of approaching them to two or three bad natures and Socrates's way of approaching them. By Xenophon's account, Socrates approached those "aristocrats" who thought they were, because they were reputed to be, by nature good but despised learning in one way: by arguing that they were in need of an education (IV.1.3–4). And he approached those "oligarchs" who were proud of their wealth and who supposed they did not need any education in addition in another way: by arguing that they were foolish and naïve (IV.1.5). Socrates, therefore, approached these bad natures as an exhorter to education, learning, or knowledge, and, almost by implication, as a teacher himself. And this is strange. For it means that, when Socrates approached natures who were *not* educable, he all but did so as a teacher, while, on the other hand, when he approached natures who *were* educable, he did so not as a teacher, but as a lover. Stranger still, after descending from good natures to these two bad natures, Xenophon descends yet again to a youth named Euthydemos, who will prove to be worse even than the latter two bad natures.[15] And after describing the way Socrates approached this youth, too, but at much greater length and in much greater detail (IV.2.1–8), Xenophon goes on to describe for the first and only time the Socratic education itself—or, at any rate, the Socratic education of Euthydemos—from start to finish (IV.2.9ff.). Thus, in addition to the fact that Xenophon lets us see far more of the way Socrates approached Euthydemos than of the ways he approached any of the better natures, the one and only time Xenophon lets us see Socrates as a teacher, Socrates is the teacher of a youth who is not even remotely fit for an education.

Now, just when it seems Book IV could not get any stranger, Xenophon tells us that, although Euthydemos's soul was unfit for an education, the youth's body was beautiful (IV.2.1, I.2.29–30). So in the wake of the disclosure that Socrates "loved," not youths whose bodies were beautiful, but youths whose natures were fit for virtue of the soul (because he desired their education), Xenophon goes on to describe an attempt on the part of Socrates to educate a youth whose body was beautiful,[16] but whose nature was not fit for virtue of the soul.[17] Do we have here, in lieu of a serious Socratic education, an exact parody or caricature of one? If so, to prove that Socrates's joking way of treating a matter was no less beneficial than his serious way of treating it (IV.1.1), Xenophon has recourse especially to Socrates's joking way of educating bad natures—not, or not merely, to Socrates's joking way of approaching good natures as a lover (IV.1.2).

How then does a joking education of a bad nature differ from a serious education of a good nature? Only at the conclusion of the greater part of the *Memorabilia* (I.3–III)—which, to repeat, tended to confirm that Socrates could benefit others by treating different matters in different places—did Xenophon say in plain terms that Socrates distinguished between good natures, who were educable, and bad natures, who were not. And yet with this, writes Leo Strauss, "[he] compels us to consider whether all interlocutors of Socrates who were presented in the preceding Books were good natures and which, if any, were not: we easily could have read those Books without wondering at all whether the interlocutors presented there were good natures."[18] Likewise, only at the conclusion of the education of Euthydemos—which, to repeat, tends to confirm that the many ways of Socrates were beneficial to others—does Xenophon say in plain terms that Socrates conversed with or spoke to others in two different ways. And yet with this, too, he compels us to consider whether all Socrates said in the preceding Book or Books was said in one way and what, if anything, was said in the other. For, at the conclusion of the education, Xenophon says that if someone contradicted Socrates about something without being able to say anything clear himself, then Socrates led the speech up toward the assumption or hypothesis on which it was based by asking "what is" questions. And in this way, Xenophon says, "the truth" became clear also to the contradictors themselves. So much for when Socrates "examined" (*epeskepsato*) something (IV.6.13–14). On the other hand, Xenophon says that when Socrates would "go through" (*diexioi*) rather than "examine" something in speech by himself (compare IV.7.8 with IV.6.15 and IV.6.14)—that is, when he would "teach" (consider *Oeconomicus* 6.2–3, 15.13, 16.1)—he made his way "through" things generally agreed upon, believing this to be "safety" in speech. Xenophon knew no one, therefore, whose speeches produced so much agreement, which is not to say complete agreement (see, for the best example of this, *Symposium* 4.56–60), among those who merely (thoughtlessly) listened. But, in this, Socrates was following in another's footsteps: those of Odysseus, "the man of many ways" (*anēr polytropos*) himself (Homer, *Odyssey* I.1). For Socrates used to say that Homer, too, said of Odysseus that he was a safe rhetor, since Odysseus could lead his speeches "through" the opinions of human beings (IV.6.15).[19] According to Xenophon, then, Socrates conversed with contradictors in such a way as to reach the truth; yet he spoke to noncontradictors in such a way as to remain safely within the confines of their own, generally accepted opinions.

Euthydemos, who contradicts Socrates hardly at all and feebly at that, is a noncontradictor. This much is obvious. Equally obvious is the fact that the education Socrates conveys to Euthydemos amounts to little or nothing more than a recapitulation of safe, generally accepted opinions. Xenophon seems to say that before making his companions skilled in speaking, acting, and contriving, Socrates taught them "moderation." For, as the examples of Alcibiades and Critias suggest, the just—or, more exactly, the less unjust—use of the former arts or capacities requires the latter virtue (IV.3.1, I.2.15–17). But "moderation," which thus seems to be the end for the sake of which the arts or capacities in question should be used, consists in piety (IV.3.1–2, IV.3.17–18) and justice (IV.3.1, IV.4.1, IV.4.25), each of which consists, in turn, in obedience to the laws (IV.3.16, IV.6.2–4; IV.4.12, IV.4.25, IV.6.5–6). So the education Socrates conveys to Euthydemos amounts to little or nothing more than the teaching of the city: obey the laws. And is any teaching safer or more representative of generally accepted opinions than this? Small wonder that so many sophisticated, modern readers have mistaken Xenophon's Socrates for "a fatuous giver of conventional moral advice."[20] However, insofar as Euthydemos is a noncontradictor, and insofar as the teaching Socrates conveys to him remains safely within the confines of generally accepted opinions, the education of Euthydemos meets Xenophon's description of Odyssean speech or, as Socrates or Homer put it, rhetoric.[21] The joking education of a Euthydemos is accordingly little or nothing more than a rhetorical recapitulation of generally accepted opinions for the sake of a youth whose natural needs and capacities ensure that it would not be safe—both for the teacher and, in another way, for the student (IV.2.40)—to make a go at the truth.[22] If Xenophon's Socrates was sometimes a "giver of conventional moral advice," he was by no means "fatuous." That said, given that good natures reach the truth through their Socratic education, they are bound to be contradictors. Rather than go "through" generally accepted opinions, the serious education of a good nature leads from generally accepted opinions up toward the truth or up toward true answers to one or more "what is" questions (I.1.16). Earlier, Xenophon said that Socrates was accused of frequently reciting verses of Homer to the effect that Odysseus—to whom Socrates compared himself (I.3.6–7, *Apology* 26)—spoke in one way to extraordinary people, in another way, if at all, to ordinary ones (I.2.58). Xenophon neither denied the accusation nor accounted for Socrates's purpose in reciting the verses so frequently (contrast I.2.56–57 with I.2.58–59). Now we know better why.

On the other hand, if a joking education of a bad nature differs from a serious education of a good nature as much as generally accepted opinions differ from the truth, how could the former education be as beneficial as the latter? Xenophon offers the education of Euthydemos as proof that Socrates revealed his thought "simply" or "straightforwardly" (*haplōs*) "with a view to" his interlocutor (IV.7.1). Socrates had a reputation for concealing his thought, which he may well then have deserved (IV.4.9–11, I.2.36). Indeed, Xenophon—to whom it was clear that Socrates was a man of many ways (IV.1.1), a man who, among other things, did not approach all natures in the same way (IV.1.3)—perceived that precisely because Socrates revealed his thought *ad hominem*, or "with a view to" the needs and capacities of his interlocutor, he frequently knew more than he taught and taught others to learn less than he knew (IV.7.3; IV.7.5; IV.7.6–7, I.1.11–15, I.4, IV.3). But somehow, in spite of this, Socrates revealed his thought at the same time. And it is hard to fathom how Socrates could do both at once, conceal and reveal, unless Xenophon's apparently unintelligible formulation means that by revealing his thought "with a view to" someone—"with a view to" Euthydemos, for example, whose weak mind and soft heart set the limits beyond which Socrates would not go (IV.2.39–40)[23]—Socrates simultaneously revealed his thought unstraightforwardly to someone else. On occasion, Socrates would indeed speak to someone, not by speaking to him, but by speaking in his presence to another or others (IV.4.25; I.3.8, II.5.1, III.14.2–4, IV.2.2, IV.2.6–7, consider III.8.1–2; *Oeconomicus* 1.1, 3.1), or by speaking in his absence to another or others who could be counted on to circulate reports of his remarks (I.2.30, I.2.38).[24] Was the education of Euthydemos just such an occasion? If the education recapitulates safe, generally accepted opinions, and not the truth, then it will be open to contradiction. And we can be sure that one contradictor (consider I.3.8–13) in particular was present for at least some of the education, and even if he was not present for all of it, we can be sure that he received reports of the rest: Xenophon (IV.3.2; IV.4.5, IV.5.2). While Socrates was teaching "with a view to" Euthydemos, was he also or especially teaching, through him, a good nature such as Xenophon who might reach the truth, first, by silently contradicting the teaching, then, by thinking through the assumptions or hypotheses on which the contradiction and the teaching were, each of them, based? In other words, granted that the education of Euthydemos was a joke, which Euthydemos was in no position to "get," could a good nature who managed to "get" the joke—for example, by coming to see the problems that prevent whoever sees them from taking the (city's) teaching too seriously—not thereby come to see what Socrates thought in all seriousness? However that may be, only if a joking education amounted in this way to a serious education could the former be as beneficial as the latter. For an education is, by Socrates's account, nothing less than the greatest good for a human being (*Apology* 21). Here, too, Socrates would joke and be serious simultaneously (consider I.3.7–8ff., III.11.16).

If a joking education of a bad nature is as beneficial as a serious education of a good nature because it amounts to one itself, another question arises. For why would Socrates leave good natures to think through for themselves (the problems with) what he told bad natures to believe and do, when he could just as well tell good natures the truth in the simplest and clearest manner (consider IV.2.40)? Why would he take this long, roundabout way to the object of his desire when he could just as well take a short, straight way to it? One answer was given already, when Xenophon said that Socrates was concerned with safety. But another answer, which goes together with the first, implies that Socrates could not take a much shorter, straighter way even if it were safe to do so, for example, in private. Xenophon indicates that, after having been educated, good natures became good friends to Socrates and to one another for as long as they lived (I.2.8, I.6.14, IV.1.2).[25] So to say that Socrates desired to educate good natures is almost to say that he desired to make good friends. Now, in pursuit of good friends, Socrates availed himself of the erotic art (II.6.28), the rudiments of which he once imparted to the beautiful courtesan Theodote.[26] To approach human beings "according to nature and correctly" (III.11.11, consider IV.2.1), he told her, she should not offer herself to anyone who does not already desire her, lest she appear repulsive rather than attractive (III.11.13). Instead, she should first arouse desire for herself by approaching friends as if to gratify them, then, all of a sudden, fleeing (III.11.14). True to his word, Socrates behaved no differently. When it came to the pursuit of good friends, he proceeded according to nature and correctly. To tell good natures the truth in the simplest and clearest manner would have been contrary to nature and incorrect, violent (III.11.11), and, in effect, repulsive to them, *unless* they already desired to know this. But did they, even they, already desire to know this? Recall that, with respect to its end, this knowledge was not exactly the knowledge good natures desired (IV.1.2). By "force feeding" them the truth, which they did not yet desire, Socrates would only repulse good natures (consider III.11.13). So he first aroused desire for *his* knowledge (of the truth) by approaching them as if to gratify *their* desire for knowledge (on account of which it is possible to manage a household and a city nobly), then, all of a sudden, leaving them to think for themselves. That is, to connect the dots somewhat, the more good natures strove in response to Socrates's erotic art to gratify their desire for knowledge all by themselves—while thoughtfully listening to Socrates jokingly arouse and gratify a bad nature's desire—the more they would come to see with their own eyes the problems with, and hence the undesirability of, such knowledge as they desired to begin with. Would their desire for knowledge, or, rather, for knowledge so-called, not accordingly undergo a change for the better—a distillation into the desire for genuine knowledge? In any case, on account of the difference between the state reached by good natures who receive an education and the state good natures desire to reach prior to receiving an education, which follows from the difference between the truth and generally accepted opinions, there is no shorter, straighter way to the education of good natures.[27] To take this way is according to nature and correct. To do otherwise, violent and repulsive.

CHAPTER 2

Can Politics Be Taught?

I

Socrates approached both those bad natures who thought they were by nature good and those who were proud of their wealth as an exhorter to education or to learning. Euthydemos, however, was one of those bad natures who thought they had already obtained the best education and were proud of their wisdom (compare IV.2.1 with IV.1.3–4 and IV.1.5). By means of that education or wisdom (that is not to say learning) Euthydemos hoped to make good on his political ambitions. He hoped to surpass everyone in the capacity "to speak and to do" (IV.2.1)—in the capacity, that is, to engage in political affairs—and he hoped, with that capacity, to do what was, according to Socrates, the greatest "deed" or "work" of all (IV.2.2, contrast I.2.7): to rule the city (IV.2.36, IV.2.11, consider IV.2.3). If, however, Euthydemos had this much in common with Alcibiades and Critias (I.2.15–16, I.2.39, I.2.47), he hoped to become fit for gentlemanship (*kalokagathia*) by means of his education or wisdom as well (IV.2.23; compare I.2.47 with I.2.48, consider II.9.1). Much like good natures (IV.1.2), he hoped to rule not only with an unsurpassed capacity to do so, but also as a good citizen would, namely, with justice (IV.2.11). Finally, while Euthydemos hoped to make good on his political ambitions and thus to be worthy to do so by means of his education or wisdom, that education or wisdom was itself obtained, he thought, by means of collecting—merely collecting—books of men reputed to be wise (IV.2.1, IV.2.8–9, consider IV.2.23).[1] Book collecting was, then, supposed to be the means to that education or wisdom whose end was great statesmanship with gentlemanship at its core.

Because Euthydemos was one of those bad natures who thought they had already obtained the best education for (being worthy of) making good on their political ambitions, Socrates could not approach him, too, as an exhorter to education. That would have been worse than useless. So Socrates approached Euthydemos, instead, by calling his attention to the need the politically ambitious have for teachers (IV.2.2–7). That is, instead of exhorting Euthydemos to education on the grounds that it is the means to great statesmanship and gentlemanship, Socrates took it for granted that education is indeed the means to great statesmanship and gentlemanship, and then exhorted Euthydemos to adopt another, different means to education itself. Reading, much less collecting books, he suggested, is no substitute for having teachers. That exhortation—to turn from books toward teachers—was of course not enough to turn Euthydemos from books toward teachers all by itself (IV.2.3, IV.2.6; IV.2.9). But justice, Euthydemos says, is what a good citizen or gentleman should know above all, while the good is what even a slave should know (IV.2.11ff.). And Socrates goes on, after calling the youth's attention to the need the politically ambitious have for teachers, to refute Euthydemos about justice as well as the good. By making Euthydemos realize, as a result of this refutation, that he had not really obtained the best education for making good on his political ambitions—after all, to repeat, he did not hope to rule without justice—Socrates made Euthydemos realize, in turn, that education is not really obtained by means of collecting books (IV.2.23). And, not only was Euthydemos taught to this extent that he had been going the wrong way to education, but he was also, so to speak, "taught" as much by a man whose constant refrain just so happened to be that the right way goes through a teacher. No wonder he turned without further ado toward Socrates, as if Socrates were the very teacher whom, his own exhortations would seem to say, the politically ambitious need. Socrates approached Euthydemos in such a way as to do just this. Socrates approached Euthydemos, that is, in such a way as to lead him to believe that, with Socrates as his teacher, he would obtain at least the core of that education which he thought he had already obtained, up until Socrates refuted him (compare IV.2.40 with IV.2.6).

Socrates called Euthydemos's attention to the need the politically ambitious have for teachers, specifically, over the course of three exhortatory or protreptic speeches, which he made in the youth's presence on three separate occasions (IV.2.2, IV.2.3–5, and IV.2.6–7). When Socrates approached other bad natures, however, he made other exhortatory speeches. And only after giving a brief description of the exhortatory speeches that Socrates made to other bad natures does Xenophon go on to describe, at much greater length and in much greater detail, the ones made to Euthydemos. The fact that Xenophon describes how Socrates approached not only Euthydemos but also, in the first place, politically ambitious "aristocrats" and "oligarchs" is no accident. Just because Euthydemos had no clue that Socrates approached other bad natures in different ways does not mean, after all, that good natures were not watching with rapt attention as Socrates approached, in very different ways, one bad nature after another. And, by including descriptions of how Socrates approached other bad natures, too, Xenophon suggests that the latter makes up the first part of a good nature's education. For some reason, only after thoughtfully listening to Socrates jokingly arouse the desire for knowledge of those bad natures who despised education or learning (IV.1.3), on one hand, and paid it no mind (IV.1.5), on the other, were good natures fully prepared to listen thoughtfully to Socrates jokingly arouse the desire for knowledge of one of those bad natures who thought they had already obtained the best education. Given their unfavorable stances toward learning, Socrates could not approach "aristocrats" or "oligarchs" by calling their attention to the need the politically ambitious have for teachers any more than he could approach Euthydemos as an exhorter to education. That would have been useless. It was, therefore, to the need the politically ambitious have for *education* (IV.1.3–5), and not to the need they have for *teachers*, that Socrates called their attention. But that means, when Socrates approached them, he began from a point farther back. Rather than exhort them to adopt another, different means to education, he exhorted them to education itself. Hard-pressed to beg the question, begged in one form or another by Euthydemos and good natures alike, Socrates had to make the case that education is necessary for the politically ambitious. So perhaps thoughtfully listening to Socrates jokingly arouse the desire for knowledge of other bad natures made up the first part of a good nature's education because, when Socrates approached other bad natures, he was enabled or compelled to begin back at the beginning. That would add up—after all, first things first—if not for the fact that, to repeat, good natures beg the question already. For why should the choir have to listen thoughtfully to Socrates preach to the scoffers? Nothing would come of that. Or nothing would come of that if the preaching of Socrates left nothing to be desired. But if, on the other hand, Socrates failed miserably to make his case, then, by preaching to the scoffers within earshot of the choir, he would simultaneously be sowing seeds of doubt in the choir. And since an education changes for the better even or precisely their expectations of what an education is or does, this long, roundabout way to the education of good natures would be according to nature and correct. Rather than flout their expectations of what an education is or does, which would only repulse them, Socrates would in that case give good natures the opportunity—too good for them, with their self-sufficiency when it came to education, to pass up—to see with their own eyes the problems with their expectations.

II

When Socrates approached Euthydemos, for one (consider IV.1.5), he used to treat the matter of education as if it were akin to teaching other human beings, "by speech," medicine (IV.2.2–5) or horsemanship (IV.2.6–7). However, when he approached politically ambitious "aristocrats," he used to treat the matter of education as if it were akin to breaking good-natured horses by deed, with a carrot and stick (*On Horsemanship* 8.13–14). To them, that is, Socrates pointed out that, just as good-natured horses and dogs become best and most useful to their (human) masters if they have been habituated by them, worst and most useless to them if they have not (IV.1.3), "similarly," those reputed to be by nature good become best and most beneficial to their (divine) masters if they have been educated by them, worst and most harmful to them if they have not (IV.1.4). Although Socrates did not say *why*—only *that*—unbroken, good-natured horses and untrained, good-natured dogs become the worst and least useful of all, while broken and trained ones become the best and most useful, he did not have to. Unbroken, good-natured horses and untrained, good-natured dogs are the worst horses and dogs when it comes to the willingness, rather than the ability, to be useful to their masters (IV.1.3). And what colt breaking or dog training drills into the "most uncontrollable" horses and the "most disobedient" dogs is of course just that: in a word, obedience (*Oeconomicus* 13.6–9). Colt breaking or dog training will be similar to education, then, if what education drills into the most uncontrollable, most disobedient youths is the willingness to be beneficial to their divine masters (consider IV.3.17). That education is a matter of training or habit, like colt breaking and dog training, was bound to go over well with those politically ambitious bad natures who, again, despised learning. Casting education in the mold of colt breaking and dog training meant, however, that little or no role was leftover for learning or knowledge to play in an education.[2] And, whereas "aristocrats" would perhaps do as Socrates apparently did and practice greater continence (*enkrateia*) (I.2.1–3; I.2.17–18, I.3.1), good natures, who desired to learn, were bound to be taken aback by this. Now, to be sure, Socrates did say why—not only that—unlearned, uneducated, "good-natured" youths become the worst and most harmful of all, while learned, educated ones become the best and most beneficial. And what he said of learned, educated, "good-natured" youths was that they become best and most beneficial of all because, having learned what they should do, they do the most, greatest good works. However, in accord with the fact that he spoke of *both* learning *and* education, he went on to say of unlearned, uneducated, "good-natured" youths that they become the worst and most harmful of all. And they become the worst and most harmful of all *not only* because, in their ignorance of how to judge what they should do, they frequently (not always) try to do bad deeds, *but also* because, given how "hard to control" they are, they do the most, greatest evils (consider III.1.3). "Good-natured" youths would not, therefore, do the most, greatest evils, despite their ignorance of how to judge what they should do, if they were easy to control or, in a word, obedient. And insofar as ignorance of how to judge what one should do does not make one an evildoer, at least when the will to do what one should is there too, does learning or knowledge of what one should do make one a do-gooder when the will to do what one should is lacking (consider IV.2.19–20)? According to what Socrates said of why unlearned, uneducated, "good-natured" youths become worst and most harmful, two things go into doing the most, greatest good works, apart from ability, which "good-natured" youths have in spades (IV.1.4): the knowledge of what one should do and the will to do it. Justice is not necessarily beneficial, injustice not necessarily harmful, for which reason knowledge of *what* one should do is not necessarily knowledge of *why*—for what benefit, to avoid what harm (consider IV.1.5)—one should do what one should. And so, just as colt breaking or dog training drills obedience into good-natured horses and dogs, what education, as distinguished from learning or knowledge, drills into "good-natured" youths is the willingness to do what they should, in obedience to their divine masters, their ignorance of how beneficial or their knowledge of how harmful doing so may be to their own lives notwithstanding. Now, according to their masters, the gods, what they should do is obey the laws (IV.3.16; I.3.1, IV.4.13), which means that what education, training, or habituation drills into "good-natured" youths is more specifically piety and justice or, in a word, "moderation." For "moderation," as we have seen, consists in piety and justice, each of which consists, in turn, in obedience to the laws.

Therefore, good natures were moved by what Socrates said to "aristocrats" to entertain the possibility that the politically ambitious have little or no need for learning or knowledge. Despite or because of this, when Socrates approached "oligarchs," he used to treat the matter of education in a very different way (IV.1.5). To them, he did not so much as allude to any similarity between education and colt breaking or dog training. Nor did he make any mention of "education" itself, which, when he approached "aristocrats," he cast in their mold. Here, instead, he spoke only of "learning" or "knowledge." Along with this striking difference in what education is—a matter of learning or knowledge rather than training or habituation—came an equally striking difference in what education does. According to what Socrates said to "aristocrats," the end of an education was obedience (to the laws), whereas according to what he said to "oligarchs," learning (how to distinguish between the beneficial and the harmful) is necessary for the ability to do what is advantageous, an ability which is necessary, in turn, for the sake of one's own life. Few things are more noble than the first end (without the second), Socrates said elsewhere, or more shameful than the second (without the first) (III.2.3–4, contrast III.2.2). By the same token, according to what Socrates said to "aristocrats," the opposite of a do-gooder was "hard to control" or disobedient, whereas according to what he said to "oligarchs," the opposite of a wise man was foolish or naïve (IV.1.5). Already moved by what Socrates said to "aristocrats" to entertain the possibility that little or no learning or knowledge is necessary for the politically ambitious, good natures were moved still farther in this direction by the striking differences between what Socrates said about education to "aristocrats" and, then again, to "oligarchs." They were bound to be taken aback by the fact—bound to go over well enough with those bad natures who were proud of their wealth—that, in the exhortatory speech to "oligarchs," Socrates arranged for one's own life to take the place occupied, in the exhortatory speech to "aristocrats," by obedience to the laws. And seeing as how he arranged at the same time for learning or knowledge to take the place occupied there by training or habituation (consider I.5.5), good natures were moved by the striking differences between the two exhortatory speeches to entertain also the further possibility that learning, knowledge, or the wise man's favorable stance toward learning or knowledge is incompatible with that education, training, or habituation which drills obedience to the laws into "good-natured" youths. That is, although the exhortatory speech that Socrates made to "oligarchs" was apparently about them and them alone, in fact he spoke of two "foolish" beliefs, only one of which was their belief (that, by means of their wealth, they would do whatever they wanted or be advantageous to themselves), before he went on to speak of two "naïve" beliefs, only one of which was their belief (that, by means of their wealth, they would be honored or well reputed by others). And of the two remaining beliefs, one foolish, the other naïve, neither of which belonged to "oligarchs," both or each belonged to "aristocrats" instead, even or precisely to the educated, habituated, or trained among them. For the belief that learning or knowing (how to distinguish between the beneficial and the harmful) is *not* necessary for the ability to do what is advantageous or, in turn, for the sake of one's own life is foolish, Socrates said. And the belief that while learning or knowing *is* necessary for the ability to do what is advantageous, the ability to do what is advantageous is not necessary, in turn, for the sake of one's own life is naïve, he said (IV.1.5). Blind obedience is either foolish or naïve or both foolish and naïve. Even, or precisely, those "good-natured" youths who have been educated, habituated, or trained to do what they should, *either* foolishly take it for granted that, by doing what they should, they do what is advantageous and, in turn, what makes themselves happy *or* they naively hope against hope that somehow, even though they do what is disadvantageous by doing what they should, they do what makes themselves happy. Again, just as colt breaking or dog training drills obedience into good-natured horses and dogs, what education, training, or habituation drills into "good-natured" youths is obedience to the laws. The more obedient to the laws, however, the more foolish, more naïve, or both more foolish and more naïve they become; the wiser, the less obedient to the laws.

Regarding good natures, it was their expectation that an education is a matter of learning or knowledge, and that what education, learning, or knowledge does is make it possible to do nobly the greatest deed or work of all: manage a city. But there is a difference, as we saw, between what an education is or does, on one hand, and a good nature's expectations of what an education is or does, on the other. And thoughtfully listening to Socrates jokingly arouse the desire for knowledge of bad natures other than Euthydemos made up the first part of a good nature's education, in the first place, because what Socrates said to "aristocrats" and to "oligarchs" gave good natures the opportunity to ask themselves whether their expectations were reasonable. By failing miserably to make the case, *their* case, that learning or knowledge is the handmaid of political ambition, bearing the torch before her mistress, Socrates sowed seeds of doubt in good natures. The "oligarchs," who paid learning no mind, and the "aristocrats," who despised it, were perhaps onto something. And if indeed it is neither necessary nor possible for the politically ambitious, as such, to possess learning, knowledge, or the wise man's stance toward learning or knowledge, then good natures were confused. Their expectations of what an education is were not compatible, to begin with, with their expectations of what an education does. *Either*, as Socrates said to "oligarchs," an education is a matter of learning or knowledge (and what education does is make it possible for one's own life to be a happy one) *or*, as Socrates said to "aristocrats," (an education is a matter of training or habituation and) what education does is make it possible to obey the laws, one's ignorance of how beneficial or one's knowledge of how harmful doing so may be to one's own life notwithstanding. And the more good natures strove to gratify their desire for knowledge all by themselves, while thoughtfully listening to Socrates jokingly arouse the desire for knowledge of bad natures other than Euthydemos, the more they would come to see as much with their own eyes.

Of the two educations into which Socrates split the one that good natures had come to expect, only one can be serious, and the other must be a joke. As for which is which, besides the fact that the joking education of Euthydemos first took place, tellingly, in a *bridle-maker's* shop (IV.2.1, IV.2.8),[3] Xenophon has already told us what Socrates thought: only those who desire to learn would, after having been educated, be happy themselves and manage (only) their own households nobly (IV.1.2; consider *Cyropaedia* I.6.7 and *Oeconomicus* 11.10–11). Good natures, to be sure, had no one to tell them what Socrates thought. And yet how could they possibly overlook the fact, almost too obvious to mention, that Socrates did not himself engage in political affairs (I.6.15)? Even what Socrates did, to say nothing of what he thought, flew in the face of what Socrates said to "aristocrats." The thought would thus have been inescapable for good natures that Socrates was only joking when he exhorted them to education on the grounds that it is the means to making good on their political ambitions. By approaching one bad nature after another as an exhorter to education, however, Socrates approached them, almost by implication, as a teacher himself. And the thought that Socrates was only jokingly approaching bad natures as an exhorter to education could not have occurred to good natures without the thought also occurring to them that Socrates was not being entirely serious or straightforward in approaching them as a teacher either. In short, by making good natures realize that it is perhaps neither necessary nor possible for the politically ambitious, as such, to possess learning, knowledge, or the wise man's stance toward learning or knowledge, Socrates made them realize, in turn, that it is perhaps neither necessary nor possible *for them* to have a wise man, *like him*, as a teacher. After all, what on earth did a wise man, like Socrates, have to teach politically ambitious youths, like them, if learning, knowledge, or the wise man's stance toward learning or knowledge is unnecessary for and incompatible with engaging in political affairs? Not coincidentally, that was the force of the question which "someone" asked Socrates next, when the latter came with his entourage in tow to the bridle-maker's shop frequented by Euthydemos (IV.2.2). Was it on account of his association with some wise man or by his nature—still very much in the running after what Socrates had said to "aristocrats"—that Themistocles so surpassed the citizens that the city looked to him whenever it had need of a serious man? That "someone," whose name Xenophon keeps to himself, was not just anyone. Bad natures thought that, on account of their "wisdom," wealth, or nature, they were going to make good on their political ambitions; yet that "someone," who asked Socrates whether Themistocles so surpassed the other citizens by his nature, thought nothing of wealth, on one hand, and did not know what to think of nature or wisdom, on the other. And Euthydemos, because he was on guard lest he appear or be reputed to admire Socrates's wisdom, was no less loath to speak or to listen to Socrates than other bad natures (IV.2.3, IV.2.6, IV.2.8); yet that "someone," because he desired to learn, was eager to do both. That "someone," who asked Socrates the very same question that the latter's exhortatory speeches had only just led good natures and good natures alone to ask, who desired at the same time to learn how to make good on his political ambitions, had to be a good nature like Xenophon for both of these reasons. Thus, if it was to the need the politically ambitious have for teachers and not to the need they have for education that Socrates called attention next (IV.2.2–7), perhaps this had less to do, in the end, with the fact that to do otherwise, with Euthydemos, would have been worse than useless and more to do with the fact that good natures, after coming to see with their own eyes the problems with their expectations of what an education is or does, came to question Socrates's carefully cultivated image or reputation as teacher of the (use of the) kingly art (consider II.1.17, I.6.15). Perhaps in his long, roundabout way, that is, Socrates was now going to answer their question, now that it was, in fact, *their* question.

III

Socrates, as we saw, approached Euthydemos in such a way as to lead him to believe that he himself was the very teacher whom, his own exhortations would seem to say, the politically ambitious need, but was he? Or was his carefully cultivated image only part of an elaborate joke? The thought that Socrates was not being entirely serious or straightforward is even more inescapable for us, Xenophon's readers, than it was for good natures, watching with rapt attention as Socrates approached, in very different ways, one bad nature after another. There was, after all, a written and oral criticism of Socrates, mentioned by Xenophon earlier, according to which Socrates, with his protreptic (exhortatory) and elenctic (refutative) speeches, was particularly able to urge human beings (*anthropoi*) to virtue, yet insufficient to lead them all the way toward it (I.4.1). Now, to be sure, the moment Xenophon mentioned this extralegal criticism, he made as if to speak up in Socrates's defense. Xenophon, however, did not "wonder" at the criticism (contrast I.4.1 with I.1.1 as well as I.2.1). And instead of going straight to the source and contradicting what the critics themselves wrote or said of Socrates, Xenophon only addressed those who, having no firsthand knowledge of Socrates, based their judgment of him on what the critics, who did, wrote or said. Then, instead of contradicting at least their judgment of Socrates, Xenophon only asked them to test—or examine (consider I.5.1, I.7.1)—whether Socrates made his companions (*sunontes*) better. And he asked them to do so by considering not only Socrates's protreptic and elenctic speeches but also his speeches to his companions, in which he would "go through" something by himself, at which point he offered in his own writing three Socratic dialogues (I.4, I.6, II.1) and two Socratic monologues (I.5, I.7) for their consideration. In the course of doing so, however, Xenophon discreetly lowered the bar: from Socrates leading his companions all the way toward virtue to making them "better" (either more virtuous than they already somewhat were, in other words, or better in some other way, or perhaps both). Even if Socrates did not fail *that* test, would the critics be silenced? In the very speech through which he came closest to passing the test,[4] Socrates said that, whatever good things he may have taught his friends (I.2.3, I.2.8), he introduced them *to others* from whom they will be helped in some respect toward virtue (I.6.14, consider IV.4.5). Xenophon's defense of Socrates, if we can even call it that, thus left so much to be desired that it strengthened rather than weakened the position of the critics who wrote or said that Socrates was insufficient to lead human beings all the way toward virtue. More to the point, leading human beings all the way toward virtue is tantamount to teaching them virtue or making them virtuous. But Socrates was perhaps, by Xenophon's account, too, insufficient to do that. How for that matter could anyone be sufficient to teach human beings virtue, according to Xenophon, if indeed he understood virtue to be a matter of training or habit rather than learning (I.2.23, consider III.9.5)? So far from contradicting Xenophon's indications to the effect that neither he nor anyone else was a teacher of this, Socrates *never* claimed to teach *anyone* gentlemanship or virtue (I.2.2–3, I.2.7–8).[5] But why not, if indeed Socrates taught most eagerly of all whatever he knew of the things fitting for a gentleman to know (IV.7.1), unless he himself did not know what justice is? Does the fact that he was "always" examining the question (I.1.16, consider IV.8.4) mean, as Callias put it, that he—or he, too, along with Xenophon?—was "perplexed" or "at a loss" for an answer (*Symposium* 4.1)? However that may be, besides the fact that he never claimed to teach anyone what a good citizen or gentleman should know above all, Socrates "always" used to say that, while teachers of the arts are easy to come by, "there is no place" where teachers of justice can be found (IV.4.5–6).[6] But then, despite knowing full well that neither he nor anyone else was a teacher of virtue, Socrates approached Euthydemos in such a way as to lead him to believe that, with Socrates as his teacher, he would learn this from him! Was Socrates "pulling a bait-and-switch"? With that thought in mind, we come to the three exhortatory speeches over the course of which Socrates called Euthydemos's attention to the need the politically ambitious have for teachers (IV.2.2, IV.2.3–5, and IV.2.6–7).

The first of them (IV.2.2) was occasioned by the question, which "someone," almost certainly "someone" named Xenophon, once asked Socrates in the presence of Euthydemos, whether it was on account of his association with some wise man or by his nature that Themistocles so surpassed the citizens that the city looked to him whenever it had need of a serious man. Euthydemos imagined Socrates, in answer to this question, said that Themistocles was a great statesman on account of his association with some wise man—some wise man from whom he learned, as from a teacher, some art of politics or statesmanship. As a matter of fact, however, Socrates said nothing of the sort. For, on one hand, he avoided the subject of Themistocles, no doubt because Themistocles was "a serious man" (*spoudaios anēr*) by his nature (Thucydides, *History of the Peloponnesian War* I.137.3).[7] On the other hand, although Socrates was asked what made Themistocles "a serious man," or what made him—just as others are "serious" (*spoudaious*), or good, when it comes to the arts—"serious," or good, when it comes to the "work" or "deed" (*ergon*) of ruling the city, he avoided that subject too. Asked how Themistocles came to be a good ruler, Socrates replied that it would be foolish to believe that "human beings" (*anthropoi*) come to be rulers spontaneously. However, by denying that human beings come to be rulers spontaneously, which goes without saying anyway (III.9.10), Socrates did not deny that they come to be *good* rulers spontaneously (consider IV.2.3–5). Not only did Socrates decline to rule out the possibility that Themistocles was a great statesman by his nature, then, but he also declined to rule out the possibility that human beings generally become great statesmen spontaneously (consider *Cyropaedia* I.1.6, II.1.1–2, and III.1.38). That Socrates had not said what Euthydemos, to say nothing of other bad natures, imagined he had—that, again, "since teachers are needed for the lesser arts, surely skill in the greatest of the arts, that of governing a city, does not come automatically to men"[8]—was clear to good natures, like Xenophon, who perceived, in turn, that Socrates wanted "to move" Euthydemos rather than reveal his thought straightforwardly to him; to move him, specifically, toward learning politics or statesmanship from a teacher, as if politics or statesmanship were one of the arts. Not for the last time, by revealing his thought "with a view to" Euthydemos, Socrates simultaneously revealed his thought unstraightforwardly to Xenophon.

At least for the time being, however, if Euthydemos was moved by what Socrates had apparently said, he was not moved much. When Socrates returned to the bridle-maker's shop, the youth kept aloof and was on guard lest he be reputed to admire Socrates's wisdom (IV.2.3). For this reason, because Euthydemos was loath to be reputed to listen to Socrates, the latter, to catch the former's attention (compare IV.2.3 with IV.2.6), made him the butt of a joke. Euthydemos, Socrates said in the joke's first part, wanted to rule Athens on the grounds that he had fled, not only learning (anything from anyone), but also a reputation for having learned (anything from anyone); yet that, he said in the joke's second part, is no less ridiculous than if he wanted to do the medical work in Athens on the grounds that he had guarded against, not only learning (the medical art) from a doctor, but also a reputation for having learned the medical art (from a doctor) (IV.2.4–5). Two claims were apparently made here, each straining credulity. First of all, just as learning the medical art from a doctor *is* necessary for doing the medical work, learning some art of politics or statesmanship from a teacher *is* necessary for ruling. Second, just as learning the medical art from a doctor is *reputed to be* necessary for doing the medical work, learning some art of politics or statesmanship from a teacher is *reputed to be* necessary for ruling. However, notwithstanding the fact that Euthydemos, to say nothing of other bad natures, imagined that Socrates was seriously making the first claim, no good nature could fail to perceive that, whereas Socrates had spoken of medicine as an "art," which can be "learned," as such, even without a teacher, he had not spoken of ruling accordingly (compare IV.2.4 with IV.2.5). Nor could a good nature fail to perceive that Socrates had spoken of expert practitioners of medicine, or doctors, as "teachers" of medicine; yet he had spoken of (nonpracticing) experts or "knowers," in contradistinction to reputable (inexpert) practitioners of politics, or statesmen, as "teachers" of or, rather, about politics (compare IV.2.4 with IV.2.5). Xenophon, putting two and two together, would have perceived that ruling cannot be learned, according to Socrates, for ruling is not a work of art; and those who cannot teach (because they have not learned) as much do politics, while those who can (because they have) do not. That Pericles, who could not teach (because he had not learned) what law is (apart from brute force) (I.2.40–46), did politics, while Socrates, who could (consider I.2.34), did not (I.6.15) is a case in point. Now, as for the second claim, notwithstanding the fact that Euthydemos imagined that Socrates was seriously making it too, the fact of the matter was that only the joke's second part made the "men" (*andres*) gathered round him laugh. To such "men," there is nothing funny about wanting to rule without wanting, in addition, to learn or to be reputed to have learned some art of politics or statesmanship. Politics, unlike medicine, does not appear to them to be an art. And Xenophon would have perceived that this was only to be expected. For Socrates prefaced the joke by saying that guarding against a reputation for learning is "noble," and thus perfectly normal, preparation for engaging in political affairs (IV.2.3). Normally, to be sure, "those longing for the noble things" (III.1.1) either despised learning or paid it no mind (consider III.6). The Athenians in particular, because they were democrats, were so far from believing that (just as learning the medical art is necessary for doing the medical art) learning some art is necessary for ruling that Socrates was, they believed, a corruptor of the youth partly for teaching that it is (I.2.9, consider III.9.10). Socrates seriously thought that learning *both* is *and* is reputed to be incompatible with doing politics. The joke he made at Euthydemos's expense—to catch his attention rather than to reveal his thought straightforwardly to him—was, then, not entirely serious. That was the serious joke, however, which Xenophon managed to "get."

As for Euthydemos, who was in no position to "get" the joke, everything went pretty much according to plan. He was no longer so loath (consider IV.2.8) to (be reputed to) listen to Socrates. Another obstacle remained, however. For Euthydemos, who thought that he covered himself in a reputation for moderation by keeping silent, was still loath for this reason to speak to Socrates.[9] To put a stop to this, too, Socrates took a much softer tone with Euthydemos, as if to catch him with honey, now that he had already caught his attention with vinegar. Instead of ridiculing him for his stance toward learning, Socrates expressed general bewilderment at those who, for all their political ambition, do not prepare or take care (to obtain the capacity) to make good on them. Euthydemos, to say nothing of other bad natures, imagined that Socrates was merely repeating himself in all essentials.[10] But was he? Was he really just saying, what he had apparently said before, that there is some "art" of politics or statesmanship, which, like the medical art, human beings obtain by "learning" from "teachers" or "knowers" (IV.2.2–5)?

Socrates was not even apparently saying more than that there is some "capacity" to do political affairs well, which, like the capacity to ride a horse or play the flute well, we obtain by practicing, "trying to do," the work in question alongside "those reputed to be best (at doing it)." And good natures, like Xenophon, who did not let their imaginations get the better of them, would have perceived that Socrates was not even apparently saying more than this—that, rather than learn from "some wise man," such as Socrates, the politically ambitious should try to rule alongside a reputable statesman, such as Pericles—and, in addition, that he was only apparently saying even this much. To obtain the capacity to ride a horse, to play the flute, or to do anything else of that sort, Socrates said, it is all but sufficient to try to do the work in question alongside those reputed to be best at doing it; accordingly, those who have taken the trouble to obtain such capacities do, for the most part, do their work well (*oi katergazomenoi*). And yet that (unteachable: *Oeconomicus* 12.10) "care" (*epimelia*), which is all but sufficient to obtain such capacities, is not the least bit sufficient, Socrates said, to obtain the capacity to rule well; accordingly, hardly any of those who have taken the trouble to become great statesmen, only "some" of whom, he said, do not try or take care to do their work well (IV.2.6), do, in fact, do their work well (IV.2.7). That Socrates himself never tried to rule alongside a reputable statesman—that, in other words, he did not practice what he only apparently preached—does not therefore make him a hypocrite.

Socrates's three exhortatory speeches seemed to Euthydemos to mean that, since politics is and is reputed to be an art, "it is important for aspiring politicians to find eminent teachers."[11] Accordingly, they prepared Euthydemos to turn toward Socrates once the youth had been refuted by him, as if Socrates were the very teacher whom, he seemed to say, Euthydemos needed (compare, again, IV.2.40 with IV.2.6). In fact, however, they meant just the opposite of all this and more, indeed, much more. Over the course of the three exhortatory speeches, Socrates answered somewhat the same question put to him in Plato's *Meno* (70a1–4): is the capacity to engage in political affairs teachable (IV.2.3–5), or is it obtained by practice (IV.2.6–7), or does it come to human beings by nature (IV.2.2)? As he put it in his long, roundabout way, either the capacity to engage in political affairs comes to human beings by nature rather than by practice, which is not the least bit sufficient for obtaining the capacity to engage in political affairs, or it comes to human beings by teaching and learning, with which, however, the use of the capacity to engage in political affairs is not even compatible. Just as we thought, Socrates was "pulling a bait-and-switch." Neither he himself nor anyone else was a teacher of some art of politics or statesmanship. And the education of Euthydemos was for this reason a joke.

IV

Good natures, while thoughtfully listening to Socrates call a bad nature's attention to the need the politically ambitious have for teachers, had the question of Socrates as teacher answered now that it was, in fact, *their* question. To them, Socrates's three exhortatory speeches meant that, since politics is neither an art, like medicine, nor even a practice, like horsemanship, "it is important for aspiring politicians to find eminent," or at least adequate, "teachers" of this truth, which is as much as to say, it is important for them to have a wise man, like Socrates, as a teacher of this truth. Good natures were fully prepared to listen thoughtfully to Socrates jokingly arouse the desire for knowledge of Euthydemos only after thoughtfully listening to Socrates jokingly arouse the desire for knowledge of "aristocrats" and "oligarchs" partly for this reason, partly for another.

In the first place, the former exhortatory speeches answered the question raised by the latter ones. And Socrates, approaching good natures according to nature and correctly, did not answer questions—not even in his long, roundabout way—unless, already gripped by the questions, they already desired the answers (consider III.9.11–13). In the second place, however, even as the three exhortatory speeches answered the question raised by what Socrates had said to "aristocrats" and to "oligarchs," the question of Socrates as teacher, what Socrates had said to "aristocrats" and to "oligarchs" answered, also in his long, roundabout way, a question raised by the three exhortatory speeches. Granted, after all, that Socrates seriously thought that, since learning, knowledge, or the wise man's stance toward learning or knowledge is unnecessary for and incompatible with doing politics, a wise man, like him, had to teach the politically ambitious this truth, on what basis did he think that this was indeed the truth? To this question, the exhortatory speeches that Socrates made to Euthydemos gave no answer. And yet, according to the exhortatory speeches that Socrates made to other bad natures, because justice and piety or, in a word, "moderation" consists in obedience to the laws (notwithstanding ignorance of how beneficial or knowledge of how harmful obedience to the laws may be), human beings become "moderate" if and only if they have been habituated, like horses or dogs, by the gods. That was of course the very same, highly questionable, and even dangerous answer (consider Plato, *Apology* 18b3) that Socrates gave to the question put to him in Plato's *Meno*: virtue, if not the capacity to engage in political affairs, comes to human beings by divine lot, without intellect or mind (*Meno*, 99e4–100b4, 99d1–5). But for Socrates and Xenophon (IV.3.1, I.2.15–17) as well as for Euthydemos and good natures, who hoped to rule with justice (IV.2.11, IV.2.23) or nobly (IV.1.2), "moderation" or virtue is apparently the end for the sake of which the naturally occurring capacity to engage in political affairs should be used. And the use of the capacity to engage in political affairs cannot possibly be any more rational than virtue itself. If, in other words, gentlemanship or good citizenship is the core of great statesmanship, or the whole of which great statesmanship forms a part, the rationality or irrationality of the whole has some bearing on the rationality of the part. And that means, for those who desired one, an answer to the question raised by the three exhortatory speeches that Socrates made to Euthydemos was theirs for the taking. All they had to do was remember Socrates jokingly arousing the desire for knowledge of other bad natures.

The protreptic teaching is at an end. What happened next, the refutation of Euthydemos and the lead-up to the refutation, happened in private, away from prying eyes (IV.2.8ff.). Enough has been said about how the second part of the protreptic teaching would have affected Euthydemos. All by itself, that teaching was not sufficient to turn Euthydemos from books toward teachers in general, Socrates in particular. That teaching did its job only after the Socratic refutation made Euthydemos realize that he had not really obtained the best education for making good on his political ambitions. Only then did Euthydemos turn from books toward Socrates. But how would the whole protreptic teaching—both the exhortatory speeches that Socrates made to Euthydemos and the ones that Socrates made to other bad natures—affect good natures? According to the protreptic teaching, Socrates was quite possibly a teacher of the truth that, because learning, knowledge, or the wise man's stance toward learning or knowledge is unnecessary for and incompatible with political or vulgar virtue, learning, knowledge, or the wise man's stance toward learning or knowledge is unnecessary for and incompatible with doing politics. In that case, if Socrates refuted good natures much as he refuted Euthydemos, the protreptic teaching would *not* have prepared them to turn toward him in the belief that, with Socrates as their teacher, they would learn from him what they had learned they did not know, as a result of the refutation. The protreptic teaching would have prepared good natures, in that case, to learn from the refutation that they did not know, or could not learn, what they believed they knew, up until Socrates refuted them. If only Socrates refuted good natures about the just, in other words, the protreptic teaching would have prepared good natures to realize that the refutation, the elenctic or "negative" teaching of Socrates, so far from being just another propaedeutic to the "positive" teaching,[12] was nothing less than (the basis of) the Socratic teaching itself. But did Socrates refute good natures? Xenophon tells us that, much as Socrates refuted Euthydemos, he refuted others, many of whom—the more slack, he thought—no longer approached him after the fact (IV.2.40, consider I.2.47). We saw that good natures were confused about the object of their desire. It only remains to be seen whether, in their confusion, they were in the same boat as Euthydemos. If they were, much the same refutation that Socrates brought to bear against Euthydemos would have to be brought to bear against good natures too.[13]

V

Socrates could not possibly teach Euthydemos, even assuming that he was a teacher about, if not of, what a good citizen or gentleman should know above all, if Euthydemos had little or no desire to learn, much less a desire not to. And just how favorable was Euthydemos's stance toward learning really? Although Socrates understood the "education" to which he exhorted bad natures as "learning" or "knowledge" rather than "wisdom" (IV.1.3–5, consider IV.2.2–7), Euthydemos understood the "education" he thought he had already obtained as "wisdom"—or "virtue" (IV.2.9)—rather than "learning" or "knowledge" (IV.2.1).[14] And to this observation, which was already made in passing before, we may now add the further one that, although good natures were distinguished in Socrates's eyes not least by their desire for "learning" rather than "wisdom" (IV.1.2), Euthydemos—Xenophon and Socrates both suggest—was distinguished by his love of "wisdom" rather than "learning" (IV.2.1, IV.2.9, IV.2.23, consider IV.2.3). Enough light has been shed already on how that "learning" which Socrates thought so much of differs from that "wisdom" which Euthydemos was proud of that we are not surprised to find that they differ so much, according to Xenophon's indications, that Euthydemos, in his "wisdom," fled and was on guard against "learning." Euthydemos fled and was on guard against "learning," not only the arts and sciences (IV.2.22, IV.2.10, IV.3.3), but also any and all subjects on account of which it is possible to manage a household and a city nobly (IV.2.3–5). But then, precisely assuming that he was a teacher about, if not of, what a good citizen or gentleman should know above all,

Socrates would teach Euthydemos despite knowing full well that Euthydemos had, at best, little or no desire to learn! Was Socrates "casting his pearls before swine"?

At the outset, when Socrates made protreptic speeches of that sort which seemed (to bad natures) to say that, since politics is an art, "it is important for aspiring politicians to find eminent teachers,"[15] Euthydemos only listened (IV.2.8). Eventually, however, Socrates went by himself to the bridle-maker's shop and, alone with Euthydemos, struck up a conversation with the youth. Having heard that Euthydemos had already collected many books of men reputed to be wise, and also having seen that Euthydemos thought himself to be so wise on this account as to be bound to make good on his political ambitions (IV.2.1–7), Socrates asked the youth whether what he had heard of him was true. Was he collecting the books of men reputed to be wise? Euthydemos replied that, not only had he already collected many such books, but he was still collecting them, and he would continue to collect them, until he owned as many as possible. Swearing, like a woman, "by Hera,"[16] Socrates expressed admiration for the youth's, so to speak, "philosophizing" or "philosophy" (compare IV.2.9 and IV.2.23 with III.11.16–18). Euthydemos, Socrates said, would rather own treasures of wisdom than treasures of silver and gold because clearly, whereas the youth did not believe that silver and gold make human beings better, he believed that the (written) thoughts (*gnōmas*) of wise men make their owners rich in virtue. If, however, Prodicus the wise is any indication, the thoughts (*gnōmas*) of wise men—their hidden thoughts (*Symposium* 3.6: *tas huponoias*)—are not the same thing as their written words (compare *Memorabilia* II.2.34 with II.2.21). And the fact that Euthydemos was willing and able to spend "treasures of silver and gold" on "treasures of wisdom," something to which Socrates draws our attention here, reminds us that books do not come cheap. In order to own as many as possible, did Euthydemos not require as much wealth as possible (consider IV.2.36–39)? However that may be, Euthydemos was gratified to hear this praise, which led him to believe that, according to Socrates, by collecting the books of men reputed to be wise, he was pursuing wisdom correctly.

By praising Euthydemos for collecting by himself the books of men *reputed* to be wise (IV.2.8, consider IV.2.1), just as if *they* were "treasures," which make their *owners* rich in virtue (IV.2.9), Socrates already revealed to us that the youth was not pursuing wisdom correctly. "Xenophon implicitly reminds us here of the Antiphon passage, where," very roughly speaking, "Socrates reported that his erotic intercourse with his associates involved picking out the treasures (*thesauroi*) from the books of the wise men of the past."[17] As that passage would have it, however, Socrates and his good friends *read*—together, *not* by themselves (contrast IV.2.2–7)—the books of wise men who were *not* necessarily reputed to be wise. And they did so for the sake of the "treasures" their authors left behind *in* them (I.6.14). Was, then, what Xenophon praised Socrates for doing not almost totally and completely at odds with what Socrates praised Euthydemos for doing?[18] And do the deeds of Socrates not give the lie to his speech (consider *Symposium* 4.27; *Oeconomicus* 6.12, 11.6–7)? According to Socrates, because Euthydemos was collecting some books just as if they were "treasures," the youth required considerable wealth,[19] and because he was doing so without any inkling of the "treasures" their authors may have left behind in them, the youth was forced to bow to the authority of generally accepted opinions about the wisdom of their authors. According to Xenophon, however, because Socrates was reading other books for the sake of the "treasures" their authors left behind in them, he was free to make up his own mind about the wisdom of their authors (consider II.1.21, *Symposium* 4.62), and because he was not laboring under the delusion that they were "treasures," too, he did not require any wealth of his own (consider *Oeconomicus* 1.14, II.8). Euthydemos, who believed that the written thoughts of wise men make their owners rich in virtue, believed that wealth is necessary, if not sufficient, to make human beings better; yet Socrates, whose total net worth was only about five mina (*Oeconomicus* 2.3; consider Plato, *Apology* 38b1–5), could not have disagreed more (I.6.1–10, *Oeconomicus* 11.3–6). And, also, Euthydemos bowed to the authority of generally accepted opinions about the wisdom of this or that author; yet Socrates, who made up his own mind about which natures were good, which authors were wise, and which natures or authors were merely reputed to be good or wise, did not (contrast IV.1.2 with IV.1.3–4; I.2.56, consider II.1.21 and *Symposium* 4.62). Euthydemos needed to follow conventions; Socrates did not.

That Euthydemos was not pursuing wisdom correctly according to Socrates—that Socrates's praise of Euthydemos was only "flattery" or a joke, which Euthydemos was in no position to "get"—is obvious enough.[20] But how, by what means, Euthydemos was pursuing wisdom was inevitably determined by what he understood wisdom to be. And it is no less obvious that his understanding of wisdom was confused. Earlier, Socrates had praised Euthydemos for believing that the written thoughts of wise men make their owners rich in virtue and consequently, Xenophon said, Euthydemos had been led to believe that he was pursuing wisdom correctly according to Socrates. But virtue is not necessarily wisdom (consider I.6.12)—what Socrates had said to "aristocrats" and to "oligarchs" makes this abundantly clear—and Socrates had spoken only of virtue. Such virtue was, if not necessarily wisdom, necessarily not knowledge. After all, besides the fact clear as day to all but the least perceptive that his stance toward learning was not favorable, Euthydemos was collecting the books of men reputed to be wise just as if they were "treasures," without any inkling of the "treasures" their authors may have left behind in them. That means, just as Xenophon understood virtue or everything noble and good to be a matter of training or habit rather than learning (I.2.23, consider III.9.5), Socrates understood virtue or the virtue Euthydemos was after (IV.2.23) to be one thing, knowledge another. If Xenophon understood wisdom to be nothing but knowledge, too, just as Socrates evidently did (IV.6.7), then Xenophon's suggestion would have to be this: Socrates and his good friends distinguished between wisdom and virtue, whereas Euthydemos, failing to do so, understood wisdom to be, not (only) knowledge, but (also) a virtue. Socrates all but suggested as much himself. For, after flattering Euthydemos, Socrates asked him what he wanted to become good at by collecting the books of men reputed to be wise. As if the question had never even crossed his mind, however, Euthydemos did not have an answer ready to hand. So Socrates asked him whether he wanted to become a doctor, an architect, a geometer, an astronomer, or a rhapsode, because of course the youth did not want to learn any of *these* arts (contrast IV.7.9, III.8.8–10, IV.7.3, IV.7.5, I.2.56ff.) and a moment's reflection on the difference between those who do, on one hand, and Euthydemos, on the other, leaves no doubt that the youth did not really want to learn *any* art. Those who want to learn an art—from artisans (knowers) of the sort they themselves want to become or, alternatively, from their books (compare IV.2.10 with IV.2.5)—are able, if asked, to say what they want to learn. They are well aware of their ignorance of something, which they feel the need to know. Not so Euthydemos. Although he was collecting the books of men reputed to be wise, or because he was merely collecting them, Euthydemos did not really want to learn anything from them. And therefore, last but not least, Socrates asked Euthydemos whether he wanted to become good, not (only) at an art, but (also) at a virtue: "that virtue," namely, "on account of which human beings become skilled politicians (possessors of the art of politics or statesmanship), and skilled household managers (possessors of the art of economics or household management), and able to rule, and beneficial to other human beings and to themselves" (IV.2.11). Euthydemos answered that he did want this virtue, very much so; and yet, since on account of possessing this virtue, human beings apparently come to possess, in addition to the virtue itself, the political and the economic arts or art, Socrates rejoined that what the youth wanted to become good at was in fact *both* the noblest virtue, the virtue of kings, *and* the greatest art, the "so-called" kingly art.[21] Euthydemos was confused. Was the object of his desire (only) an art, learning, knowledge, or wisdom so understood? Or rather, although he was collecting the books of men reputed to be wise or, again, because he was merely collecting them, was it (also) a virtue? Euthydemos did not distinguish between "these (two) things" (IV.2.11), which means, if Socrates understood wisdom to be nothing but knowledge, then Euthydemos, according to Socrates, did not really desire wisdom. Socrates was "casting his pearls before swine," just as we thought. Euthydemos did not really desire learning or knowledge. And the education of him was for this reason, too, a joke.

VI

In this, his stance toward learning or knowledge, Euthydemos was by no means alone. The other bad natures Xenophon saw fit to mention were, like him, not a little politically ambitious. Euthydemos understood his own good to be bound up with the good of others (IV.2.11, IV.2.23, IV.2.36) and so did they. For those who thought they were by nature good desired to be best themselves and most beneficial to others (IV.1.4). And those who were proud of their wealth, albeit not so noble-minded, desired to be advantageous to themselves and well reputed by others (IV.1.5)—others to whom they were beneficial (consider III.6.3, II.1.28). Of course, in desiring to be good for themselves and others, neither desired learning or knowledge, which those who were reputed to be by nature good despised and those who were proud of their wealth supposed they did not need. And what they understood the object of their desire (not) to be inevitably determined how, by what means, they pursued it. To make good on their political ambitions, the former bowed to the authority of generally accepted opinions about their natures; the latter required, they thought, only wealth. In other words, since to be good did not seem to these bad natures to be a matter of learning, the roads they took to become good were paved with conventions. And Euthydemos was, at bottom, no different. Since he was pursuing, not (only) the "so-called" kingly art, but (also) the virtue of kings, he required only wealth and the authority of generally accepted opinions, which guided him in spending his wealth, to become good. Little or no thought was needed for such an education or wisdom. Bad natures, to be good for themselves and others, followed conventions; they were mere listeners, who did not feel the need to think for themselves, not contradictors.

As for good natures, they desired all subjects of learning on account of which it is possible to manage a household and a city nobly (IV.2.11). And yet Euthydemos, Socrates said, wanted that virtue on account of which human beings come to possess the political and the economic arts or art (IV.1.2). Although knowledge came before virtue for good natures, while virtue came before knowledge for Euthydemos, neither the former nor the latter distinguished between "these (two) things."[22] Good natures were, to begin with, confused about the object of their desire: yet again, the knowledge they desired was, with respect to its end (noble management of a household and a city), not exactly genuine knowledge. Even if they were in the same boat as Euthydemos, however, good natures were at the bow, Euthydemos at the stern. Because knowledge came before virtue for good natures, while virtue came before knowledge for Euthydemos, they pursued "these (two) things" very differently. Good natures, to make good on their political ambitions, did not bow to the authority of generally accepted opinions about their own natures, for example, or about the wisdom of others. Nor did they require any wealth. For them, since they were pursuing, not (only) the virtue of kings, but (also) the "so-called" kingly art, following conventions was almost entirely out of the question; they were contradictors, who felt the need to think for themselves, not mere listeners.

The stance of Euthydemos toward learning or knowledge is the stance of our nature, in its lack of learning or knowledge, toward learning or knowledge: the stance not only of bad natures, if especially of them, but even, at the end of the day, of good ones. All of us have, at best, little or no desire to know to begin with.

VII

Having said all that, what sense does it make to say that Socrates was *both* "pulling a bait-and-switch" *and* "casting his pearls before swine"? If Socrates was "pulling a bait-and-switch," then Euthydemos had some desire to learn and Socrates was no teacher. On the other hand, if Socrates was "casting his pearls before swine," then Socrates was a teacher and Euthydemos had, at best, little or no desire to learn. Either Socrates had no education to give Euthydemos, who (as a result of Socrates's protreptic and elenctic speeches) had some desire to receive one from him, or Euthydemos had, at best, little or no desire to receive an education from Socrates, who had one to give him; yet we said both at once. And this makes no sense, of course, unless Socrates was (in one sense) and (in another sense) was not able to teach, and Euthydemos was (in one sense) and (in another sense) was not willing to learn. But precisely that—that Socrates was able to teach what Euthydemos was not willing to learn and was not able to teach what Euthydemos was willing to learn—does, in retrospect, make sense. For on account of the difference between the truth and generally accepted opinions, the state reached by those good natures who receive an education is not exactly the state they desire to reach prior to receiving an education. And, when it comes to those bad natures who are not educable, the difference between what an education is or does, on one hand, and their expectations of what an education is or does, on the other, proves to be too great. What Socrates could teach about justice, Euthydemos would not learn. And what Euthydemos would learn, Socrates could not teach.

That gulf between the truth and generally accepted opinions makes sense not only of how Socrates could both "pull a bait-and-switch" and "cast his pearls before swine," in all seriousness, but also of why he would jokingly do just the opposite of this and jokingly educate Euthydemos. Disaster struck the Socrates of Aristophanes's *Clouds* because of his ignorance of just this, the unbridgeable gulf separating the wise man from foolish or naïve human beings. The Socrates of the *Clouds*, knowing neither himself nor others, made a go at the truth with a student, Strepsiades, whose nature ensured that it would not be safe for either of them to do so. Strepsiades bore a grudge against Socrates for not teaching what he would learn and Socrates, in turn, lost his temper with Strepsiades for not learning what he could teach. By contrast, Xenophon—who, in his *Memorabilia*, or his *Grudge-Bearing*, as he indicates the title should really be translated (I.2.31), takes the place of Strepsiades in the *Clouds* (compare I.3.11, I.3.13 with Aristophanes, *Clouds* 68, 398)—only jokingly bore a grudge against Socrates for not teaching him virtue, and Socrates, in turn, only jokingly lost his temper with Xenophon for not learning virtue from him (I.3.8–13, II.1.30). For Xenophon's Socrates, as we saw, the difference between the truth and generally accepted opinions was not so much a recipe for disaster as an opportunity for "inside jokes" among lifelong, good friends or good friends in the making. Disaster was all but averted because, rather than make a go at the truth with bad natures in a hopelessly misguided attempt to bridge the unbridgeable gulf separating them, Xenophon's Socrates, knowing himself and others, concealed that gulf as much as possible by means of Odyssean speech or rhetoric. But a concern with safety was just one of the reasons why Socrates would not be entirely serious or straightforward with Euthydemos about the gulf separating them. The other reason, which, as we saw, goes together with the first, was his desire to educate good natures or to make new, good friends—to whom he would simultaneously reveal that he was not being entirely serious or straightforward with Euthydemos, among others, without "force feeding" them the truth about what a good citizen or gentleman should know above all. That Socrates took this long, roundabout way to the education of good natures was, again, according to nature and correct. To do otherwise would only repulse them.

To say that Socrates was, in all seriousness, both "pulling a bait-and-switch" and "casting his pearls before swine" is as much as to say somewhat more precisely that there was, according to him, a difference between the truth and generally accepted opinions or between education strictly and loosely speaking. Likewise, to say that Socrates was doing just the opposite of this and jokingly educating Euthydemos is as much as to say somewhat less precisely that telling the truth in the simplest and clearest manner was, according to him, neither safe nor the shortest and straightest way to the education of good natures. But then, at least on these last points, we have only—or almost only—been repeating ourselves more or less precisely on the basis of new evidence. And the new evidence, however much more plausible it may make them, still leaves at least one too many questions unanswered. First and foremost, what is the truth? Or what is the truth (about justice) as distinguished from generally accepted opinions? The most we can say for now is that the difference between the truth and generally accepted opinions may have something to do with this: whereas Socrates and his good friends knew that they were "perplexed," "at a loss," or ignorant of justice, which they distinguished from knowledge, bad natures and even, to begin with, good ones did not know that they were ignorant of justice, which they understood to be, not (only) knowledge, but (also) something else—namely, dogged obedience. As a result of Socrates's refutation of him, Euthydemos was left, at least for the moment, at least somewhat "perplexed" or "at a loss" as to what a good citizen or gentleman should know above all. And by reading Socrates's refutation of Euthydemos we, too, can come to know something of the lasting, complete ignorance of Socrates and his good friends.

PART TWO

CHAPTER 3

Justice and the Weakness of Writing

I

As readers of Socrates's refutation of Euthydemos, we are not in the same situation as Euthydemos, who was refuted by Socrates. In fact, insofar as we are reading a book rather than having a teacher refute us, are we not at a severe disadvantage? For even reading books, Socrates suggested, is no substitute for having teachers when it comes to an education in or to gentlemanship, the whole of which great statesmanship forms a part. Now that would not wash, it should go without saying, if there really were some art of politics or statesmanship, which is no less teachable and learnable than the medical art, for example. Nor would that wash even if politics really were some capacity which, like the capacity to ride a horse, we obtain by practice. There are, after all, many books written by doctors, the reading of which, no less than an adequate teacher, could make someone into a knower of the medical art (compare IV.2.5 with IV.2.10). Xenophon himself wrote a book by means of which, he said, he wished to shed light on horsemanship (compare IV.2.6 with *On Horsemanship* 1.1). And yet, however absurd it may be to say *both* that reading books is no substitute for having teachers, when it comes to an education in or to gentlemanship, *and* that politics or statesmanship is some art, or even some practice, the fact remains that Socrates only apparently said the latter. In reality, he said just the opposite. If, then, reading books is no substitute for having teachers when it comes to an education in or to gentlemanship, perhaps this is because learning about gentlemanship, which is not to be confused with learning gentlemanship, differs from learning an art. After all, whereas those who want to learn an art are well aware of their ignorance of something, something which they feel the need to know, bad natures and even, to begin with, good ones believe they know already what a good citizen or gentleman should know above all (IV.2.21, IV.2.36; IV.2.12, IV.2.31). And, for those who want to learn an art, reading books by knowers of the sort they themselves want to become is surely not much or any worse than having an artisan of that sort become their teacher. But can the same be said for those who, because they believe they know already what a good citizen or gentleman should know above all, do not yet desire to know the truth about gentlemanship?

More than once perhaps, Euthydemos had read the words written on the temple of Apollo at Delphi, "Know yourself." And, although he had learned, as a result of his reading, that this was written there, like a rhapsode (IV.2.10), he had not learned who or what he was (for and able to be for). Euthydemos had not attempted, as a result of his reading, to examine himself and he had not attempted to do so because, as he put it, this was something he believed he knew already (IV.2.24, consider IV.2.36; *Cyropaedia* VII.2.20–21). Writing, even the writing on the temple of Apollo at Delphi, is scarcely able to lead readers toward such knowledge as they believe they have already, much less give such knowledge to them. By means of speech, however, Socrates could do at least for the moment, at least somewhat what Apollo or the temple of the god at Delphi could not do by means of writing. At any rate, by refuting his opinions about justice, Socrates could give Euthydemos cause to pause and ask himself whether he knew himself (compare IV.2.24 with IV.2.21–23, IV.2.30, and IV.2.39). What Socrates said, when he suggested that having teachers is better than reading books, was borne out by what he did. For although Socrates always conversed, he never wrote anything. And the fact that Socrates, by means of speech, succeeded where Apollo or the lapidary writing on the temple of the god at Delphi failed suggests that he never wrote anything at least partly because writing pales in comparison to speaking as a means of teaching those who believe they know what they do not know the truth, namely, that they do not know what they believe they know.

Xenophon makes it hard to overlook the fact that, as compared with Socrates, Apollo was a very inadequate teacher of self-knowledge. And perhaps the fact that he taught self-knowledge only very inadequately follows from the fact that his understanding of self-knowledge was very inadequate too. To know oneself is, Socrates says, to know and to do what one (can and) should do (IV.2.25–26). And so, if only Apollo and Socrates were on the same page to this extent, it would come as no surprise that Apollo—whose "know yourself" neither showed readers how to begin examining themselves (consider IV.2.30) nor, for that matter, made them feel the need to do so—taught "self-knowledge" by exhortation alone, as if it were not much or any more difficult to obtain (given the will to do so) than knowledge of one's name (IV.2.25). For Apollo would tell those who asked what they should do, or what they should do in order to please the gods, that they should obey the laws (I.3.1, IV.3.16). And to know the laws it is enough to be told what they are (I.2.41–42). No less than to know one's name, to know the laws it is enough merely to listen or—since laws, like names (IV.4.7), are written (I.2.42; IV.4.13, IV.4.19)—to read them and, having done that, to remember them.[1] Little or no thought is needed to "know yourself" (to be under the divine or divinely sanctioned laws) or to do what you should according to Apollo. Only, or especially, the dogged will to do as you are told is needed. For this reason also, just as he did not feel the need to refute others (in order to teach them that they do not know what they believe they know about what they should do), Apollo did not let others refute him (in order to learn from him that they should do what he told them to do). Apollo, gentleman that he was, did not take kindly to those—like Socrates, perhaps (*Apology* 15)—who questioned his authority (*Cyropaedia* VII.2.15–17). But it would then come as a surprise and even as something of a shock if what Socrates taught was no different from what Apollo taught, considering how differently they taught. For why in the world would Socrates feel the need to teach the laws by contradicting the generally accepted opinions of others about justice especially, on one hand, and by setting others up to contradict his own (rhetorical recapitulations of) generally accepted opinions, on the other? Unless he was teaching just the opposite—that the laws are not truly just, notwithstanding the authority of Apollo and generally accepted opinions—the form of the teaching is hard to square with its content.[2] Alcibiades, while still a companion of Socrates, had asked Pericles the question "what is law?" and then, after refuting his adoptive father's answers one by one, had brought him to the brink of concluding that law is nothing but brute force. And, it is true, the question (consider I.1.16), the refutation (consider IV.2.11ff.), and perhaps even the answer (I.2.34) bore the mark of Socrates (I.2.40–46, consider I.2.47). But, whether this really was what Socrates taught good natures, we will just have to wait and see from the refutation itself.

II

The refutation was preceded by a brief back-and-forth between Socrates and Euthydemos, which began when Socrates asked the youth if, in his opinion, it is possible to become good at the virtue of kings and the "so-called" kingly art, both of "these (two) things," without justice. Euthydemos answered that, without justice, it is impossible even to become a good citizen, much less a great statesman, at which point Socrates asked him if he himself had done the work of becoming just (*su de touto kateirgasai*). Then, when the youth answered that by and large he had, Socrates asked him if the just can "explain"—or, insofar as to know something is to be able to explain what it is (IV.6.1, I.2.52), if they know—their works or deeds, just as carpenters can "display" or "point out" theirs, and Euthydemos answered somewhat indignantly that of course he, for his part, can "explain" not only the works or deeds of justice but also, he added, those of injustice, "since not a few of the latter can be seen and heard every day." Euthydemos was confident both in his justice and in his ability to display or explain the works or deeds of justice and injustice; yet he was, Xenophon makes clear, somewhat less confident in the former than he was in the latter. In his opinion, knowing what they should do is easy enough for the just; the hard part is doing what they know they should do (consider IV.2.19). And, at the same time as we get some indication that in Euthydemos's opinion justice was not (only) a matter of speaking, explaining, or knowing but (also) doing, we get some indication of the source of this generally accepted opinion (consider IV.4.10–11) of his. For the just, Socrates suggested, cannot "explain" their works any more than carpenters can "display" theirs. But of course, although carpenters are able to "display" their works, only architects—to whom Socrates called our attention just a moment ago (IV.2.10)—are, properly speaking, able to "explain" them. Carpenters can "display" a house built to an architect's exact specifications; unless they are architects themselves, however, they do not have the ability to "explain" whether a house built to an architect's exact specifications (or not) is good or bad. And so, by likening the just to carpenters, Socrates suggested of them that, although they can "display" or "point out" a work or deed done to Apollo's exact specifications—that is, in obedience to the laws—they do not have the ability to "explain" whether a work or deed done in obedience (or disobedience) to the laws is good or bad. Indeed, however confident Euthydemos may have been in his ability to "explain" both the works of justice and injustice, if his answer to Socrates's question is any indication, he understood by to "explain" nothing more than to "display," which confirms that the just do not have "architectonic" knowledge of their works or deeds. So far as Euthydemos was concerned, no (further) explanation was possible or necessary. But, then, Socrates's question suggested and Euthydemos's answer confirmed in advance Aristotle's great "discovery" that the just do not know *why* they should do *what* they have been told they should do.[3] Injustice is good, for all they know, and justice bad. And does the youth's generally accepted opinion that justice is not (only) a matter of speaking, explaining, or knowing but (also) of doing not have its source, to put two and two together, in just this: his no less generally accepted opinion that justice is not necessarily good, injustice not necessarily bad? Ignorance, according to generally accepted opinions, bears little or no blame for the many unjust works or deeds seen and heard every day. The laws—everything the (ruling part of the) city writes about what should and should not be done (I.2.42; IV.4.13, IV.4.19), if not the answers to questions like "What is law?"—are easy enough to know (consider I.2.41–42). So the blame for the many unjust works or deeds falls rather squarely on the shoulders of those who give in to the temptation to do good (not just) works or deeds for themselves—in spite of the fact that they, so to speak, "know better" (consider IV.2.19). By the same token, whereas the unjust give in to temptation, according to generally accepted opinions, the just do just (not good) works or deeds, however hard they may be to do (II.1.20). More than that, justice is the whole of which great statesmanship forms a part. If, then, the generally accepted opinion that justice is not necessarily good and injustice not necessarily bad is the source of the generally accepted opinion that justice is not (only) a matter of speaking, explaining, or knowing but (also) of doing, the fact that, for politically ambitious bad natures, virtue comes before—or, for good ones, with—art has its source, in turn, in their opinion that justice is not necessarily good and injustice not necessarily bad.[4] Now this, the complex relation between the just and the good, proves to be the heart and soul of the refutation of Euthydemos. And the brief back-and-forth preceding the refutation goes to show, therefore, just how much is at stake in the refutation itself. Should it turn out that Euthydemos's confidence in his ability to "display" or "point out" the works or deeds of justice and injustice was not well-founded, owing to his inability to "explain" whether the former are good and the latter bad, then his confusion about the object of his desire—was it (only) an art or (also) a virtue?—would come down, in the end, to confusion about justice: was justice (only) good or (also) not?

When Euthydemos said that he could explain or display the works or deeds of justice and injustice, Socrates proposed that "we" write under the heading *J* whatever is, in "our" opinion, a work or deed of justice and under the heading *I* whatever is, in "our" opinion, a work or deed of injustice. Euthydemos, vouchsafing to the proposal, believed he knew that lying, deceiving, evildoing, and enslaving were unjust works or deeds; not only that, he also felt that it would be "terrible" if any of these works or deeds were to be just (IV.2.13–15). But then, after writing out the youth's opinion accordingly, Socrates asked

Euthydemos a series of questions, in response to which Euthydemos found himself contradicting necessary consequences of his opinion and, consequently, his opinion itself. Would it be unjust, Socrates asked him, if a general were to enslave an unjust enemy city? Or if he were to deceive them? And what if, while at war, he were to steal from them or rob them of their belongings? Forced to choose between the opinion that enslaving, deceiving, and stealing or robbing are unjust deeds, an opinion whose necessary consequences he could not bring himself to accept, and another opinion, whose necessary consequences he apparently did accept, Euthydemos opted for the latter. Enslaving, deceiving, and stealing or robbing are unjust deeds, he said, only on the condition that they are done to friends, meaning fellow citizens or allies (I.3.3, *Hiero* 11.15, *Cyropaedia* II.2.15). As long as such things are done to enemies—Socrates silently drops the requirement that they be "unjust" enemies (contrast IV.2.16 with IV.2.15)—they are just deeds. The moment "their" opinion changed, so did "their" writing. From under the heading *I*, that is, Socrates erased enslaving, deceiving, and stealing from or robbing enemies, then wrote them in under the heading *J*, leaving behind under the heading *I* only lying to, deceiving, stealing from or robbing, and enslaving friends. Only with friends, according to the youth's new and improved opinion, is it just to be as straightforward as possible (IV.2.15–17).

Socrates pressed on. To the opinion left behind from the first round of questioning, he devoted a round of questioning of its own. Would it be unjust, he asked Euthydemos, if a general were to lie to and deceive his army when they are "depressed," both for his own and for his army's safety? Or if a father were to lie to and deceive his son when the youth will not take his medicine, for his son's own good? And what if someone were to steal a depressed friend's sword or rob him of it—or, for that matter, any of his belongings, which he was not in a position to use well—lest he destroy himself with it? Once again, forced to choose between the opinion that lying to, deceiving, stealing from or robbing, and enslaving friends are unjust deeds, an opinion whose necessary consequences he could not bring himself to accept (because they were bad), and another opinion, whose necessary consequences he apparently did accept (because they were good), Euthydemos opted for the latter. Lying to, deceiving, and stealing from or robbing friends are just deeds, he said, on the condition that they are done for their good (consider II.4.6). And, once again, from under the heading *I*, Socrates erased lying to, deceiving, stealing from or robbing, and enslaving friends (for their good), then wrote them in under the heading *J*, leaving behind under the heading *I* only the harming of friends. Even with friends, according to the youth's still newer, still more improved opinion, it is just not to be entirely straightforward all the time (IV.2.17–18).

In summarizing the results of the first round of questioning (IV.2.16), Socrates had said that enslaving, deceiving, and stealing or robbing are just deeds as long as they are done to enemies. The requirement that they be "unjust" enemies was silently dropped. And this, together with his summary of the results of the second round of questioning (IV.2.18), made it clear that works or deeds are just, according to Euthydemos, insofar as they are beneficial to or good for friends, harmful to or bad for enemies.[5] But that means, when there is no common good between Athens and another city, the other city would not be "unjust" for harming Athens (in order to benefit itself). More to the purpose, Athens or an Athenian general would not be "unjust" for harming the other city (in order to benefit Athens). In harming one another, both of them would be just. And, however depressing it may seem to be to say that justice means harming the just (enemies) (II.6.17–18ff.), to say otherwise—that it would be just for someone to benefit another city and harm his own, when there is no common good between them—is, among other things, no longer to speak the language of the good citizen. And so here on the verge of the third and final round of questioning we have justice according to good citizens as such, always and everywhere. But if, when there is no common good between one city and another, it would be just for either one of them to harm the other (in order to benefit itself), then, when there is no common good between fellow citizens or allies, the question arises: would it be just, in that case, for one of them to harm the others (in order to benefit himself)? At first, Socrates had dodged the question by asking Euthydemos about two "white lies," which were, each of them, turned to everyone's advantage. That the question could not be dodged for long, however, was indicated by what Socrates asked Euthydemos about next. For would it still be just for someone to rob a depressed friend of his sword, lest he destroy himself with it, if that meant putting *himself* in harm's way? In other words, the one and only work or deed left behind under the heading *I* after the second round of questioning was the harming of friends, and Xenophon gives us every reason to expect that Socrates would devote to that opinion, too, a round of questioning of its own.

What happens next, therefore, happens contrary to all expectation. Instead of asking Euthydemos if it would be just, when there is no common good between fellow citizens or allies, for one of them—for an individual, that is, no less than for a city in similar straits—to harm the others, Socrates put another question to him. Who is more unjust, he asked, someone who deliberately deceives his friends so as to harm them or someone who does as much involuntarily? Owing to the substitution of the latter question for the former, writing (under the heading *J* whatever is, in "our" opinion, a work or deed of justice and under the heading *I* whatever is, in "our" opinion, a work or deed of injustice) was missing from the third and final round of questioning.[6] Also owing to that substitution, the truth and the way to the truth, too, was missing. If someone contradicted Socrates about who is more just, for example, whether it is the one the contradictor praised or the one Socrates himself praised, Socrates led the speech up toward the assumption or hypothesis on which it was based by asking what is (the work of the) just. In that way, according to Xenophon, the truth became clear (IV.6.13–14). But then, after having gone the right way (to the truth) in rounds one and two, Socrates turned back around and went the wrong way in the third and final round of questioning. That is, after having turned, in the brief back-and-forth preceding the refutation, from the less fundamental question "Who is just?" to the more fundamental question "What is (the work of the) just?" Socrates broke off the examination of the latter, more fundamental question, although—or because—the examination was drawing to a close, only to turn back around and examine, instead of the latter question, the former question.[7] Because of this, the third and final round of questioning—in contrast to the first two, which, though they bear a striking resemblance to one another, look absolutely nothing like the third—never rose to the level of a true, dialectical refutation of Euthydemos.

To be sure, when Euthydemos answered Socrates that someone who deliberately deceives—and, Euthydemos added, lies to (IV.2.19)—his friends so as to harm them is more unjust than someone who does as much involuntarily, Socrates asked the youth a series of follow-up questions, in response to which Euthydemos found himself contradicting himself. But the refutation was more apparent, that is, more sophistical, than real. First of all, Socrates got Euthydemos to agree that, in the same way as there is learning or knowledge of writing, there is learning or knowledge of justice. Now, he who deliberately writes—and, Socrates added, reads (IV.2.20)—incorrectly is literate, whereas he who does as much involuntarily is illiterate: for the former, rather than the latter, knows how to write correctly. So far, so good. But then, on the basis of an analogy between justice and the art of writing, Socrates got Euthydemos to agree that, contrary to the answer he had given at first, he who deliberately deceives and lies about the just things is more just and he who does as much involuntarily is less just: for the former, rather than the latter, knows the just things. And was that basis solid? Socrates admitted to us, even as he pulled the wool over Euthydemos's eyes, that it was not. The analogy was faulty.[8] To repeat, someone who knows how to write correctly is (rather than only relatively more literate than someone who is ignorant of how to write correctly) absolutely literate, according to what Socrates said, while someone who is ignorant of how to write correctly is (rather than only relatively less literate than someone who knows how to write correctly) absolutely illiterate; yet, according to what Socrates also said, someone who knows the just things is (rather than absolutely just) only relatively more just than someone who is ignorant of the just things, while someone who is ignorant of the just things is (rather than absolutely unjust) only relatively less just than someone who knows the just things. By Socrates's own admission, justice is not (only) learning or knowledge, like the art of writing (compare *Cyropaedia* I.2.6 with I.2.7 and I.3.16–18), but (also) something else. If the ill-intentioned knower is only relatively just, the well-intentioned nonknower only relatively unjust, then the well-intentioned knower is absolutely just and the ill-intentioned nonknower absolutely unjust. And, that means, what makes knowers still more just is the *will*, the *intention* to do justice, and what makes nonknowers still less just is the lack thereof. Two things go into justice, Socrates tacitly admits: knowledge and intention—the knowledge of just and unjust things, and the intention to do the former not the latter (consider IV.4.12). And which of the two comes first, whether knowledge comes before intention or intention comes before knowledge, remains a wide-open question. Euthydemos, in whose opinion intention comes before knowledge, was therefore never truly, dialectically refuted; he was only deceived on the basis of an admittedly faulty analogy. The generally accepted opinion of Euthydemos that the just have good, and the unjust bad, intentions, though apparently refuted, was in reality only brushed aside without any real basis. And the victory of the Socratic paradox over generally accepted opinion was apparently unjustly gained, by hook or by crook.

What is going on here? Xenophon gave us every reason to expect from the third and final round of questioning a *written, dialectical* refutation of the *fundamental* opinion that it is unjust, when there is no common good between fellow citizens or allies, for one of them to harm the others. But what we get instead, contrary to all expectation, is an *unwritten, sophistical* refutation of the *less fundamental* opinion that someone who deliberately harms his friends (by deceiving them) is more unjust than someone who does as much involuntarily. The latter has some bearing on the former. Even apart from the fact that one is evidently interchangeable with the other, Socrates asked Euthydemos, "Who is more unjust?" on the grounds that "we should not leave even this behind, unexamined," and what is "this," in that case, if not the opinion left behind from the second round of questioning, that harming friends is an unjust work or deed (IV.2.19)? The unwritten, sophistical refutation of the less fundamental opinion is not completely beside the point. Far from it; according to the indications given in the brief back-and-forth preceding the refutation, the fundamental opinion is the source of the less fundamental one and indeed, on reflection, the assumption or hypothesis on which the latter, which is its necessary consequence, is based. Only because justice is not necessarily good, injustice not necessarily bad, in other words, is justice not (only) knowledge but (also) good intentions. And so, instead of a written, dialectical refutation of the fundamental assumption or hypothesis that justice is not necessarily good and injustice not necessarily bad, we get an unwritten, sophistical refutation of its necessary consequence. Something is missing: the unwritten, sophistical refutation's written, dialectical basis. "The peak," to quote Leo Strauss, "is missing."[9] For some reason, Xenophon was deliberately writing incorrectly.[10]

As soon as we see this, we see why. Were the written, dialectical refutation of the assumption or hypothesis that it is unjust for one of them to harm the others, when there is no common good between fellow citizens or allies, *not* in fact missing, Euthydemos would have fallen victim to it just as he fell victim to the unwritten, sophistical refutation of its necessary consequence. For the doer of justice is in that case, on that assumption or hypothesis, bad for himself (and good for friends). But it turned out, from the first two rounds of questioning, that Euthydemos's confidence in his ability to "display" or "point out" the works or deeds of justice and injustice was not well-founded owing to his inability to "explain" whether the former are bad and the latter good *for enemies* (IV.2.14–16) and, *for friends*, whether the former are good and the latter bad (IV.2.17–18). And if, among other things, his opinion that it would be just for a city to benefit itself (at another's expense) is any indication, Euthydemos's confidence in his ability to "display" or "point out" the works or deeds of justice and injustice was not well-founded owing, also, to his inability to "explain" whether the former are good and the latter bad for the doers *themselves*. Euthydemos was indeed confused about justice. The youth did not know what he believed he knew about what one should do. According to Socrates, like a man who wants to give directions to one and the same place yet, not knowing his ignorance of the right way, sometimes points east, other times west, Euthydemos wanted to speak the truth about what justice is yet, in his confusion, sometimes said that it is good (and injustice is not), other times that it is not (and injustice is). Hence, like a man who wants to answer one and the same math problem correctly yet, not knowing his ignorance of the right answer, sometimes says the answer is more, other times less, the youth wanted to speak the truth about who is just yet, in his confusion, sometimes said that someone who deliberately harms his friends is more just than someone who does as much involuntarily, and other times that he is less just than the latter (IV.2.21). And yet, since he was only for the moment, only somewhat "perplexed" or "at a loss" as to what justice is, Euthydemos did not feel forced to choose between the two assumptions or hypotheses. To the bitter end, he believed he knew that justice was not (only) good, but (also) obedience to the laws.[11] Had Socrates actually gone through with the third and final round of the written, dialectical refutation of Euthydemos, all this and more would have been brought out. But at what cost? Lying, deceiving, evildoing, and enslaving were, in the beginning, written under the heading *I*, and, under the heading *J*, nothing was written. Twice, however, Socrates erased works or deeds from under the heading *I*, then wrote them in under the heading *J*, leaving behind, after the second round of questioning, one and only one work or deed under the heading *I*. And, had Socrates actually gone through with the third and final round, nothing would have been left behind, in the end, under the heading *I*. Each and every work or deed written, in the beginning, under the heading *I*—lying, deceiving, stealing, robbing, and enslaving—would have been erased and written, in the end, under the heading *J*. But that, according to Euthydemos—and not only Euthydemos (consider IV.4.5–6) but "all" Greeks and their laws (compare, in context, Plato, *Lesser Hippias* 372a6–c1 with 365c7, 375d3–4)—would have been "terrible." Had Socrates, in Xenophon's *Memorabilia*, actually gone through with the third and final round of the written, dialectical refutation of Euthydemos, Xenophon would have put in writing that his teacher Socrates had put in writing the very same thought he was accused of teaching others and harboring himself (consider I.2.56–57). No wonder the peak—the nadir, according to generally accepted opinions—is missing or, rather, all but missing. If, throughout the third and final round of questioning, Xenophon deliberately wrote incorrectly, he did not do so without reason.[12]

Still, if the peak is all but missing from Xenophon's writing for this reason, to conceal his teacher's wisdom, with what right was Xenophon swayed by it? Or with what right, to put this differently, did Socrates deceive Euthydemos, in much the same way as Xenophon pulled the wool over the eyes of not a few of his readers by writing incorrectly? Perhaps, if it is just for a general to lie to his army when they are "depressed" (IV.2.17), both for his own and for his army's safety, it is no less just for a wise man, like Socrates, to lie to Euthydemos (about the just, or the divine, things) when he, too, is "depressed" (IV.2.23, IV.2.39; IV.3.15), both for his own and, in another way, for Euthydemos's safety. And yet, in the immediate sequel, Socrates will go on to say that those ignorant of the noble, the good, and the just things are "called" or "named" slaves (IV.2.22, contrast IV.2.39: *tō onti andrapodon*). We have only just seen that nobody other than Socrates—least of all Euthydemos, to repeat, in whose opinion intention comes before knowledge—would call those ignorant of (and willing to do) the just things slaves. Even or precisely if, however, Socrates and Socrates alone was right to call nonknowers of the just things slaves, and to call knowers (rather than willing doers) of the just things gentlemen (IV.2.23, I.1.16), then, at least on the assumption or hypothesis of Euthydemos, justice demands that Socrates go for broke and make a good faith effort at liberating the youth, however depressing to Euthydemos or dangerous to himself (consider IV.2.33) that may be. The necessary consequences of the general's lie are indisputably good, after all, whereas the necessary consequences of withholding from human beings the truth that will set them free, if they come to know it, are not. And so with what right, to repeat, did Socrates do that? It was no coincidence that, by arguing that he who deliberately deceives and lies to his friends *about the just things* is more just than he who does as much involuntarily, Socrates was deliberately deceiving his friend Euthydemos about the just things and Euthydemos was lying to Socrates about them involuntarily (IV.2.20). With that argument, Socrates invited a few of Xenophon's readers to entertain the thought that he is more just than Euthydemos. Now, that Socrates (who deliberately deceived his friend Euthydemos about the just things so as to harm him if, that is, to be ignorant of the just things is to be a slave) is more just than Euthydemos (who lied to his friend Socrates about the just things despite the fact that he, for his part, "wanted to speak the truth"), there can be no doubt whatsoever. Unless justice defies all comprehension, Socrates was just, absolutely just, and Euthydemos was absolutely unjust (IV.2.12, consider I.2.41). For the victory of the Socratic paradox over generally accepted opinion, although gained by hook or by crook in the third and final round of questioning, was not entirely without basis; it was only all but missing. But then, by laying a merely apparent, merely sophistical basis for his eponymous paradox, that virtue is knowledge, Socrates was only doing what a virtuous man, so understood, would do. And *either* to get the good-natured reader to think through for himself the Socratic paradox's real, all-but-missing basis *or*, if he had already thought this through, to give the reader some idea of the paradox's implications for what one should do—or, rather, to do both at once—Xenophon calls attention in this way to the (just or unjust) works or deeds done right here, by Socrates and Euthydemos, before our very eyes. For this reason, too, Xenophon deliberately wrote incorrectly: to reveal his teacher's wisdom.

III

Although or because, as we will soon see, he had a deeper appreciation than just about any other writer for the weakness of writing, Xenophon had mastered the art of writing more completely than just about anybody else. And his mastery is on full display here. As we saw, when Socrates said that he who deliberately writes incorrectly is literate and he who does as much involuntarily is illiterate, he added that he who deliberately *reads* incorrectly is literate, too, and he who does as much involuntarily is illiterate (IV.2.20). From there, however, Socrates went on to speak of writing and writing alone. And, by leaving us in the lurch, Xenophon invited us to do some thinking on our own. What does it mean to read incorrectly, deliberately as well as involuntarily?[13] No sooner do we accept Xenophon's invitation than we discover that reading was added to writing for a reason. To read incorrectly is, of course, to read some writing or other incorrectly. On one hand, if the writing has been written correctly, deliberately reading incorrectly and involuntarily reading incorrectly both have perfectly obvious meanings. But, in the very same breath as Socrates spoke of reading incorrectly, he spoke of writing incorrectly; and both deliberately reading incorrectly and involuntarily reading incorrectly have somewhat less obvious meanings if, on the other hand, the writing—the writing read incorrectly—has been written incorrectly. Deliberately reading incorrectly means, in that case, reading some (incorrectly written) writing knowing full well that the writing is, in fact, incorrectly written. And then involuntarily reading incorrectly means reading some (incorrectly written) writing or other in ignorance of the fact that it is incorrectly written. It was, therefore, no coincidence that, by having Socrates argue that he who reads some (incorrectly written) writing or other knowing full well that the writing is, in fact, (deliberately) incorrectly written is more literate than he who reads some (incorrectly written) writing or other in ignorance of the fact that it is (deliberately) incorrectly written, Xenophon was writing incorrectly and the reader was reading incorrectly. No, with that argument, Xenophon invited a few of his readers to entertain the thought that only the functionally illiterate would read his (deliberately) incorrect writing incorrectly involuntarily. Following closely in his teacher's footsteps, the writer Xenophon first aroused the good-natured reader's desire for Xenophon's knowledge (of the truth) by approaching the reader as if to gratify his desire for knowledge, then, all of a sudden, leaving the reader to think for himself. And either to get the reader to see for himself that he, Xenophon, had been writing incorrectly throughout the third and final round of questioning or, if the reader had already come to see this, to give the reader his stamp of approval—or, rather, to do both at once—Xenophon added reading to writing. But nothing, not even the fact that he was deliberately writing incorrectly by writing about deliberately writing incorrectly, betrays Xenophon's mastery of the art of writing more than the fact that, for the reason already mentioned, Socrates was deliberately deceiving his friend Euthydemos about the just things (who was lying to Socrates about them involuntarily) by arguing that he who deliberately deceives and lies to his friends about the just things is just (relative to someone who does as much involuntarily).

As bad—unsafe and contrary to nature—as it may be to tell the truth in the simplest and clearest manner, to write the truth in the simplest and clearest manner is worse, much worse. The written word is readily available to the reading public for centuries perhaps; the spoken word need not be available to more than one, single interlocutor for a brief moment in time. And the steps that Xenophon took when writing down his recollections of Socrates (I.3.1), both to conceal from bad natures and to reveal to good ones his teacher's wisdom, have made it abundantly clear that he did not take his responsibility lightly. Xenophon's writing, like Socrates himself, did not approach all natures in the same way. And yet, however masterful his writing may have been, the fact remains that, according to what Socrates said and did, reading the books of wise men is no substitute for having teachers when it comes to an education. And, although he let himself write, Xenophon shared his teacher's deep appreciation for the weakness of writing, even that which does not approach all natures in the same way.

Reading the words written on the temple of Apollo at Delphi had absolutely no effect on Euthydemos (IV.2.24). By means of speech, however, Socrates succeeded where the writing on the temple of Apollo at Delphi failed: after dragging the youth kicking and screaming from the generally accepted opinion that lying, deceiving, evildoing, and enslaving are unjust works or deeds and leading him blindfolded up toward the truth that they are not, Socrates left Euthydemos "depressed" (IV.2.23, IV.2.39). And Xenophon lets it be known that, so far from having been a one-off, Socrates had this effect on all those who fell victim to his refutations (IV.2.40). So we have to ask, if reading the refutation of Euthydemos found here in Xenophon's *Memorabilia* does not have much the same effect on us as the refutations had on all those who fell victim to them, then are we any better than Euthydemos reading—again, like a rhapsode (IV.2.10)—the words written on the temple of Apollo at Delphi? In proportion as Apollo is a worse teacher than Xenophon's Socrates, we are even worse. And yet, without a doubt, the refutation of Euthydemos found here in Xenophon's *Memorabilia* has had much the same effect on not a few readers as the words written on the temple of Apollo at Delphi had on Euthydemos: absolutely none. And that means, whereas Socrates had a profound effect on all those who fell victim to his refutations, reading the Socratic refutation found here in Xenophon's *Memorabilia* has had absolutely no effect on many of us. As readers, then, we have to face the fact that for some reason reading Xenophon does not bring out the best in us much, if any, more than reading Apollo brought out the best in Euthydemos. For what reason?

Thematically, while the complex relation between the just and the good took center stage, the weakness of writing played a supporting role throughout the refutation.[14] Even as he carried out the refutation of Euthydemos by means of speech, Socrates also wrote the youth's answers to his questions as they went (IV.2.13ff.). As a rule, however, Socrates never wrote anything. And the already striking fact that, in writing out the refutation of Euthydemos, Socrates was breaking his rule against writing is only made more striking by the fact that the refutation had not a little to do, by the end, with writing itself (IV.2.20). Now, to be sure, how Socrates wrote the refutation of Euthydemos was still a very far cry indeed from how Apollo "wrote" the lapidary words on his temple at Delphi. As the youth's answers changed, the writing of Socrates changed to reflect them; and the youth's answers changed, in the first place, because Socrates asked him direct, perfectly tailored questions, which were for their part, unlike the youth's (changing) answers to them, unwritten (consider IV.2.15, IV.2.18). Socrates was, therefore, not writing—not really, for writing neither asks the reader questions nor changes to reflect the reader's answers—so much as he was coming as close as he would let himself come to doing so. But if, then, Socrates was teaching Euthydemos that he did not know what he believed he knew by means of speech, all the while specifying what would have to be true of writing for him to teach as much by means of it, was Xenophon showing us what held his teacher back from writing? What would have to be true of writing for Socrates to teach by means of it was, after all, *not* in fact true of it: writing, again, neither asks the reader direct, perfectly tailored questions nor holds up a mirror to the reader's changing answers. And, that means, Socrates's rule against writing followed from the fact that, if Socrates was going to bring out the best in us, it was of the utmost importance for him to do both. To say this, however, is only to answer one question with another, more specific question. Granted that Socrates never wrote anything for this reason, because alteration and interrogation are of the utmost importance for bringing out the best in us and writing allows neither, for what reason are they of the utmost importance for bringing out the best in us?

To Euthydemos's opinions about the works or deeds of injustice Socrates put direct, perfectly tailored questions whose only acceptable answers forced the youth to choose, again and again, still newer and more improved opinions, which Socrates wrote as they went. The Socratic refutation found here in Xenophon's *Memorabilia*, to give the example of reading and writing most relevant to our purpose, can only give us the opportunity to come to see with our own eyes that the opinions of Euthydemos to which Socrates put his questions are also our opinions; that the answers given by the youth upon questioning are also our answers; that, altogether, the new and improved opinions forced upon Euthydemos by his own answers are indeed, if not true, closer to the truth. And yet, without Socrates there to push the youth from generally accepted opinions and to pull him up toward the truth with direct, perfectly tailored questions, Euthydemos would have passed up the opportunity to examine justice for the exact same reason that reading the words written on the temple of Apollo at Delphi did not result in any attempt on his part to examine himself: this was something he believed he knew already (compare IV.2.12–14 and IV.2.21 with IV.2.24). And, in this, Euthydemos was by no means alone. Learning about gentlemanship differs from learning an art, as we saw, in that all of us are, to begin with, more or less firm in our belief that we already know what justice is. But that means, so far from forcing the issue, the books of wise men can do no more than give us the opportunity to examine how well-founded our confidence in our ability to "display" or "point out" the works or deeds of justice and injustice really is. And our very confidence in our ability to do so leaves us with little or no desire to take advantage of the opportunity. Interrogation is of the utmost importance for bringing out the best in us for this reason, because we have to be dragged kicking and screaming from generally accepted opinions. Now that—that the wise man casts a weaker, albeit wider net by means of writing than he would otherwise do by means of speech—is bad enough. What makes matters worse is that writing signals the wise man's approach in advance, scaring off his quarry before it comes within reach of his net. For the truth, to begin with, appears "terrible" (IV.2.15). And the closer opinions come to the truth, the more "terrible" they appear to become. Had the writing of Socrates not merely held up a mirror to Euthydemos and changed as his answers changed, therefore, but even got ahead of him—for example, had Euthydemos read the opinion, closer to the truth, that it is just not to be entirely straightforward all the time even with friends *before*, rather than after, the opinion was forced upon him by his own answers to Socrates's questions—that would have only repulsed him. That, of course, is not at all what happened . . . to Euthydemos. And yet, precisely if the writing of Socrates did not repulse Euthydemos because, changing to reflect his answers, it did not get ahead of him, does the Socratic refutation found here in Xenophon's *Memorabilia* not repulse us because, without changing, it does get ahead of us? Ready or not, there is the opinion that it is just not to be entirely straightforward all the time even with friends, rearing its ugly head. In the course of giving us the opportunity to take advantage of the opportunity to examine justice, by giving us too much information too soon, the books of wise men arouse in us the desire not to take advantage of the opportunity to do so. And for this reason, because we have to be led blindfolded up toward the apparently "terrible" truth, alteration is of the utmost importance for bringing out the best in us.

How Socrates taught, how differently from Apollo Socrates taught, followed from what he taught. The form of the teaching followed from its content. For our confidence in generally accepted opinions together with our terror of the truth about justice means that all of us are, to begin with, stuck between a rock and a hard place. With overconfidence on one hand and fear on the other, the odds of starting, much less finishing the uphill climb from generally accepted opinions toward the truth are stacked against us. And so much so according to Xenophon's indications that, without a teacher to drag us kicking and screaming from the former and to lead us blindfolded up toward the latter, we have little hope of success. Reading, though better than nothing, does not bring out the best in us. The treasures of wisdom left behind in the books of wise men are, rather, a lot like Jonathan Swift's Struldbrugs—lasting for centuries perhaps, but toothless and ghastly to behold.

CHAPTER 4

Self-Knowledge and the Hope for Happiness

I

His opinions about justice refuted, Euthydemos became "depressed." Collecting the books of men reputed to be wise had gotten him nowhere. And it was at this point in the conversation, just when Euthydemos was bewailing the fact that there was apparently no other road or way for him to take to become better (IV.2.23), that Socrates brought up self-knowledge. But what does self-knowledge have to do with becoming better (more virtuous)? At least to Euthydemos, Socrates seemed to offer no explanation. Partly for this reason, even after listening to Socrates go on for a while in his own name about the good or noble things that are acquired by those who know themselves (IV.2.26, IV.2.28) and the bad or base things that are encountered by those who do not (IV.2.27, IV.2.29), Euthydemos was no more aware of how to become better than he was before. And Euthydemos was no more aware of how to become better than he was before partly also for another reason. Namely, although Euthydemos felt some need to know himself after all that Socrates had said, Socrates had not yet shown him, or so he thought, how to begin examining himself (IV.2.30). And when Euthydemos requested from Socrates an explanation of this, rather than grant the youth's request, Socrates requested from Euthydemos an explanation of what sorts of things are good and bad, before launching into yet another refutation of Euthydemos, a refutation whose main target was the good as Euthydemos understood it and not the just (IV.2.31ff.). But what does self-knowledge have to do with the good? Again, Socrates seemed to offer no explanation. The Socratic monologue concerning self-knowledge (IV.2.23–30) therefore falls in between two Socratic conversations or dialogues, one whose subject matter is justice

(IV.2.11ff.), the other whose subject matter is the good (IV.2.31ff.). And, it may be asked, what is the meaning of this? What does self-knowledge have to do with the good, on one hand, and justice or virtue, on the other?

According to Socrates, only those who know themselves know "the good things," which is just another way of saying, from among the things suitable to them, the things they have the "power" or "capacity" to acquire (IV.2.26–28). Knowledge of the good things arises from self-knowledge. As for self-knowledge, just as horse buyers do not believe they know a horse until they have examined how useful—first and foremost, how obedient or disobedient—it is to its (human) masters, human beings should not believe they know themselves, according to Socrates, until they have examined how useful they themselves are to their (divine) masters (IV.2.25), "the gods" (IV.2.23, IV.2.36). Self-knowledge, from which our knowledge of the good things arises, itself arises therefore from an examination of how useful, obedient, or disobedient we are to the gods. And what is that, thinking back on what Socrates said to "aristocrats" now, if not an examination of justice and, by implication (consider IV.6.13–14), how just we are? To spell this out a bit, Euthydemos believed he knew himself (IV.2.24); that is, he believed he knew himself to be just (IV.2.12). But since, to the bitter end, he believed he knew that justice was not (only) good, but (also) obedience to the laws—ignorance of how beneficial or knowledge of how harmful obedience may be to one's own life notwithstanding—this means that Euthydemos believed he knew himself to be useful and obedient to the gods (IV.3.16; I.3.1, IV.4.13). In his confusion about justice, Euthydemos did not know himself. He did not know himself, at any rate, *to be a self.* For he believed he knew himself to be, not (only) a self, but (also) the property of another or others (consider *Cyropaedia* VII.5.44), for which reason Socrates, just a moment ago, "called" or "named" Euthydemos a slave on account of the youth's ignorance of the noble, good, and just things (IV.2.22; consider I.1.16 and *Oeconomicus* 6.16, 7.2–3). Not knowing the truth about justice, Euthydemos did not know himself, and not knowing himself, he did not know the good things either. If, then, the second Socratic dialogue brings out the youth's ignorance of the good, just as the first brought out his ignorance of the truth about justice, the Socratic monologue in between offers to explain that the former arises from the latter.

II

At first, when Socrates requested from Euthydemos an explanation of what sorts of things are good and bad, Euthydemos did not anticipate having any difficulty granting the request. Health is good, he said, and sickness is bad; the causes of the former are good, he said, and the causes of the latter are bad (IV.2.31). But, to this, Socrates was quick to reply that, according to Euthydemos, when health and sickness "come to be" causes of something good, they would be good; when they "come to be" causes of something bad, they would be bad. And although Euthydemos was not in the least bit surprised to hear that health sometimes comes to be a cause of something good and sickness of something bad—for he had already seen as much with his own eyes (consider IV.2.32)—he was very surprised indeed to hear that health sometimes comes to be a cause of something bad and sickness of something good. Socrates, therefore, gave one or two examples of pursuits in which the healthy can participate only to perish and from the ill effects of which the sick are spared: "shameful" military campaigns and "harmful" voyages (IV.2.32). Of the reference to the "shameful," so out of place here, we will have more to say later. For now, even if the distinction between "harmful" and "shameful" pursuits was completely lost on Euthydemos, the distinction between *being* and *coming to be* a cause of something good or bad, or the distinction between *being* and *coming to be* "beneficial" or "harmful," as Socrates put, was not. Nor was the distinction between a cause *of something good or bad* and a cause *of a cause of something good or bad* completely lost on him either. For the causes of which Euthydemos first spoke were drinks or foods or pursuits (IV.2.31), examples of which—medicine (IV.2.17) and unwise military campaigns (IV.2.29)—were perhaps still fresh in his mind. In the one or two examples given by Socrates, however, health comes to be a cause of something bad, sickness of something good, only insofar as the former state of being comes to be a cause of participating, and the latter of not participating, in pursuits that are themselves causes of something bad. Of course, one of these things is not like the other. And the attempt to blur the lines between that pursuit which is itself a cause of something good or bad, on one hand, and that state of being which comes to be a cause of participating or not participating in that pursuit (which is itself a cause of something good or bad), on the other, was so feeble that even the noncontradictor Euthydemos came to health's defense. Taking the highly unusual step of contradicting Socrates, the youth argued that, however true it may be for Socrates to say that the healthy perhaps participate not only in beneficial pursuits but also in harmful ones, Socrates can see with his own eyes that the sick definitely do not participate in either beneficial or harmful pursuits (IV.2.32). Against this, Socrates did not utter a word; after all, how could he? Health *is* a potential, remote cause of death, and sickness *is* a potential, remote cause of life—sometimes, when the latter comes to be a cause of not participating, and the former of participating, in harmful, death-causing pursuits, they actually are remote causes of life and death, respectively—whereas sickness always, actually *is* a proximate cause of slavery, and health of freedom (III.12, IV.7.9).[1] And so, instead of contradicting Euthydemos in turn, Socrates merely checked to see how prepared the youth was to accept the conclusion of his own, perfectly reasonable argument. Seeing as how health and sickness sometimes actually are remote causes of bad and good things, he asked Euthydemos, are they more good than bad (IV.2.32)? And, just like that, the youth admitted defeat. "According to this argument," Euthydemos said, the question admits of only one answer: neither health nor sickness is more good than bad (IV.2.33). The burden of responsibility for this answer falls squarely on the shoulders of Euthydemos, however, whose "worthlessness" and not the argument (compare IV.2.32 with IV.2.39) led him to conclude that not only the actual, proximate causes of something bad, but also *their* potential causes—or the potential, remote causes of something bad—are not more good than bad. For the argument led to just the opposite conclusion. Only when health and sickness come to be causes of something good are they good, according to the argument, and only when they come to be causes of something bad are they bad (IV.2.32). And since health is a remote cause of death and sickness a remote cause of life sometimes, whereas sickness is a proximate cause of slavery and health a proximate cause of freedom always, that means, for the most part, if not always, health is good and sickness is bad. Or health is more good than bad. Add to this that, after only a moment's reflection, the youth's answer gives way to a reductio ad absurdum. If health is not more good than bad because the healthy can participate in harmful, death-causing pursuits from which the sick are spared, life is not more good than bad too, for the living can participate in harmful pursuits (compare IV.2.32 with II.2.3); yet health is not more good than bad, Euthydemos agreed, because life is more good than bad. And thus, Socrates saw, Euthydemos was so unprepared to accept the conclusion of a perfectly reasonable argument about what sorts of things are good that, if he could not reject the argument's conclusion without absurdity, then he would do so with it. Of good things, that is, Euthydemos believed he knew that they are not even potential, remote causes of bad things. The only sorts of things that are good are, therefore, always good, never bad. And the distinction between that state of being which is for the most part, if not always, good and that state of being which is for the most part, if not always, bad was bound to seem like a distinction without a difference in comparison with the youth's supposed knowledge that there was something of this sort. To him, "whose thoughts are more than the Sands," to quote Locke's *First Treatise of Government* (§58), "and wider than the Ocean," how big of a difference can there be between a mountain and a molehill, a pond and a puddle, health and sickness, life and death? But only if there was something of this sort, just as Euthydemos thought, can there really be none to speak of. And perhaps there was, but where?

When Euthydemos agreed that, because health is sometimes bad, it is not more good than bad, he offered to explain, in almost the same breath, that wisdom or knowledge is indisputably good (IV.2.33). Coming from him just now, this makes some sense. For if health is sometimes bad, in the first place, because the healthy can participate not only in beneficial pursuits but also in harmful ones, the trick lies in knowing with absolute certainty, in each and every case, which is which. Or if the otherwise good things are sometimes bad, to put this more generally, absolutely certain knowledge of them—of when they are either good or bad—is alone always better to have than not to have. To this, then, Socrates replied that wisdom or knowledge would seem to be sometimes bad, too, on account of the political power as well as the envy of other men (IV.2.33). Unlike the youth's explanation, however, the reply makes little sense. By pointing out that wise men are sometimes enslaved by kings or tyrants and forced to put their wisdom or knowledge to work for them or for the common good of their cities or nations, sometimes destroyed by other men envious of their wisdom, Socrates pointed out that a well-deserved *reputation* for wisdom or knowledge (consider IV.2.34, IV.2.35) and not wisdom or knowledge itself is sometimes bad. A wise man who successfully conceals his wisdom from others has nothing, or nothing special, to fear from them, unless he gets a reputation for concealing his wisdom (consider IV.4.9–11, I.2.36; but consider III.9.13).[2] And, as for a "wise" man who does not make any effort to conceal his "wisdom," is he perhaps "not wise" (consider I.6.11)? Of the reference to lying and deceiving, no less out of place here in the second round of questioning than the reference to the shameful was in the first, we will have more to say soon enough. For now, because it did not occur to Euthydemos that shameful pursuits, like lying and deceiving, are sometimes beneficial or good, he was again too quick to admit defeat. This time, however, he was not entirely wrong to do so. For of Palamedes Socrates said that, it is said, he was destroyed by Odysseus who was envious of his wisdom; then, of other wise men he said that many of them are enslaved by the Great King. First of all, however, he said of Daedalus *not only* that, it is said, he was enslaved by Minos, *but also* that, it is said, he tried to escape together with his son, Icarus, only to be recaptured after his son perished in the attempt (IV.2.33). And to point out that (a reputation for) wisdom or knowledge is sometimes bad on account of the political power of others no more needed to be said than that, it is rightly said, Daedalus was enslaved by Minos. Instead, by throwing the flight of Daedalus and Icarus into the mix, Xenophon's Socrates points out that wisdom or knowledge itself, and not a reputation for wisdom or knowledge, is sometimes bad. For Daedalus took to the skies in the first place only because Minos barred him from participating in any voyages by sea, for fear that he would reach Athens, his fatherland, and obtain his freedom. Even knowing with absolute certainty which pursuits will cause something good, and which will cause something bad is of no use to a wise man so long as he does not have the freedom to participate in the one and not the other. No less than an enslaved wise man, for example, a wise man too sick to participate in a voyage that he knows will cause something good is worse and not better off than an ignoramus in a position to make the trip—except, of course, insofar as the wise man accepts and the ignoramus does not accept that all of us are slaves, in the end, to circumstances beyond our control. Still, knowing with absolute certainty which pursuits will cause something good and which will cause something bad does mean that, all else being equal, the wise are always either better or (at worst) no worse off than the ignorant (consider IV.2.33). That is, while no amount of knowledge of "the outcome" (consider I.1.6ff.) means that we will never suffer bad things unless we are all-powerful, too, having absolutely certain knowledge does mean that we will always experience as much good and suffer as little bad as possible, given the circumstances. And yet, for all his wisdom or knowledge, how well did Daedalus fare? Cut off from the sea, he did what no ignoramus could: he built a flying machine and, together with his son, took to the skies. But then, since doing so cost him his only son and profited him nothing, would he not have been better off had he been ignorant (of how to build a flying machine) rather than wise? Just as the healthy can participate in harmful pursuits from which the sick are spared, the wise can participate in harmful pursuits from which the ignorant are spared. For no man, not even a wise man, knows with absolute certainty which pursuits will produce good, and which will produce bad, outcomes.

That said, just because wisdom or knowledge is sometimes bad does not necessarily mean that it is not indisputably good—any more than the fact that health is sometimes bad meant that it is not more good than bad.[3] As Socrates put it elsewhere, not even a ship's pilot knows with absolute certainty which voyages will be beneficial, and which will be harmful (I.1.6–8). And yet, unless we are nearly mad, all of us know with absolute certainty that a pilot, with his less then absolutely certain knowledge, and not a nonknower, should be given the run of the ship (I.1.9; compare III.9.14–15).[4] For the most part, if not always, learning or knowledge is good, and ignorance is bad (consider IV.2.26); and, however bad learning or knowledge may sometimes be, if learning or knowledge is our "only Star and compass," to quote Locke's *First Treatise* (§58) again, the wise man's stance toward learning or knowledge is beyond dispute. Is it really, though, our *only* "Star and compass"? In almost the same breath as he agreed that wisdom or knowledge is sometimes bad, Euthydemos offered to explain that happiness, not wisdom or knowledge, runs the risk of being the least disputable good (IV.2.34). This too, coming from him just now, makes some sense. For if wisdom or knowledge is sometimes bad because not even a wise man knows with absolute certainty which pursuits will produce good, and which will produce bad, outcomes, then we are at the mercy of circumstances beyond our control—either "the natural" or, for all we know with absolute certainty, "the divine things" (consider I.1.11–15). And happiness (*eudaimonia*), good luck (consider III.9.14), is what Euthydemos prayed to the gods for (IV.2.36). In other words, although having wisdom or knowledge definitely does not even mean that we will always experience as much good and suffer as little bad as possible, if the all-powerful gods answer our prayers, perhaps we will never suffer bad things nevertheless.[5] And rather than accept that reason, which is sometimes bad, is our "only Star and compass," Euthydemos continued to believe he knew that the only sorts of things that are good are always good, never bad; that there was, somewhere, something of this sort. He did so at a price, though, the price of a favorable stance toward learning or knowledge. And when Euthydemos said, with some trepidation, that happiness "runs the risk of being the least disputable" good, he betrayed some inkling of this. Laying aside reason as if it were impudence or madness, giving the prayers of the "undefiled" (III.8.10) and not the pilot's knowledge the run of the ship, for example, is neither without risk nor beyond dispute according to Euthydemos. Still, when push came to shove, Euthydemos would sooner give up small needs that were definitely within his power to satisfy than great, imagined ones that were perhaps not (consider IV.2.37–38).

But to lay aside reason, to lay aside reason altogether, that is, means to lay aside the end or ends of reason no less than reason as a means. And so, with the question of the usefulness of praying to the gods for happiness left hanging, Socrates took up the question of the makeup, the meaning of happiness itself. Socrates politely asked Euthydemos whether, in his opinion, happiness is made up of beauty or strength or wealth or reputation or anything else of this sort, and the youth answered in the affirmative on the grounds that, without such things, it is impossible to be happy (IV.2.34). Of the reference to these "disputably good things," no less out of place here in the third and final round of questioning than the references to the shameful were in the first two, we will have more to say in just a moment. For now, because it did not occur to Euthydemos that "many" human beings suffer ill effects from things of this sort, many more than suffer ill effects, "sometimes," from health or knowledge (compare IV.2.35 with IV.2.32), Socrates had only to recall the conclusion of the first two rounds of questioning. So far as we know, the disputably good things are no less often bad—they are, Euthydemos was not surprised to hear (contrast IV.2.32), much more often bad—than the latter sort (IV.2.34–35). Affirming or reaffirming that happiness is made up of the (disputably or indisputably) good things that we know would have the effect of making happiness known, but definitely at least sometimes bad, while denying as much would have the effect of making happiness never bad perhaps, but unknown. And Euthydemos, although he did not for a moment deny that happiness is made up of the good things that we know, still continued to believe he knew that the only sorts of things that are good are always good, never bad. Once it had been settled that happiness is at least sometimes bad, if or since it is known, he agreed that he did not know what to pray to the gods for (IV.2.36). Rather than accept that this far-from-perfect happiness is to be prayed for or good, Euthydemos still continued to believe he knew that the only sorts of things that are good are always good, never bad; that there was somewhere, he knew not where, something of this sort.[6] But that was the last straw, the end of the line for reason. In this situation, the youth would have to give up the great, imagined needs whose satisfaction was perhaps not within his power in favor of still greater ones whose satisfaction was even beyond his ken, just as he gave up the small needs that were definitely within his power to satisfy in favor of the great, imagined ones that were perhaps not. And yet, while the price to be paid for laying aside reason (as a means) and praying to the gods for the happiness of which we know was not prohibitively high for Euthydemos, the price to be paid for laying aside (the end or ends of) reason altogether and praying to the gods for what they and they alone know to be good was, it turns out, prohibitively high for him. Socrates used to pray to the gods "simply" for the good things, rather than for gold or silver or tyranny or anything else of this sort, on the grounds that the gods have the most beautiful knowledge of what sorts of things are good (I.3.2; contrast I.5.5, II.2.10). However, not only praying to the gods for the good things of which we know, but also praying to the gods after the fashion of Socrates, "simply" for the good things of which they have the most beautiful knowledge, was ruled out by the youth's agreement that he did not know what to pray to the gods for. "The sacrifice of the intellect," although necessary for Euthydemos, was not altogether possible for him either. For praying to the gods "simply" for the good things of which they have the most beautiful knowledge means not praying to the gods for anything of which we know. And, as for not praying to the gods for anything of which we know, either this means, in turn, not praying to the gods for anything at all, if we stick to what we know, or praying to the gods for something in which we can only believe, if we do not. And although Euthydemos for his part could not bring himself to stick to what he knew (consider IV.2.26–27), he could not bring himself to hold fast to the very risky, very disputable belief that "the wisdom of this world is foolishness with God" either (1 Corinthians 3:19). To explain what sorts of things are good was, therefore, too difficult for him after all. And so, for a third and final time, he admitted defeat. But was he not, yet again, too quick to do so?

There were apparently two ways out of the difficulty in which Euthydemos found himself. On one hand, if he had stuck to what he knew, Euthydemos would have had no difficulty explaining what sorts of things are good. For the argument of the first round of questioning led to the conclusion that the good is that which is for the most part, if not always, beneficial (IV.2.32). Now, to be sure, to say that the good is the beneficial is to say that, since the beneficial is the good's cause, the good is the cause of the good. But then the good of which the good is the cause is itself the cause of the good, which is, in turn, the cause of the good. And this cannot be allowed to go on forever. Unless the good or beneficial things are eventually good *for something*, there can be no explaining what sorts of things are good. That said, according to the argument of the dialogue, they are indeed good for—or, rather, against (consider III.8.3)—something. In the first round of questioning, health was said to be harmful or bad when it came to be a cause of death, and sickness beneficial or good when it came to be a cause of life (IV.2.32). And then again, in the second and third rounds of questioning, wisdom and happiness were said to be harmful or bad when they came to be causes of death, ignorance and unhappiness beneficial or good when they came to be causes of life. Are the good or beneficial things good, then, against the greatest evil: death (II.2.3, consider I.2.54)? The only thing holding us back from this explanation is that, in the second and third rounds of questioning, wisdom and happiness were said to be harmful or bad when they came to be causes not only of death but also of slavery and corruption, respectively, while ignorance and unhappiness were said to be beneficial or good when they came to be causes not only of life but also of freedom and corruption's opposite (IV.2.33–35). However, in the second round of questioning, slavery was said to be beneficial or good, for Daedalus, when it came to be a cause of "safety" or life (compare IV.2.33 with IV.2.29), while corruption did not mean "the corruption of the youth," in the third and final round of questioning, but rather not minding one's own business (compare IV.2.35 with I.2.24, I.2.22, and I.3.8–13). Everything points to this: "the good things" are "the things (human beings) need" for the sake of our own lives (IV.2.26–28, IV.2.29), to say nothing of the lives of our nearest and dearest (IV.2.33). And had Euthydemos stuck to the good things of which we know, he would have had no difficulty explaining, along these lines, what sorts of things are good. But of course, since none of the good things of which we know are always good against—in fact, all of them are potential, remote causes of—death, had Euthydemos stuck to the good things of which we know, he would have had to accept that it was not within his power to satisfy his great, imagined need for a state of being where, according to John the Apostle, "there shall be no more death, neither sorrow, nor crying, neither shall there be any more pain: for the former things are passed away" (Revelation 21:4). And Euthydemos could not bring himself to do this (consider IV.2.26–27).[7] On the other hand, if he had held fast to the belief that "the wisdom of this world is foolishness with God"—that is, if he had prayed to the gods for a state of being of which they have the most beautiful knowledge, where "there shall be no more death," but in which we can only believe—Euthydemos would have had less difficulty explaining what sorts of things are good. Note that, throughout the whole course of the private conversation between Socrates and Euthydemos, Socrates swore "by Zeus" thrice (IV.2.11, IV.2.32, IV.2.35), which is one fifth the total number of times Euthydemos swore "by Zeus" (IV.2.8, IV.2.10, IV.2.12, IV.2.17, IV.2.18, IV.2.21, IV.2.24, IV.2.31, IV.2.33, IV.2.34, IV.2.37, IV.2.38); although the dialogue concerning the good took up one fifth of the whole, private conversation, however, Socrates swore "by Zeus" there twice (IV.2.32, IV.2.35), which is half the number of times Euthydemos swore "by Zeus" there (IV.2.31, IV.2.33, IV.2.34) and twice the number of times he himself swore "by Zeus" elsewhere (IV.2.11)—by every measure, that is to say, Socrates swears "by Zeus" far more there than elsewhere. And rightly so; after all, the question of the usefulness of praying to God, the question on which the question of the makeup, the meaning, of the good hangs, was left hanging. But of course, since all of the good things of which we know are potential, remote causes of death, had Euthydemos prayed to the gods for a state of being where "there shall be no more death," he would have had to believe that, however risky, however disputable this may be, it was within his power to satisfy his great, imagined need for a state of being beyond his ken. And Euthydemos could not bring himself to do this either.

III

The difficulty Euthydemos had explaining what sorts of things are good—his ignorance of the good—arose because he could not bring himself *either* to accept the fact that it was not within his power to satisfy his great, imagined need for the good things, *or* to believe, contrary to the fact that it was not within his power to do so, that it was within his power. In other words, although he did not believe he had the power or capacity to obtain the good things he wanted, he did not accept the fact that he did not have that power or capacity either. Like Eros, who all day, every day goes from rags to riches, death to life, and back again (Plato, *Symposium* 203a9–204a1), the youth went back and forth: his great reach now exceeding, now apparently not exceeding, his grasp. Absurdity was, as we saw, the result. But there was another difficulty looming in the background all along and, although Socrates did not bring it into the foreground for Euthydemos to see, too, Xenophon did let the reader catch a glimpse of it. This difficulty had to do with the fact that, although they were out of place in a dialogue concerning the good, references to the noble and the shameful were made in each of the three rounds of questioning. In the first round of questioning, it did not occur to Euthydemos that shameful pursuits are not always harmful. Nor did it occur to him, in the second round of questioning, that shameful pursuits are sometimes beneficial. And finally, in the third round of questioning, the youth let it be known that he could not even imagine happiness without the disputably good things, which is to say, the noble things: beauty, strength, wealth, and reputation. To the bitter end, Euthydemos believed he knew that shameful pursuits are harmful, not beneficial, while the noble things are good. And yet, to say nothing of the youth's complete lack of surprise at hearing Socrates say that they are often harmful to one's own life, did not the Socratic refutation of his opinions about justice go to show that the noble things are not always good, according to Euthydemos, also or instead? In accord with this, the youth had said, at the start of the Socratic dialogue concerning the good, that the good is what even a slave should know (IV.2.31, IV.2.39), whereas he had said, at the start (IV.2.11) and at the finish (IV.2.23) of the Socratic dialogue concerning justice or nobility, that the just or the noble is what a good citizen and gentleman should know above all. So then, even apart from the difficulty arising from the youth's supposed knowledge that there was something always good, there was the difficulty of the complex relation between this good and the just or the noble. Are the just or the noble things always good or not? The conversation has gone from a dialogue concerning justice, in the first place, to a dialogue concerning the good, in the second. And the third and final dialogue, which we come to just after Xenophon let us catch a glimpse of this difficulty in the second, is therefore both an opportunity to think through the difficulty looming in the background of the second dialogue and, at the same time, a most fitting conclusion to the conversation as a whole. For the subject matter with which it was concerned was not only democracy, as it seemed to Euthydemos at least, but also, and especially, the good and the just or the noble.

"Since you are preparing to rule a democracy," Socrates said to Euthydemos in the next place, "it is clear that you know democracy, what it is, at least." Now of course, since Euthydemos was not in fact "preparing" to rule Athens (compare IV.2.36 with IV.2.3 and IV.2.6), it was not in fact clear that he knew what democracy is. But he clearly believed he knew this too (IV.2.36). So Socrates put a series of questions to him, in response to which Euthydemos agreed that it is impossible to know democracy without knowing a demos; that a demos is the poor among the citizens; and that those who do not have enough to spend on what they need are called "poor," while those who have more than enough are called "rich" (IV.2.37). And then, having made the youth's supposed knowledge of democracy depend on his supposed knowledge of the poor, Socrates put his supposed knowledge of the poor to the test. Socrates asked Euthydemos whether he had learned that, for some, not only are the few things they have enough to satisfy their needs, but they even put away savings from what little they have, while for others many things are not enough. The former are rich, the latter poor, strictly speaking. About the poor in the strict sense, the youth had only forgotten. For the question reminded him of tyrants, in particular, some of whom, he had learned, have to do injustice in spite of their vast resources, power, or capacity because their imagined needs are so great, just as others have to do injustice in spite of their small needs because they are most lacking in resources, power, or capacity (IV.2.38). As for the rich in the strict sense, those to whom Socrates referred in passing as "skilled household managers" or "possessors of the art of economics" (IV.2.39), the question did not remind Euthydemos of any of them in particular. Of the "skilled household managers," if not of the tyrants, had Euthydemos not learned anything? But of course, although this escaped the notice of Euthydemos, Socrates was talking *about himself.*

The tyrants are to be included among the poor or the demos; Socrates and other "skilled household managers," those with few things at least, are to be included among the rich. Thus, the argument led to the conclusion that democracy is the rule of tyrants (among others, perhaps, without even a few things) over Socrates and other "skilled household managers," or, at least, those with few things. And Euthydemos agreed, but only in a manner of speaking, with the conclusion that democracy is tyrannical. "Only in a manner of speaking," that is, because this time around Euthydemos held his own "worthlessness," and not the argument, responsible for making it necessary for him agree (IV.2.39). So completely convinced was he of democracy's justice that even or precisely when the argument led him to the conclusion that democracy is unjust, Euthydemos would rather think ill of himself than think ill of democracy (contrast III.7).[8] Nevertheless, the conclusion followed from the premise, which Euthydemos granted, that rich and poor have to be taken, each of them, in the strict sense. And the fact that he clung to democracy's justice, contrary to an argument whose sufficient premise he himself granted, means that he was a partisan of democracy. Euthydemos—whose very name ("Straight-to-the-demos") is a clear indication of this—was a good democratic citizen who, as such, was not about to lose faith in the justice of democracy merely on account of an indefeasible argument to the effect that democracy and tyranny are one and the same thing. Of politically ambitious "aristocrats," who thought they were by nature good because they were reputed to be, and of politically ambitious "oligarchs," who were proud of their wealth, we have already heard. And we are now in a position to see that Euthydemos was one of the politically ambitious "democrats" who, because they bowed to the authority of generally accepted opinions and lived in poverty, thought they had already obtained the best education (in the noble, the good, and the just things) and were proud of their wisdom or virtue. But if, strictly speaking, Socrates is to be included among the rich, and Euthydemos among the poor or the demos, Socrates was not only talking about himself, when he was speaking of the rich and the poor in the strict sense, but also, although this escaped the youth's notice, too, *about Euthydemos.*

Euthydemos, as we saw, did not hope to rule without justice (IV.2.11, IV.2.23). But the conversation's turn from the good to democracy was called for in the first place on the grounds that Euthydemos was hoping to rule Athens, even if he was not preparing to do so (IV.2.36). And just before mentioning this fact, the fact that Euthydemos was hoping to rule, Socrates had tagged on at the end of the list of disputably good things, without which Euthydemos could not even imagine happiness, "political power" (IV.2.35, contrast IV.2.34). To make good on his political ambitions was then, according to Euthydemos, both just and good. And yet, insofar as it was on account of their great, imagined need for the good things that the poor or the demos desired to do injustice, does the same go for Euthydemos, whose own imagined need for the good things was so great that he himself went back and forth as to whether his resources, power, or capacity would ever be vast enough to satisfy this desire of his? If so, the youth's political ambitions would perhaps tempt him, too, away from justice, toward the good (consider *Oeconomicus* 1.15, reading with the manuscripts; Machiavelli, *Prince* XVII; Montaigne, *Essays* I:14), whereas Socrates and other "skilled household managers," by contrast, would be as resistant to the temptations of tyranny as human beings can be (I.3.5, *Apology* 16). Now, just as the peak was all but missing from the first dialogue, Socrates was not about to drive a wedge between the just and the good in the second or third, at least, not here in Xenophon's *Memorabilia*. But it was especially to give us the opportunity to think through for ourselves how easy it would have been for Socrates to do so that Xenophon wrote, after the second, the third and final Socratic dialogue.

When Eckermann told Goethe that one of the latter's works had become clear to him only by degrees, after he had read it so many times that he knew it almost by heart, Goethe replied, "I can well believe that; for all its parts are, as one may say, wedged one within another."[9] And the same can be said for the one and only private Socratic conversation found in Xenophon's writings: its two dialogical parts are wedged one within another. While the first dialogue brought out that, to the bitter end, Euthydemos believed he knew that justice was not good, the second dialogue brought out that, to the bitter end, he believed he knew that it was. At the same time, while the peak all but missing from the first dialogue brought out how easy it would have been for Socrates to get Euthydemos to agree that justice was good, the sequel to the second dialogue brought out how easy it would have been for Socrates to get Euthydemos to agree that it was not. Xenophon's work thus makes clear to a few of his readers how, exactly, Euthydemos was confused about the object of his desire.

IV

So here we have two difficulties: one in the foreground of the second dialogue, another viewed from one angle in the first dialogue and then, after looming in the background of the second dialogue, viewed from another angle in the third. And it was no accident that the latter difficulty came first, the former second.

For the Socratic monologue concerning self-knowledge, to which we will now to return, offers to explain that the former difficulty arises, via ignorance of oneself, from the latter.

That said, judging from what Euthydemos said in response to the statement with which Socrates opened his monologue, half of what Socrates said, the more fundamental half, went in one ear and out the other. In his opening statement, Socrates said that knowledge of one's power or capacity *and* knowledge of how useful one is to one's (divine) masters *both* go into self-knowledge. And he said that, while the man who has self-knowledge must have "examined" how useful he is to his (divine) masters, the man who (having examined how useful he is to them) has self-knowledge "knows," *he need not have examined*, his power or capacity. Although Euthydemos said in response that this was his opinion of self-knowledge, too, he was sorely mistaken. In his opinion, rather, knowledge of one's capacity or power alone goes into self-knowledge (IV.2.25).[10] And if what Euthydemos said in response to the statement with which Socrates opened his monologue betrayed the youth's ignorance of self-knowledge—his ignorance of the fact that the examination of justice is the beginning of self-knowledge—the monologue (IV.2.26–29) did nothing, judging from what Euthydemos said in response to it, too, to remedy the situation. Even after all that Socrates had said of self-knowledge, Euthydemos thought that Socrates had not yet shown him how to begin examining himself or, at any rate, his capacity or power (IV.2.30). In point of fact, though, not only had Socrates already shown Euthydemos how to begin to examine himself, but the youth had even already begun, when Socrates forced the issue: for to examine oneself is, to begin with, to examine justice. But then, if Euthydemos did not understand that Socrates had already shown him how to begin examining himself, through the monologue concerning self-knowledge, this was, according to the monologue itself, because he did not understand the examination of justice. The youth's irremediable ignorance of self-knowledge—again, his ignorance of the fact that the examination of justice is the beginning of self-knowledge—arose, by that account, from his failure to understand the examination of justice. And that means Socrates was not so much offering Euthydemos an explanation of self-knowledge as Xenophon was offering us, through the youth's failure to understand the explanation of self-knowledge that Socrates was offering him, an explanation of the youth's ignorance of himself. In other words, the Socratic monologue offers the reader an explanation of the fact that the youth's ignorance of himself (as a self) arose from his ignorance of the truth about justice, on one hand, and gave rise to his ignorance of the good, on the other.

Socrates, notes Strauss, "makes here a clear, if tacit, distinction between the good things and the noble ones; the former are more fundamental than the latter."[11] That is to say, in the monologue's first part (IV.2.26–27), Socrates explained that for the most part, if not always, self-knowers acquire the good and guard against the bad things (IV.2.26), because they know what sorts of things are good and bad, while the self-ignorant fail to acquire the good and encounter the bad things, because they are ignorant of which is which (IV.2.27). But then, in the monologue's second part (IV.2.28–29), he did an about-face and explained that self-knowers, if or since they acquire the good things, acquire the noble things (IV.2.28), while the self-ignorant, if or since they encounter the bad things, encounter the shameful things (IV.2.29).[12] And it was, fittingly enough, in the course of explaining that the noble things are acquired by self-knowers, too, that Socrates said of the self-ignorant that they desire not only to be taught, but even to be ruled, by self-knowers. Socrates painted Euthydemos a pretty picture of the world, one in which political power followed from philosophy, the noble things from the good ones (consider *Cyropaedia* VIII.3.48). But Socrates also said of the self-ignorant that they know neither themselves nor others. They fail utterly to know the things they need, what they are doing, and all others with whom they have dealings (IV.2.27). And how then, if the self-ignorant know neither themselves nor others, can they possibly know both themselves (to be ignorant of themselves and others) and others (to be knowers of themselves and others)?[13] If they fail utterly to know the things they need and what they are doing, they cannot possibly know that they need advice-givers or rulers, that they are doing themselves no good without them. On the other hand, if they fail utterly to know all others with whom they have dealings, they cannot possibly know which of the others with whom they have dealings are, and which are not, self-knowers. Although Socrates said that the self-ignorant desire to be taught or ruled by self-knowers, everything else he said, when thought through, contradicted this. And so, too, did the second Socratic dialogue—according to which, as we saw, unwise men were so far from desiring to be ruled by wise men that they enslaved or destroyed them (IV.2.33, consider *Symposium* 2.10). Even as the self-ignorant do not desire to be taught or ruled by self-knowers, do self-knowers desire to advise or to rule the self-ignorant? Socrates did not say so (IV.2.28); after all, if the good things are "more fundamental" than the noble things, self-knowers desire to fulfill, nobly, the hopes of others for the good things less strongly than they desire the good things (contrast IV.2.26 with IV.2.28). Nor did Socrates say of their dealings with the self-ignorant what he did say of their dealings with other self-knowers, that they take pleasure in them (compare IV.2.28 with I.6.14). There was, then, no love lost between self-knowers and the self-ignorant, who were so far from taking pleasure in self-knowers that they enslaved or destroyed them, as we saw, just as if they were their enemies. And the fact that self-knowers would have to fulfill the hopes of the self-ignorant for the good things against their will, too, only exacerbates the problem, later made famous by Plato's *Republic*, of the weakness of their own will or desire to do so. The whole problem of the coincidence of political power and philosophy—which is rationality itself—boils down to this: that wise men do not desire to advise, much less to rule their fellow citizens or allies and, since they would have to do so against their will, albeit for the sake of their fellow citizens or allies, their fellow citizens and allies do not desire to force the wise men to force them, in turn, to do as the wise men say. The tyrants included among the demos do not desire to force "skilled household managers" to force them, in turn, to rein in their great, imagined needs (for beauty, strength, wealth, reputation, and political power, for example). And with that, in the wake of the problem of the rationality of political affairs, we come at last to the one and only example of self-knowledge, or the lack thereof, to be found in the Socratic monologue concerning it.

The example both conceals and reveals what self-knowledge is. For Socrates cites, as *the* example of self-ignorance, cities that, in ignorance of their lack of power or capacity, go to war against stronger cities and are, because of this, either destroyed or enslaved. And yet, first of all, the monologue has so far been concerned with the self-knowledge of human beings, individual human beings, and not with the self-knowledge of cities or collectives of human beings. And justifiably so. After all, not only the cities but also the parts of the cities, the many, individual human beings, have (proper) names—"Athens," say, and "Chairephon" or "Chairecrates"—whereas the parts of the many, individual human beings, the parts of the parts of the cities—"hands" or "feet," say—do not (consider II.3.18–19). In any event, why divert our attention in this way from the self to the city, "too" or "also"?[14] Second, knowledge of one's power or capacity to acquire the good things was only half of self-knowledge, the less fundamental half, according to the statement with which Socrates opened his monologue. Whatever happened to knowledge of the truth about justice? By leaving the beginning of self-knowledge out of account, Socrates was intentionally making the very same mistake that was made unintentionally, not only by Euthydemos (IV.2.25), but also by "the many." For the many call "mad" those who are ignorant of the things the many know (III.9.6). So those who, in ignorance of their lack of strength, try to lift houses are called mad by the many

(III.9.7). According to Socrates, however, madness (whose opposite is wisdom) is ignorance of oneself—or, to be more precise, ignorance of oneself comes *nearest* to full-fledged madness (III.9.7). And to be ignorant of oneself is especially, in turn, to be ignorant of the things one believes one knows, the very same things the many, too, are ignorant of and believe they know (III.9.6), which is to say, the just or the noble and good things (compare III.9.6 with III.9.5). There is, by that account, only a difference of degree between the many unwise men and the few full-fledged madmen. Nearly everyone is nearly mad (III.9.7). But why, then, does the example of self-ignorance cited by Socrates give credence to the mistaken opinion of the many, according to which the many themselves are not self-ignorant, since only full-fledged madmen—those who, in ignorance of their lack of strength, power, or capacity, fail "to act," as Socrates liked to say, "according to their power" (I.3.3)—are?

The one and only example of self-ignorance is, on one hand, merely a half-finished diversion. On the other hand, we can say how the example reveals what self-knowledge is, too, precisely if we allow Socrates to divert our attention for the moment from the self to the city. For the works or deeds of generals acting on behalf of cities, the nearest thing there is to the works or deeds of cities "themselves," so to speak, made an appearance in the conversation already. At the same time, Socrates made it clear that works or deeds are just, according to Euthydemos and other good citizens, insofar as they are beneficial to or good for friends, harmful to or bad for enemies. But the will, the intention to do justice—"the virtue of a real man (*anēr*)" (II.6.35, II.3.14, II.1.28, II.2.2)—is therefore the will, the intention to go to war against stronger cities, either when the latter are unjust enemies or when there is no common good between them. And that "harmful" military campaigns are not always "shameful," that they are sometimes just the opposite, follows from the example of self-ignorance cited by Socrates. After all, not a moment after explaining to Euthydemos that the self-ignorant encounter the shameful things (disrepute, ridicule, contempt, and dishonor), if or since they encounter the bad things (destruction and slavery), Socrates cited an example of self-ignorance in which only the bad things are encountered (IV.2.29). Consider, above all, the fate of Abradatas (*Cyropaedia* VII.3.11, VII.3.16).[15] Does, then, ignorance of one's power to save oneself from destruction or slavery at the hands of the stronger, if not also to destroy or enslave them, even though they are the stronger—does hope, in a word, for one's just deserts arise from the will, the intention to do justice? If so, to put this the other way around, the truth from which self-knowledge arises would appear to be "terrible," at least, because to know yourself to be a self would be to know yourself to be condemned, by nature, to death (*Apology* 27). However that may be, the two punishments suffered by the cities lacking self-knowledge—destruction and slavery—are the very same punishments suffered by a "wise" man who does not make any effort to conceal his "wisdom." Wise men, to say it once more, do not desire to rule their fellow citizens or allies (consider III.4.1). And how this reveals what self-knowledge is should go without saying. Suffice it to say only that Euthydemos did desire to rule. For the tacit distinction between the noble things and the "more fundamental," good ones was by no means clear to him: Euthydemos did not contradict the pretty picture of the world that Socrates painted him, self-contradictory though it was, owing to the fact that he did not separate the things according to classes or kinds (IV.5.11–12). And from the fact that the youth did not separate the more fundamental things from the less it arose that he could not even imagine happiness without political power. Political power is a disputably good thing if ever there was one (IV.2.35), on which it would be immoderate to pin his "hopes for the good things," unless he hoped for his just deserts from the all-powerful gods (IV.2.28, IV.3.17).

PART THREE

CHAPTER 5

"Natural Theology"

I

Through the Socratic monologue concerning self-knowledge, Xenophon offers the reader an explanation, also, of how the elenctic or "negative" teaching of Socrates would have affected good natures. With their opinions about justice refuted, their knowledge of the truth about justice would have given rise, via knowledge of themselves, to knowledge of their lack of power or capacity. According to Xenophon, Socrates took the liberty of adding to that mischievous (I.5.56, contrast IV.3.16 with IV.3.17) verse of Hesiod which he used to praise so highly, "according to one's power, offer sacrifices to the immortal gods," that "to act according to one's power" is good advice, not only toward gods but also toward friends and foreigners or allies and enemies (I.3.3). And only now that the effects of the Socratic refutation have slowly begun to make themselves felt would good natures have been in any position at all to know what Socrates meant by that—by saying that "to act according to one's power," toward enemies, for example, is good advice (IV.2.29). As Socrates put it elsewhere, too, despite the fact that "the good men" and Virtue herself say that "whatsoever a man soweth, that shall he also reap" (Galatians 6:7), the weak are often destroyed, enslaved, or otherwise harmed by the strong (contrast II.1.20–21, II.1.27–28 with II.1.10–15; I.1.8, *Oeconomicus* 5.7, 5.13, but contrast 5.12), which is just another way of saying the (cosmic) gods are often gratified by bad, not good, men (I.3.3). And good natures would have felt their desire to rule their fellow citizens and allies and to harm their enemies weaken insofar as they came to know that they lacked the power, for this reason, to acquire the good things by doing so. So far from being just another propaedeutic to the "positive" or nonelenctic teaching, the "negative" or elenctic teaching of Socrates was indeed, then, nothing less than (the basis of) the Socratic teaching itself—according to which learning, knowledge, or the wise man's stance toward learning or knowledge is unnecessary for and incompatible with doing politics. And, just as we thought, the protreptic teaching would have prepared good natures to realize as much.

However, just because refuted, good natures knew the truth about justice and themselves, did they know with equal certainty which pursuits will not produce good, and which will not produce bad, outcomes? Bearing in mind that Socrates was a refuted good nature himself, if not *the* refuted good nature, his knowledge of the truth about justice, on one hand, and of himself, on the other, was absolutely certain and beyond dispute; his knowledge of his lack of resources, power, or capacity, however, was not. Only if we knew with absolute certainty that reason is "our only Star and compass," to repeat, would we know with absolute certainty that a ship's pilot, for instance, with his less then absolutely certain knowledge, should be given the run of the ship. And the question of the usefulness of praying to the gods was, as we saw, left hanging. So—like Ischomachus, the gentleman, who hoped and prayed for noble safety in war (*Oeconomicus* 11.7ff.)—the many youths who kept their distance from Socrates after having been refuted by him (IV.2.40) were perhaps not nearly mad, they were perhaps wise, to pin their hopes for happiness on something so disputably good as political power. The refuted good nature would have been left asking himself whether it can be known with any certainty that our less than absolutely certain knowledge is our "only Star and compass." Thanks not only to justice (compare *Oeconomicus* 1.16–17 with 1.15 and 1.23), to summarize the results of Chapter 3, but also, and especially perhaps, to piety (compare *Oeconomicus* 1.21 with 5.18–20, 6.1), to summarize the results of Chapter 4, it is highly paradoxical to suppose that virtue is knowledge. On the basis of what, then, did Socrates do so? Before venturing an answer, however, we need a better statement of the question. For this reason, before turning to the conversation between Socrates and Euthydemos concerning piety (IV.3.2), we should pause to say a few brief words about Socrates's conversation with Aristodemos ("Best-of-the-demos"), another one of "those who lived constantly" with him (compare I.4.1 with IV.1.1). That conversation, during which Xenophon was also present, was the only one explicitly devoted to the divine (*to daimonion*) (I.4.2).

II

Aristodemos was not doing pious deeds—he was neither performing sacrifices nor using divination—and he was making mocking, impious speeches about those who were (I.4.2). The source of his impious deeds and speeches were his impious thoughts. Aristodemos, simply put, did not believe in the gods in whom the city believed. For he did not see the gods themselves (compare I.4.10 with I.4.9; contrast I.4.13). And he did not believe that the divine needs anything from human beings (I.4.10). Now if, after giving thought to the evident facts, works, or deeds for which the invisible[1] gods are allegedly responsible (compare IV.3.13–14 with I.4.10), Aristodemos had come away with the view that the gods worry about particular human beings (I.4.13–14), to say nothing of human beings in general (I.4.11), then neither their invisibility nor his best guess as to what the divine is or requires of us would have prevented him from caring about them. By his account, however, we are all at the mercy of chance (I.4.4)—of chance *motions*, Socrates took him to be saying, *of bodies*: earth, water, "and each of the other great beings" (I.4.8). And it was for this reason, because he did not believe that the gods are worried about him, that Aristodemos did not care about them either (I.4.11, consider IV.3.15; contrast I.4.13). But his impious deeds and speeches were foolish according to Socrates (I.3.1), who thus, upon learning of them, struck up a conversation with Aristodemos in which he appeared to go straight to their source: his impious thoughts about the divine (I.4.2). In his conversation with Aristodemos, Socrates apparently tried to show to the latter's satisfaction—that is, by an argument from facts evident "to all human beings" (compare I.4.15 with *Oeconomicus* 17.1–3) and not just to one or another of the "cities and nations" (I.4.15–16; contrast I.1.19 with I.1.9)—how carefully the invisible being or beings responsible for the facts provide for us. Seeing as how Aristodemos was prevented from serving the gods of the city by his doubts about the fact, if it is a fact, that human beings are served by them (I.4.11), Socrates made as if to argue that we are served by them, at least when it comes to the makeup of the human soul and the human body. He did so apparently because, with his interlocutor's doubts about divine providence put to rest, there would have been nothing left to prevent him from serving the gods. But did Socrates, with his "argument from design" for the gods of the city, make Aristodemos pious or more pious than he found him? Or was he, just as some of his critics wrote or said, particularly able to urge or exhort human beings to piety, for one, yet insufficient to lead them all the way toward it (I.4.1)?

If Socrates succeeded in making Aristodemos pious or more pious, Xenophon failed to say so. Instead, as we saw, he arranged for us to make up our own minds after considering the conversation between Socrates and Aristodemos for ourselves. And what becomes clear, if we do our part, is that Xenophon was himself one of the critics who wrote or said, in his *Grudge-Bearing*, that the most that Socrates could do was urge or exhort human beings to piety among other things. First of all, when it comes to the "design" of the human soul and the bodies, the argument raises more questions than it answers. Again, we must be brief, but was the human soul's ability to be on guard against hunger, thirst, cold, heat, sickness (I.4.13), injury, revulsion (I.4.6), and death (I.4.7)—in particular, when we use our hands, which our upright posture allows us to do (I.4.11, I.4.14), to cultivate the arts and thus, doing for ourselves what the divine artisan could not do for us, pull ourselves up above the other animals by our bootstraps (I.4.11, I.4.14, IV.3.7, IV.3.10; consider Diels–Kranz 59B.21b)[2]—not beneficial only insofar as it was impossible for the god to make a *better* human body, one without the ability to suffer these and other "bad things" (IV.3.11, I.4.11)?

For example, were eyelids, eyelashes, and eyebrows not beneficial only insofar as it was impossible for the god to make eyes more resistant to injury?[3] Were eyelids, which offer the eyes protection but get in the way of their use, and eyelashes, which make way for their use but offer little protection, not beneficial only insofar as it was impossible for the god to contrive anything that would be able to protect the eyes and, at the same time, make way for their use? For each picked up the other's slack. And were eyebrows, which pick up the eyelashes' slack in the event of sweat just as the eyelashes pick up the eyebrows' slack in the event of winds, not beneficial only insofar as it was impossible for the god to spare human beings from sweating, much less from doing work, which makes us sweat in the first place (II.1.20, II.1.28; *Oeconomicus* 4.24 in context)? Were incisors, which are fit for biting but not for chewing, and molars, which are fit for chewing but not for biting, not beneficial only insofar as it was impossible for the god to contrive anything that would be able to bite and, at the same time, chew? Again, each picked up the other's slack. And besides, were teeth not beneficial to begin with only insofar as it was impossible for the god to relieve animals of the desire to eat (one another: IV.3.10)? Socrates leaves no room for doubt about any of this when, last but not least, he let slip that whereas eating takes place near the eyes and nose, excretion takes place as far away "as possible" from the senses (I.4.6); as if no more could be done, when it came to the makeup of each being, than the makeup of each (class or kind of) being allowed.

And were the god's hands tied, "by nature" (I.4.14), not only when it came to the makeup of the human body but also when it came to the makeup of the human soul? For was divination not beneficial only insofar as it was impossible for the god to make a *better* human soul: one with absolutely certain knowledge of "the outcome" (compare I.4.18 with I.1.6ff.; *Oeconomicus* 5.18)? If so, seeing as how the attributes of the human soul and the human body that were possible for the god to make were not evidently good against the evidently bad attributes of the human body that were impossible for the god to will away, "are" they purposeful works, according to Socrates, or are they "like" purposeful works (compare I.4.6, the beginning and the end, with I.4.7)? Only evidently beneficial works, works whose coming into being is evidently beneficial, can be said to be purposeful (I.4.4). So perhaps Socrates agreed with Aristodemos that he, being human, "chanced upon" the best soul and body possible by nature (compare I.4.14 with I.4.8) because—living like gods in comparison to the other animals (thanks mainly to the cultivation of the arts), but like the other animals in comparison to gods, whose better souls and bodies are by nature impossible (I.4.14)—even or precisely the best soul and body possible by nature leaves much to be desired. Add to this that, contrary to all expectation, Socrates did not so much as try to liken either what we touch (and, not only what we touch, but also what we see, hear, smell, and taste) or what we touch with, which is to say, either our own or other bodies, to purposeful works (I.4.5), and the question arises: is not the makeup of each (class or kind of) being the work of chance motions of bodies? Yet again, Socrates took Aristodemos to be saying as much. Even as he himself gave the first impression of pushing back against this, however, Socrates did not deny that—he only asked whether—earth, water, "and each of the other great beings," in the first place, the heavenly things, in the second, move by chance (I.4.8, consider I.4.14).[4] And did he not affirm, in between the only remarks he ever makes about the (many) gods of the city (I.4.15–16, I.4.18), that the (one) god is that *in* each and every body which positions or moves them in such a way as is pleasing to itself (I.4.17; contrast IV.3.9)?[5] But in that case, to put two and two together, is "the god" anything other than that motion in the bodies which is limited, "by nature," to making up from them just such (classes or kinds of) beings as are evidently made up from them?[6] And is "mother nature," while providing for the existence of the animal species, not so much a kind and loving mother as an absent father to the individuals: begetting only to abandon them to the care of their no less abandoned mothers (I.4.7; consider II.2.3)?[7]

III

It is not necessary to insist on the point. For, however many unanswerable questions the argument itself may raise about the "design" of the human soul and the bodies—unanswerable, at any rate, if the human soul is indeed the best there is (consider Plato, *Laws* 716c4–6)—the gods of the city are, as of yet, nowhere to be found (consider I.4.9). So far, to use a term that Socrates avoids like the plague all throughout the only Socratic conversation explicitly devoted to it, we find only the *daimonion* (I.4.2, I.4.10).[8] And neither Xenophon nor Socrates leaves any room for doubt: Socrates was unable to do more than urge or exhort human beings to piety or moderation concerning the gods of the city.

Xenophon's parting words were that, "by saying these things," Socrates made his "companions" believe that nothing escapes the notice of the gods and thus, by making them believe that nothing escapes the notice of the gods, Socrates made his companions resist unholy and unjust or shameful things, not only in public, but even in private (I.4.19). Then, "by saying these things," did Socrates make only those of his companions who *already* served the gods—who *already* resisted unholy (and unjust or shameful) things, at least in public—resist, even in private, unholy (and unjust or shameful) things? By his own account, only those who *already* serve the gods will judge that he was right to say that nothing escapes their notice (I.4.18). But Aristodemos, who was one of "those who lived constantly" (*tois sundiatribousi*) with Socrates (I.4.1–2; consider IV.1.1), not one of his "companions" (*tous sunontas*), did not serve the gods or resist unholy things even in public (contrast I.4.19 with I.4.2), much less in private. And thus, "by saying these things," Socrates made those of his companions who were already somewhat pious and just or noble more pious and just or noble. He did not make those who were not already somewhat pious, like Aristodemos, pious.[9] But perhaps, at the same time as he made those of his companions who resisted unholy and unjust or shameful things at least in public resist them even in private, Socrates made Aristodemos, who did not resist unholy things even in public, resist them at least in public. In that case, "by saying these things," Socrates brought Aristodemos back from the brink of madness. From the insane, extreme opinion that there is no shame in saying or doing anything either in private or even in public—which is just the opposite of the equally insane, equally extreme opinion that saying or doing anything in public is shameful—Socrates brought Aristodemos around to the sane, intermediate opinion that to say or do certain things in public, if not in private, is shameful (I.1.14).

What apparently started out as an argument for the gods of the city from facts evident to all human beings (I.4.5–14) ended up, before long, as an "argument," if we can even call it that, from generally accepted opinions (I.4.15–16). Aristodemos gave Socrates no choice but to shift his ground away from facts evident to all when, after the "natural theology" left him completely unfazed, if not confirmed in his disbelief, he told Socrates that he would not believe that the gods serve him, much less would he serve them himself, until such time as they send him, "just as you say they send you," advisors concerning what one should and should not do (I.4.14–15). Since the argument from facts evident to all failed to convince him that "the things that come to be" (*tōn gignomenōn*) (IV.3.14) is the same thing as "their (purposeful) works" (*ta erga autōn*) (IV.3.13), to put this differently, and since he did not believe that the gods send Socrates advisors, only that *he said* they did, Aristodemos would not believe in the gods of the city until such time as he saw them, or their servants, with his own eyes (IV.3.13). In this situation, Socrates asked three questions, one after another, with which he reduced Aristodemos to silence (I.4.15–16). The questions, taken together, defied Aristodemos to flout openly the opinions of the cities and nations in general, the Athenians and the Greeks in particular, and state publicly that there is no such a thing as special revelation or divine providence (I.4.15–16). Precisely because he had some prudence, however, he dared not answer (consider I.4.8). To mock those who use divination and perform sacrifices (I.4.2) was one thing, to flout openly the opinions underlying such deeds was another thing entirely. And we can be sure of Aristodemos's thought, his silence notwithstanding, because Socrates all but answered his own questions, which were anything but simple or straightforward, in the very act of asking them.

First, Socrates asked Aristodemos whether it was his opinion that when the gods make declarations to the Athenians by way of divination, or when they forewarn the Greeks by way of miracles, or when they forewarn all human beings by way of neither divination nor miracles (*Oeconomicus* 17.1–3), they include him too, or whether it was his opinion that they exclude him and him alone from this care of theirs (I.4.15). But Aristodemos could not possibly be of the opinion that the gods exclude him alone from this care of theirs if it was his opinion that they do not include him when they make declarations to the Athenians by way of divination. For they exclude the Sicilians and the Egyptians (I.4.17), in that case, too. Nor could he possibly be of the opinion that the gods exclude him alone if it was his opinion that they do not include him when they forewarn the Greeks by way of miracles. For they exclude the Egyptians, in that case, too. Rather, if and only if it was his opinion that they do not include him when they forewarn all human beings, by way of neither divination nor miracles, could he possibly be of the opinion that the gods exclude him alone. So far from being of the opinion that the gods exclude him alone from care in which all other human beings are included, however, the opinion to which Aristodemos had only just given expression was that, regardless of what Socrates said of his "*daimonion*," the gods do not include Socrates and Socrates alone in care from which all other human beings are excluded. In other words, when Aristodemos expressed his opinion that the gods do not give Socrates advice they withhold from all other human beings, Socrates took issue with the converse opinion according to which the gods withhold from Aristodemos advice they give all other human beings. And not only did he let Aristodemos's opinion off the hook, by doing so, but he also sided with it against his own expressed opinion. If the gods do not withhold from a single, solitary human being advice they give all others, do the gods withhold from the Egyptians advice they give the Greeks? Do they withhold from the Sicilians advice they give the Athenians? Last but certainly not least, if the gods do not withhold from Aristodemos advice they give all other human beings, do they withhold from all other human beings, including Aristodemos, the advice they give Socrates? So perhaps there is no such thing as "special," but only "general," revelation.[10] Second, Socrates asked Aristodemos whether he thought that the gods would have planted in human beings the opinion that they are able to do good and evil if they were unable to do so, and human beings, deceived the entire time, never perceived this (I.4.16). But of course, precisely if Aristodemos thought that the gods plant in human beings—Socrates did not say "all human beings"—the false opinion that they are able to do good and evil, he must have thought that he, for his part, so far from being deceived the entire time, perceived that they are unable to do so.[11] Moreover, precisely if Aristodemos thought that the opinion is false, he must have thought that the gods are unable to plant it in us. To plant in human beings a false opinion is, after all, to do evil. So perhaps there are those, like Aristodemos, who have seen the opinion that there is such a thing as divine providence for what it is: neither true nor god-given.[12] Third, Socrates asked Aristodemos whether he saw that both the oldest and the wisest "human things," cities and nations, are the most pious; but then, instead of asking him whether he saw that the wisest human *beings* are the most pious, Socrates asked Aristodemos, in effect, whether he saw that the oldest human beings—whose minds are not in the best shape (IV.8.1, IV.8.8, *Apology* 6)—are the most pious (I.4.16). So perhaps even the wisest human *things*, cities and nations like Athens and Greece, are less wise than the wisest human *beings* (consider I.2.52).

Now that Socrates's questions reduced Aristodemos to silence, given his thought, is as good an indication as any that he brought him around to the sane, intermediate opinion that to say or do certain things in public, if not in private, is shameful. In that case, though, Socrates won a pyrrhic victory on behalf of the cities and nations. For his questions went to show that Aristodemos thought the cities and nations in general, the Athenians and the Greeks in particular, unwise. They are unwise to believe that the gods advise those who ask the Pythia what they should do that they should obey the laws (I.3.1, IV.3.16); they are unwise to believe that the gods gratify those who gratify them (I.4.18, IV.4.16–17); and they are unwise, albeit pious, to act accordingly. And, by teaching Aristodemos not to say such things, by teaching him incontinence in speech (I.5.5–6), Socrates did not teach him not to think them. But what is one *to think* of the divine? Do the gods serve those who serve them by obeying the laws, as the cities and nations would have it, or not? That is the question with which Socrates's "argument" from generally accepted opinions leaves us. And Socrates gives us an answer in the sequel. Or rather, if and only if we separate things (like potentiality and actuality, learning and doing, one and many, hedonism and justice) according to classes or kinds, he gives us two answers, *the* two answers: one in an initial statement (I.4.17), another in a restatement (I.4.18). Xenophon thus spares readers who are not gripped by the question of the need to face its either-or, even as he gives others who desire to learn the opportunity to do so.

According to the initial statement, if Aristodemos, being "good," were to learn of his own mind that it manages his body in no other way than in whatever way it wants, then he should think that the one god's prudence, "also," is that in each thing or, rather, body which puts in place, positions, or moves all things in such a way as is pleasing to itself (I.4.17). And he followed this up by saying that Aristodemos should not think that while his eyes can see things far away, the eye of the god cannot see all things at once. Nor should he think that while his soul can worry about things "here," in Athens, and elsewhere, in Egypt, and in Sicily, the god's prudence cannot take care of all things at once (I.4.17). Now, to be clear, Socrates did not say that Aristodemos should think that the god can and does see and take care of all things at once, which is exactly what he will say in the restatement (I.4.18), but only that Aristodemos should not think that the god cannot do so. As to this, whether or not the divine attributes include seeing and caretaking, Aristodemos should suspend judgment. That is only natural. After all, because we can only see, and only worry, about one thing at a time (II.3.19), "seeing" and "caretaking" are unthinkable, for us, if or when predicated of that which sees and takes care of all things at once. Aristodemos should, then, think that there is a principle of motion in the elementary bodies—by each (bodily) thing, Socrates can only mean earth, water, "and each of the other great beings," since Aristodemos's body is managed by his own mind, not the god's—which it is safe to say is, also, "hedonistic" (II.1.8–9). However, as to whether that principle of motion does what it does by chance or by seeing all things and taking care of them at once (I.4.8–9), if only in some equivocal sense of the terms, Aristodemos should acknowledge his ignorance. "Those in Israel who were unbelievers also professed [the former] opinion," according to Maimonides; "they are those of whom it is said: *They have belied the Lord, and said, It is not He.*" On the other hand, "those who, deviating from our Law, believed in [the latter] opinion were those who said," if not in Israel, "*The Lord hath forsaken the earth.*"[13]

According to the restatement, "however" (*mentoi*), Socrates's companions will judge that the divine is so great and of such a sort as to see, hear, and take care of all things at once. And that was not what Socrates just told Aristodemos he should think—not by a long shot. Moreover, he just told Aristodemos that his thoughts about the one god should be based on learning, learning something about himself, not doing. But Socrates's companions will judge that the divine is "so great and of such a sort," in this case, if or since they serve the many gods (I.4.18, reading *autous* with all manuscripts except A). They will do so, to be exact, if or since they serve the gods in the hope (IV.3.17) that the gods are like grateful—or just (compare I.4.18 with IV.4.24, IV.4.17, and II.2.2–3) rather than "hedonistic"—human beings, who serve those who serve them, albeit by giving them superhuman advice. And for a conversation in which Socrates made as if to argue that the gods serve Aristodemos apparently because, with his doubts about divine providence put to rest, he would serve them, this is a stunning reversal. Aristodemos, to repeat, thought it unwise to act on the hope that the gods serve those who serve them, for example, by performing sacrifices. And what did Socrates say to that? His case for the gods of the city rested in the end on this word of advice: do not think, just act (on the hope that the gods serve those who serve them)! It is tempting to think that, when Socrates said that we learn who is prudent by asking advice, he was casting doubt on his own prudence. After all, in the very same breath, he advised Aristodemos to serve (human) beings whose willingness and ability to serve Aristodemos in turn was a matter of mere conjecture (I.4.18). But it is better to say that he was pointing to the fact that he himself was giving superhuman advice. Socrates was not teaching. In the first place, he was urging or exhorting to the hope with which those who "have not seen, and yet have believed" (John 20:29) that gods are willing and able to serve them serve the gods (compare I.4.18 with II.2.5).

Xenophon's parting words go to show that Socrates's conversation with Aristodemos would not have affected his already pious (and just or noble) companions one way or another if not for his own parting words. Thanks to his own parting words, however, Socrates made them believe that nothing escapes the notice of the gods (compare I.4.17–18 with I.4.19). And Socrates's parting words were borne out by the facts, in that case, or by Xenophon's parting words about the facts. For just as Socrates said, Xenophon says, those of his companions who already served the gods, who were already pious (and just or noble), came to the judgment that Socrates was right to say that the divine sees, hears, and takes care of all things at once. Since that would have been news to "the many," both in Athens and beyond, who did not think that the gods were omniscient (I.1.19, *Oeconomicus* 7.31),[14] it would seem as though Socrates was teaching his companions something new, something the Athenians and the Greeks did not already know, about the divine (consider *Symposium* 4.47–48). And this is no small feat, to say the least. But how in the world did Socrates accomplish it? He did not even try to make an argument. So, in the second place, why did his companions take his word for it that omniscience is to be included among the divine attributes? In the initial statement, Socrates let it be known that the human soul can worry about things farther away than the human eye can see. Even with his body in Athens, Aristodemos's soul can worry about things in Egypt or Sicily (I.4.17). His soul can do so, needless to say, because his ears can hear of them from others who claim, at least, to have seen them. And come to think of it, cannot the same be said for the gods? The human eye cannot see them (I.4.9, I.4.13, IV.3.13–14). But that never stopped the human soul from worrying about them (I.4.13). Since we do not get anything straight from the horse's mouth, we can take care of or worry about the gods only by hearing of them from others—others who can rightly claim, at least if they are not boasting or lying, to have seen them. Accordingly, while Socrates remarked upon divine hearing in the restatement (I.4.18), the distinction between divine and human hearing was conspicuously absent from the initial statement (I.4.17). The reason was that, earlier in the conversation, Socrates had given an account of human hearing that was so exaggerated as to erase any distinction between it and divine hearing. As if there were no limit to its receptivity, either in quality or in quantity, human hearing receives "all sounds," by that account, and is "never" filled up (I.4.6). By erasing the distinction between human and divine hearing, Socrates made our hearing out to be the divine sense—that is, the one by means of which we sense the divine. Only by hearing (and not by seeing or touching, much less smelling or tasting) can we perceive anything so great and of such a sort as the god or gods hearing and seeing and taking care of all things at once. And while Socrates tells us as much, Xenophon shows us. For here we have, right before our eyes, those of Socrates's companions who were already pious and just or noble receiving word from Socrates of the gods hearing and seeing and taking care of all thing at once. Undeterred by the fact that the divine attributes are so immeasurably greater than ours both in quality and in quantity that the terms in which Socrates described them were only equivocal, they took his word for it that nothing escaped the notice of the gods (I.4.19). And they took his word for it that nothing escaped their notice because they took his word for it that the *daimonion* gave him signs. With that, Socrates clinched the argument. Thus, to tie everything together, only those who serve the gods—who serve the gods, to be exact, in the hope that the gods are willing and able to return the favor—place their trust in Socrates's "*daimonion*" specifically, divination generally. But Socrates was indeed, after all, unable to do more than urge or exhort human beings to do such a thing.

Thomas Aquinas took a short, straight way to somewhat the same truth to which Xenophon, through the Socratic conversation with Aristodemos, took a long, roundabout way, when he said, "The sole way to overcome an adversary of divine truth is from the authority of Scripture. . . . For that which is above human reason we believe only because God has revealed it. Nevertheless, there are certain likely arguments that should be brought forth in order to make divine truth known. This should be done for the training and consolation of the faithful, and not with any idea of refuting those who are adversaries. For the very inadequacy of the arguments would rather strengthen them in their error, since they would imagine that our acceptance of the truth of faith was based on such weak arguments."[15]

Had Aristodemos singled out Socrates by name when Socrates asked him to say who it was that he admired for wisdom (I.4.2–3), Xenophon would have reinforced the popular prejudice against the philosophers (I.2.31). But Xenophon never denied that Socrates, the philosopher (*Oeconomicus* 16.9), persuaded the youth that he was the wisest (human) being (I.2.52ff., consider IV.2.3). In fact, by having the sophist Antiphon make the case that Socrates was just but not wise (I.6.11–12) in order to get Xenophon and the other "close companions" of Socrates to leave Socrates for him (I.6.1, I.6.14), Xenophon affirmed that his "close companions" admired Socrates for wisdom more than anything else. Who could deny that Socrates was wise (*Apology* 16)? And if only Aristodemos, too (IV.1.1), lived constantly with Socrates (I.4.1), in no small part because he admired Socrates for wisdom—and of course, by not performing sacrifices (compare I.4.2 with I.3.3, *Oeconomicus* 2.4–8), by not using divination (compare I.4.2 with I.1.2–4, I.1.6), by not believing that the divine needs anything from human beings (compare I.4.10 with I.6.10), by believing the gods are invisible (compare I.4.9 with IV.3.13–14), and maybe even by not praying for anything at all (I.3.2),

Aristodemos was, in keeping with Plato's description of him, following so zealously in Socrates's footsteps that he went very far astray by going much too far in the right direction—how could he have put much stock in the wisdom of the other, "pre-Socratic" philosophers? For Socrates, thinking it impossible for human beings to discover "the causes"—that is, "the necessities"—by which the heavenly things come into being, conversed about the nature of all things so differently from them that, even to this day, he enjoys in certain, less perceptive circles a reputation for doing nothing of the sort (I.1.11–15, IV.7.5–7).[16] But, in that case, Aristodemos should have known that he was no more able to show Socrates's pious companions, by an argument from facts evident to all, that the god is "hedonistic" than Socrates was able to show Aristodemos, by that same means, that the gods are not. Now Socrates, it is true, could only urge or exhort to piety; yet how could Aristodemos be sure that the gods do not take specially good care of the souls of the Pythia and Socrates by revealing to them, and to all other human beings through them, "that which is above reason" (IV.3.12; *Apology* 14)? If it is indeed impossible for human beings to discover the *daimonia* (I.1.12) that the other, "pre-Socratic" philosophers sought to discover, perhaps Aristodemos had no leg to stand on, whereas Socrates's pious companions did. For if reason is unable to settle the dispute between those who say that revelation, on one hand, and those who say that reason, on the other, "is [our] only Star and compass," then even or precisely the latter, in the very same breath as they bid farewell to revelation, bid farewell to reason.[17] In that event, the basis of "rational decision-making" is an irrational decision; the basis for "sticking with the intellect," contrary to the cities and nations, is the sacrifice of the intellect. The absurdity of such a life—the life that Rawls, for one, recommended—is well-expressed by the fact that sometimes, to paint with less broad strokes than we have so far, Aristodemos did think pious thoughts. To say that he did not believe in the gods of the city was too simple because, when he got ready for battle (to harm enemies), he relented and performed sacrifices just like everybody else (I.4.2, reading *machomenon* with the major manuscripts,[18] consider *Oeconomicus* 5.18–20). Aristodemos was something like a fair-weather friend to the gods (*Cyropaedia* I.6.3–4). Xenophon's point is not so much that there are no atheists in foxholes, although the fact that piety is at its strongest in old age certainly suggests that there is something to that (I.4.16), as it is that Aristodemos's mockery of those who perform sacrifices only made a mockery, twice over, of Aristodemos himself. For he did not even know himself (to be under the divine or divinely sanctioned laws). But Aristodemos's lack of confidence in the wisdom of the other, "pre-Socratic" philosophers was just one side of the coin—of his admiration for Socrates's wisdom—the other side of which was his confidence that, in much the same way as Homer and others whom he admired for wisdom made up (myths and sculptures and paintings of) gods (I.4.3, consider I.4.9), Socrates was not being entirely serious or straightforward about his "*daimonion*." And in the not unlikely event that Aristodemos's confidence in Socrates's wisdom was not misplaced, Socrates's conversation with him, right up until his parting words, not only brought Aristodemos around to the sane, intermediate opinion that to say or do certain things in public is shameful, but also, by reminding him of what a good man should think of the divine (I.4.17), confirmed or strengthened him in his belief in the, if not Socrates's, *daimonion*.[19] Or Socrates brought him back around to the sane, intermediate opinion that the gods are not to be feared, that temples and altars where sacrifices are performed are not to be honored any more than the rocks, wood, and animals that go into making them (I.1.14). In Aristodemos's defense, it should go without saying, he was not alone in thinking that Socrates, whose nickname Xenophon wisely refrained from mentioning along with Aristodemos's here, did not believe in the gods of the city: the Athenians, just about all of them, could not have agreed more (compare I.4.2 with *Symposium* 6.6–8, 7.2–5; compare I.1.20 with I.2.1 and *Oeconomicus* 11.3). Even if Aristodemos were onto something, however, the question would still have to be put to Socrates, too: how could he be sure that the Pythia was lying or boasting? Unless some common ground can be staked out on the basis of which there may be a way of settling the dispute between reason and revelation, there is no good answer. And Socrates, who never ceased examining what each of the beings is (IV.6.1), was not about to act on blind faith.

IV

To return to Euthydemos, his hopes for happiness were immoderate and nearly mad, according to the elenctic teaching, at least on their face. So great were his imagined needs that, unless he were to please the all-powerful gods in pious gratitude for their providence, any hope that they would be provided for, in spite or because of his gratitude for their providence, was immoderate. For justice to be good—and again, to the bitter end, Euthydemos believed he knew that it was—divine service is a must. But then, in the aftermath of the refutation, the Socratic, "positive" or nonelenctic teaching made Euthydemos and others who were already moderate in their hopes and already pious, more moderate in their hopes and more pious (IV.3.15–18). And thus the Socratic, nonelenctic teaching picked up right where his elenctic teaching left off, at least "with a view to" Euthydemos, insofar as the elenctic teaching left the goodness of justice in at least some doubt, while the nonelenctic teaching's first order of business was to bury away, if not put to rest, the youth's lingering, reasonable doubts about its goodness in the only way Socrates knew how: with more piety.

On the other hand, to make Euthydemos more pious, Socrates apparently tried to show how carefully the gods provide for us in much the same way as he did in his conversation with Aristodemos—namely, by an argument from facts evident to all human beings. In that conversation, however, "natural theology" gave way to natural philosophy, on one hand, and revealed theology, on the other.[20] Even if we had not understood a word of what Socrates said there, it was no great secret that he had deep reservations about the capacity of human beings for "natural theology" or philosophy (I.1.11–15, IV.7.6–7). For the youth's training and consolation, then, Socrates brought forth one of those "likely," merely likely, "arguments" of which Thomas Aquinas spoke. And, when all is said and done, what stands out about Socrates's "argument from design" is not that it ends in failure—that is a foregone conclusion—but that, as far as Euthydemos was concerned, it is an unmitigated success (IV.3.15, IV.3.18). Euthydemos, as we will soon see, failed to see the flaws in the argument. And that means, given that the argument this time around was mainly about how good the world as we know it is for us, he failed to see the flaws in the world. Or rather, since those flaws are naturally part and parcel of the world as we know it, he failed to see the natural world. Fresh from their refutations, while thoughtfully listening to Socrates make the already pious Euthydemos more pious, good natures would therefore have the opportunity to see that the youth saw the natural world, if at all, through rose-colored glasses. Now Euthydemos, who was praying to the gods long before he ever gave any thought to how carefully they provide for us (compare IV.2.36 with IV.3.3), was no Aristodemos. He believed in the gods of the city. In connection with this, we alluded in passing to the fact that the two answers to the question of what a god is given in the initial statement and the restatement had in common with one another that a ground of each was self-knowledge—understood in the Socratic sense in the one case, in the Apollonian sense in the other. Beyond that, however, Socrates gave no indication as to how self-knowledge grounds what one should think about the divine. Nor did he give any indication that it would not be imprudent for Aristodemos to take his advice and serve (human) beings in the hope that they are willing and able to serve him in turn. Only in his conversation with Euthydemos did Socrates go beyond issuing a call to action and at least try to make the case, in speech, for piety. At any rate, before urging or exhorting Euthydemos, too, to serve the gods in hopes of being served by them in turn (compare IV.3.16–17 with I.4.18), Socrates impressed upon him that we owe the gods a debt of gratitude for all the good they do us (IV.3.15). And while, to be sure, Socrates would not have been able to do more than urge or exhort to gratitude as well if Euthydemos had been so hard-headed as to force the issue, it is more important for our purposes to note that, before impressing upon the youth that we owe the gods a debt of gratitude, Socrates, as you would expect, made a case that they do, in fact, do us good. He made as if to argue that we are served by the gods—not so much when it comes to the makeup of the human soul (IV.3.11–12), and not at all when it comes to the makeup of the human body (contrast I.4.5–7, I.4.11–14)—when it comes to the makeup of the world (IV.3.3–10): the heavenly things (IV.3.4, IV.3.8–9), the elements (IV.3.5–7), and the other animals (IV.3.10). But again, however successful it may have seemed to Euthydemos, the argument is a complete and utter failure. And good natures, while thoughtfully listening in, would therefore see not only that Euthydemos saw the natural world through rose-colored glasses, if at all, but also that his rose-colored glasses were a ground of the pious will, the pious intention to serve the gods in gratitude for all the good that they have done us (IV.3.15–16) and also, or instead, in hope for all the good that they will do us (IV.3.17). Either the youth's extrasensory perception of another, divine world was perhaps godsent or else, to make one final suggestion before getting down to brass tacks, it was grounded in his self-understanding. And the Socratic, nonelenctic teaching picked up right where his elenctic teaching left off "with a view to" a good nature like Xenophon, too, if the conversation with Euthydemos were to give some indication as to how the latter's self-understanding grounded his piety and as to how self-knowledge grounded what the former should think about the divine. In that case, while good natures listened thoughtfully to Socrates jokingly teach Euthydemos the only way he knew how to bury away the reasonable doubts previously mentioned, Socrates was seriously teaching them the only way he knew how to reasonably doubt the only way he knew how to bury them away.

V

Socrates's conversation with Euthydemos—like its subject matter, the world—is illuminated by the sun. First of all, Socrates said to Euthydemos, "we need light." For without that, said the youth, swearing for the second time "by Zeus," "we would be like the blind." And the gods provide us with light, just as Socrates said they did, but do they always provide us with light? Not at night, they do not. As if anticipating the objection, which only a noncontradictor like Euthydemos would not think to make, that we are therefore half-blind owing to the envy of the gods, Socrates was quick to point out that they provide us with night, or do not always provide us with light, on account of our need for rest. "We need rest," to be sure. And yet, even apart from the fact that Socrates was in no better position to point to our need for rest than he was to point to our need for light as evidence of divine care—for needs are, as such, evidence against this[21]—night is not rest. And rest, not night, is what we need. Socrates spoke of night, accordingly, as "a most beautiful" time to rest. For it seems only fitting, at any rate, that for as long as we cannot do anything needful owing to the darkness, we shut our eyes (I.4.6) and satisfy our need for rest. The distinction between the beautiful (noble) things and the needful or good ones—we perceive both the beautiful things and the good ones; only from the good things, however, do we also receive benefit (IV.3.11, II.2.3)—was by no means clear to Euthydemos, of course, who did not contradict the pretty picture of the natural or divine world that Socrates painted him, for much the same reason that he did not contradict the pretty picture of the political world that Socrates painted him. In his opinion, darkness, "too," no less than light, "is deserving of gratitude" (IV.3.3). But Socrates only sharpened, in the very act of papering over, the distinction. The sun illuminates the time of day "and everything else," he said, whereas the stars illuminate the time of night alone, "on account of which," he let drop, "we do many of the things we need." In that case, however, the day is not long enough for us to do everything we need, and the darkness of night is not only good for nothing but also, like our need for rest and light, harmful or bad. And Euthydemos readily agreed, for this reason, that fire is directly useful against darkness, which is not so "deserving of gratitude," after all (compare IV.3.7 with IV.3.3–4). In keeping with this, while the gods do not provide us with the light we need, they do provide us with the stars. Of the stars, however, we have no need whatsoever. For the moon, which illuminates both the time of night and the time of month, does for us all that the stars do and more (IV.3.4). But the stars, too, are beautiful (I.4.11). And so Euthydemos did not notice this either.

From the sun (IV.3.3–4), Socrates turned to earth and other elements (IV.3.5–7), before circling back around to the sun (IV.3.8–9). For heat, too, is "needful." And the sun, by drawing close to and going away from the earth over and over again, gives and takes away heat by turns. Summer is scorching hot, and winter is bitter cold, to be sure. But Socrates asked Euthydemos to give thought to the fact, if it is one, that the sun guards against doing us any harm; after all, just before drawing too close and overheating us or going too far away and freezing us, the sun circles back around and heads in the opposite direction. And Euthydemos readily agreed that the sun moves not only in such a way as to do us no harm but also, as Socrates put it, too, in such a way as to "benefit us the most" (IV.3.8). On one hand, however, if the sun were to stay put in the middle of the firmament, so as to provide us with just the right (needful) amount of heat always, would that not benefit us more, indeed, much more than this orderly motion from one extreme to the other? If the sun were never to leave us out in the cold, now *that* would benefit us the most. And yet, in actual fact, the sun moves not only in such a way as to benefit us much less than this but also, on the other hand, in such a way as to do us harm. For Socrates asked the youth, in the next place, to give thought to the fact that should the heat of summer or the cold of winter come upon us very suddenly, neither the one extreme nor the other would be bearable. Given this, he put it to the youth: do not the gods deserve gratitude—if not for the given fact, which is evidence against divine care, that neither extreme is bearable in itself—for the fact that the sun's motion from one extreme to the other is so slow and so steady that the change of seasons escapes our notice? And Euthydemos, swearing for the third and final time, "by Zeus," took the bait. By readily agreeing that the gods do deserve gratitude for this, Euthydemos agreed, albeit without noticing the change from one opinion (IV.3.8) to the other (IV.3.9), that the heat of summer and the cold of winter are unbearable. Only a noncontradictor like Euthydemos would not think to make the objection that the *sun* does not guard against doing *us* any harm and thus, owing to the envy of the gods, *we* have to contrive ways to save ourselves from the *sun* (IV.3.11). In particular, because the orderly motion from one unbearable extreme to the other is, as luck or mysterious gods would have it, so slow and so steady that it escapes our notice, we must learn how the moon illuminates the time of month (IV.3.4). And just as we must learn astrology, if we are to keep watch over the change of seasons (compare IV.7.4 with IV.3.9), we must have fire, among other things, if we are to save ourselves from the otherwise unbearable cold (IV.3.7) about which astrologers—"forewarned," so to speak, by reasoning from facts evident to all human beings—forewarn the rest of us. But how, then, did the change from one opinion to the other, contradictory opinion go unnoticed by Euthydemos? The conversation moves from one ill effect of the sun's motion (away from us) to another, from the darkness of night to the cold of winter, and the course of the conversation imitates, in this way, the course of the sun itself. There is the difference, however, that the change of seasons escapes the notice of anyone completely ignorant of the art of astrology on account of how slowly and steadily the cold of winter takes the place of the heat of summer, whereas it escaped the notice of Euthydemos that he changed his mind about the sun—whether it does or does not always provide us with the light we need, on one hand, and the heat we need, on the other—on account of his complete ignorance of dialectic, the art of separating the things according to classes or kinds in conversation (IV.5.12, IV.6.1). That we should be provided, slowly and steadily, with heat not long after we cannot bear the cold anymore is only fitting; after all, even if the orderly motion of the sun is only very disputably good, is it not beautiful to perceive? In the same way as the night is "a most beautiful" (*kalliston*) time to rest (IV.4.3), to spell this out a bit more fully, the sun is foremost among the heavenly things, the "most beautiful" things (*kallista*) put in order by the god or gods (compare I.4.13 with I.4.8 and I.4.11). And the distinction between the beautiful things and the good ones was, to repeat, by no means clear to Euthydemos.

The youth swore for the first time, "by Zeus," when he told Socrates that he had never before given any thought to how carefully the gods provide human beings with the good things (IV.3.3). He did so twice more, when Socrates gave him the chance to give thought to how carefully the gods provide us with them by means of the sun (IV.3.3, IV.3.8). And this along with everything else leads us to wonder: Is he really so changed? Or is this just more of the same thoughtlessness? If Euthydemos's stance toward the sun is any indication, works the benefits of which were by no means evident struck him as beneficial, somehow, so long as they were beautiful. Only evidently beneficial works can be said to be purposeful, however (I.4.4). The rest are up to chance (I.4.8). And hence, if the youth's stance toward the sun is any indication, chance works struck him as purposeful, somehow, so long as they were beautiful. But for the beautiful, in which chance and purpose come together as one, does "natural theology" fall apart into natural philosophy, on one hand, and into revealed theology, on the other? In that event, Euthydemos was not about to start thinking now, and Socrates was merely indicating a ground or a cause of the thoughtlessness that not only predated, but also postdated his conversation with the youth. Again, the sun illuminates everything. We have not heard the last of it.

VI

In the meantime, "we need food," in addition to light, rest, and heat. And this the gods give us, in due season, from the earth (IV.3.4–5). However, to say nothing of the fact that the gods do not always give us the food we need either, do they always give us the food we need when we work the earth at just the right time of year, when the sun is not too far away, at least? No. For the earth needs water for that, no less than "we need it." And while Socrates said that the gods provide the earth and us with water "most unenviously" (*apthonestaton*), for they provide the earth and us with water more unenviously than they give us food or provide us with light or heat, at any rate, to say that the gods provide water "most unenviously" is to deny—*not to affirm*—that they provide water without any envy whatsoever (IV.3.6).[22] There are, after all, droughts (I.1.15, *Oeconomicus* 5.18–20). Next up, after earth (IV.3.5) and water (IV.3.6), came fire (IV.3.7). As for air, the last of "the other great beings" (I.4.8), Socrates passed over it in silence. He did so less for the reason that Strauss gives (that to mention air is to call to mind the Socrates of Aristophanes's *Clouds*) than for the reason that the gods provide air and air alone, of all the things we need, always and without envy.[23] The less perceptive Euthydemos was led "to conclude, then, that the views of . . . Socrates on *pthonos* and divine *philanthrōpia* entail a total rejection of divine *pthonos*,"[24] while good natures, thoughtfully listening in, reached just the opposite conclusion. Even or precisely if they always, unenviously provide us with air, the gods only sometimes, enviously give us food from the earth, provide us with light and heat from the sun, and with water from the (unmentionable or, at least, unmentioned) clouds.

Now, although Socrates did not say that we need fire, for we need rest (IV.3.3), food (IV.3.5) and water (IV.3.6), light (IV.3.3) and heat (IV.3.8), *not* fire, the fact that the gods do not always provide us with the things we need makes fire enormously useful, both directly and indirectly. Fire is directly useful against darkness and cold, to repeat, because the sun does not always provide us with the light or the heat we need (compare IV.3.7 with IV.3.3–4 and IV.3.8–9). And besides picking up the sun's slack, fire is indirectly useful too. For Socrates said in the first place that, provided only there is water, "all the things useful to us" come seasonally from the earth (IV.3.6); yet he went on to say in the next place that, "of the things useful for life," nothing worthy of note comes to be without fire (IV.3.7). And nothing particularly useful to us comes from the earth without fire because fire is a sine qua non for every single art (IV.3.7; Plato, *Protagoras* 321c7–d3) and nothing particularly useful to us comes from the natural or divine world without the arts (I.4.11, IV.3.10). The envy of the gods makes the arts necessary; yet they do not make up for this, in turn, by providing us with the arts we need. The gods "provide" us with light (IV.3.3), night (IV.3.3), seasons (IV.3.5), and water (IV.3.6); food they "give" or "give up" from the earth that they *do* provide us with only if human beings work the soil (IV.3.5). Fire, by contrast, was "procured" for or by us (IV.3.7). Did Socrates mean by this that fire was "procured" for us from the envious Olympian Zeus, along with the arts, by the philanthropic Titan Prometheus? Unless Euthydemos thought that the other animals receive benefit from it too, which can scarcely be imagined, he, for one, did not believe that the gods provide us with fire (IV.3.9).—After all, to say nothing more of the myth of Prometheus, to be pious is to feel gratitude for (IV.3.15) and also, or instead, to hold out hope for divine providence (IV.3.17), whereas to cultivate the arts, to pull ourselves up above the other animals by our bootstraps, is *not only* to refuse to believe that the gods deserve much or any gratitude for their works or deeds *but also* to refuse, hubristically perhaps, to let them help us (consider III.9.8). Other, "pre-Socratic" philosophers, to give just the most striking example of this sort of thing, hoped in the fullness of time to gain from advances in the arts and sciences, or technology, in a word, the god-like power to provide human beings with the things they need (winds, rains, and seasons, to name but a few) even or precisely when the gods themselves, in their envy, do not (I.1.15).—Either way, light, night, seasons, water, and earth are given or god-given; fire not so much, and the arts not at all. And so, while apparently trying to show in his conversation with Euthydemos that the gods "have equipped" us (*kateskeuakasi*) with the things we need (IV.3.3), what Socrates actually said was that, by procuring fire and cultivating the arts, human beings "equip" themselves (*kataskeuazontai*) with the only things particularly useful for life (IV.3.7, IV.3.10, consider I.4.11).

Even Euthydemos, who did not notice anything amiss, stopped short of saying that the gods have no other work than serving human beings. For the gods care for human beings and the other animals equally, if equally well, by means of the sun and the elements (IV.3.9). Socrates, therefore, tried to show that the other animals, no less than the sun and the elements, are or are born and raised for the sake of human beings. And yet, while he did so to Euthydemos's satisfaction, good natures could not help noticing that, so far from showing that the gods care for the other animals for the sake of human beings, Socrates actually showed, on one hand, that the gods care *less* for human beings than for the other animals by means of the sun and the elements and, on the other hand, that the other animals are *not* for the sake of human beings (IV.3.10).—"In my opinion," Socrates said, human beings receive more benefit from the other animals than from the plants, which come, in due season, from the earth. And the way most human beings live, in actual fact, bears out his opinion. For most of the human race lives off the other animals, he pointed out, not off the land (off which the other animals live). And in turn, while the fruits of the earth are less for our sake than for the sake of the other, plant-eating animals, do not the gods care for human beings and the other flesh-eating animals equally well by means of the plant-eating animals or their "flesh," at any rate? But Socrates was careful to avoid the subject of the flesh-eating animals entirely. They are not for our sake, after all, but even harmful. And Socrates was careful to avoid the subject of the useless animals (*Oeconomicus* 17.14–15), too, which are not for our sake either. More than anything else, it is true, what satisfied Euthydemos that the other animals are born and raised by the gods for the sake of human beings was that even though horses, for example, are so much stronger than we are, they do as we wish. That they do so not from birth, however, but only if we raise them up and break or train them, by way of the arts, also escaped the youth's notice (IV.3.10).

Socrates summed up the results of the conversation so far when, just before Euthydemos indicated that the strong often—unless there is some divine intervention (I.3.5)—enslave the weak (IV.3.10), he singled out war as *the* work for the sake of which we train or habituate horses, for example, to do as we wish. But, then, is war no less necessary according to Socrates than farming or animal husbandry? By his account, war is even more necessary. For if "most" human beings live off the other animals, while a few live off the land, "all," he said, make use of warhorses (IV.3.10). And those who live off the other animals, as well as those who live off the land, make use of warhorses to defend themselves from those who, living off neither the other animals nor the land, live off other human beings by force or fraud (consider *Oeconomicus* 5.7ff., 7.25; *Cyropaedia* III.2.25). As for those who live off other human beings by enslaving, deceiving, and stealing or robbing, there need to be such people—people from whom those who live in peace and quiet need to defend themselves, in turn—owing to the envy of the gods. Nothing sums up their envy like the fact that the arts of war are necessary, if not good, for human beings (*Oeconomicus* 1.15).

At the same time, while making good natures take notice of the envy of the gods, Socrates made them take notice of the fact that their envy escaped Euthydemos's notice. If the youth's stance toward the sun was any indication, the envy of the gods escaped his notice on account of the beautiful things with which they provide us. Now since then, to be sure, Socrates made no reference to anything beautiful. With his very next breath, however, he distinguished the beautiful (noble) things, which we perceive, from the good ones, which we not only perceive but also receive benefit from (compare II.2.3). Only by reasoning about the things we perceive, he said, do we learn how each of them is advantageous, on one hand, and contrive ways to benefit from the good things and to save ourselves from the bad ones, on the other (IV.3.11). And not only do we learn, but also, by expressing ourselves, we teach the good things. But we neither teach nor learn that cities and nations, laws, and citizenship are good things, Socrates indicated, by expressing ourselves about them (IV.3.12). For they are, as we saw, noble (beautiful). Not a moment after war made its appearance, and just before divination did so, law entered the conversation. If the envy of the gods tempts human beings away from justice, toward enslaving, deceiving, and stealing or robbing, their envy gives us the opportunity to resist rather than give in to the temptation to do such things, which is as much as to say, their envy gives us the opportunity—the freedom—to do noble works or deeds. And thus, while the envy of the gods escaped the youth's notice in the case of the sun on account of the beauty of "the starry sky above," to bring to mind the famous last words of Kant's *Critique of Practical Reason*, did their envy escape his notice more generally on account of the nobility of "the moral law within," with which they provide us? As was to be expected, in giving thanks to the gods no less for the fact that, by expressing ourselves, we set down laws than for the fact that, by doing so, we teach and learn the good things (IV.3.12), Euthydemos did not notice the distinction Socrates clearly, if tacitly, made between cities and nations, laws, and citizenship, among other noble things, and the good ones.

VII

If we are powerless to know which things are advantageous for the future, Socrates asked Euthydemos, do the gods, "the gods themselves," not come to our assistance, namely, with divination (IV.3.12)? Now that is a big "if," of course, which E. C. Reiske, surprised, I take it, to hear Socrates say that human beings are not necessarily incapable of knowing which things are advantageous, "corrected" to read "insofar as." And modern editors have followed suit.[25] But Socrates had only just said that, by reasoning about our memories of the things we perceive, we learn how each of them is advantageous (IV.3.11). And in *Memorabilia* IV.2, as we saw, Xenophon explained to the reader that knowledge of the good things arises, via self-knowledge, from knowledge of the truth about justice (consider also IV.5.6, IV.5.11–12, IV.8.11). So we should not be surprised to hear Socrates say that human beings are not necessarily incapable of knowing which things are advantageous; after all, whereas the self-ignorant are incapable of knowing as much, by his account, self-knowers are not (IV.2.26–27). And Socrates broached the subject of divination right after referring to political affairs precisely because Euthydemos's ignorance of the truth about justice—his failure to notice the distinction Socrates made between law, among other noble things, and the good ones—left him not only ignorant of himself but also wanting more than "human wisdom" (IV.7.10). As Socrates put it elsewhere, too, those intending to manage a city nobly are in special need of divination. For, to the farmer, it is clear that to reap the fruits of his labor is advantageous, even though it is not clear to him if he himself will do so, yet it is not clear to the statesman if it is even advantageous to rule a city nobly (I.1.7–8). And, that means, it is not so much our less than absolutely certain knowledge of "the outcome" as the problem of the rationality of political affairs that makes divination necessary for the likes of Euthydemos.[26] No wonder cities and nations are so pious (I.4.16). Even as the youth's opinions about cities and nations, laws, and citizenship made divination altogether necessary for him, however, it was not altogether possible for him to give up on human wisdom either. When Socrates refuted his opinions about the good, the youth could not bring himself either to stick to the good things of which we know or to place his trust in the most beautiful knowledge of the gods. And for the same reason, when Socrates asked Euthydemos if the gods themselves come to the assistance of the lawful, on one hand, by declaring "the outcome" through divination to those who ask them questions, and on the other hand, by teaching those who do not how to achieve the desired outcome, the youth was slow—unusually slow—to agree. In effect, he replied that whereas the diviners "declare" the future to other human beings in general, the gods themselves "teach" human beings what we should and should not do only in very special cases. Only in the case of the diviners in general and Socrates in particular do the gods perhaps take such good care of the human soul as to teach us how to benefit from the good and to save ourselves from the bad things in the same way as we, by expressing ourselves, teach other human beings how to do so (IV.3.12). Other human beings, to whom the gods are less friendly, do not get anything straight from the horse's mouth. And since, then, "the gods themselves" do *not* in fact come to the assistance of the lawful, how can we be so sure that the diviners speak the truth? The youth's need for the truth, for knowledge of the truth, was just barely enough to make him contradict Socrates—if not before, when he referred to political affairs, at least when he broached the subject of divination (consider, on the other hand, IV.2.12).

But that he himself was speaking the truth about his "*daimonion*" specifically, divination generally even Euthydemos would judge, Socrates said, if the youth were to rest satisfied with fearing and honoring the invisible gods upon seeing the facts, works, or deeds for which they are allegedly responsible (IV.3.13). In the next place, however, Socrates asked Euthydemos "to give thought" to a couple of things (IV.3.13, IV.3.14). And what began as an attempt to urge or exhort the youth to rest satisfied with fearing and honoring the invisible gods ended, before long, on a very different note. "Giving thought to these (two) things," Socrates said, one should honor the one god (*to daimonion*) by learning the power or capacity of the invisible things, and the many gods (*oi theoi*), from the things that actually come to be (IV.3.14). We have seen all this before: in the conversation with Aristodemos, when we saw that Socrates made two statements, not one, since we separated one thing from another (compare I.4.17 with IV.3.14, and I.4.18 with IV.3.13). To learn, by reasoning from "the things that come to be," is not the same thing as to fear the gods upon seeing "their works." The latter is required by law (IV.4.19); the former, to put it mildly, is not (I.1.11). And the one god is not the same thing as the many gods. And yet, not only did Euthydemos fail to notice the distinction Socrates clearly, if tacitly, made between the one god (*to daimonion*) and the many gods (*oi theoi*),[27] but he also came away with the view that he should "care" for the gods in gratitude for their good deeds (IV.3.15). Of learning, he said not a word. And Socrates did not press the issue. As if he himself had not only just said that one should honor the one god by learning, he urged or exhorted the youth to show his gratitude to the many gods by obeying them or the laws and thus, by doing so, to honor them (IV.3.16–17). Euthydemos, who had never before given any thought to how carefully the gods provide human beings with the good things (IV.3.3), was not about to start now. To honor the one god by learning was not an option for him. And a favorable stance toward learning was not an option for him, according to what Socrates had said, because Euthydemos did not give enough thought to either of the things to which Socrates asked him to give thought. Because he did not give them enough thought, that is, he did not honor the one god by learning. And did he judge that Socrates was speaking the truth about his "*daimonion*" because he did not honor the one god by learning? If he were to fear the gods, Socrates said, Euthydemos would judge that he was speaking the truth about divination (IV.3.13); however, he never said that he would do so if he were to honor the one god by learning (IV.3.14). Perhaps then, even as Socrates was asking Euthydemos jokingly, he was asking good natures seriously to give thought to a couple of things. And perhaps, having done that, they would honor the one god by learning from the things that actually come to be the power or capacity of the many gods, before going on to judge that Socrates himself honored the *daimonion* accordingly—by reasoning about the things we perceive, learning what we should and should not do and, by expressing himself incontinently, teaching as much to others.

But we have gotten ahead of ourselves. To what did Socrates ask Euthydemos jokingly, and good natures seriously, to give thought? He asked them to give thought, first, to the fact that the gods themselves indicate by deed, if not by speech, that one should rest satisfied with fearing and honoring the invisible gods upon seeing the facts, works, or deeds for which they are allegedly responsible (IV.3.13). But then, not entirely unexpectedly, he distinguished the many gods from the one god. And although the many gods and the one god both indicate that one should fear the gods upon seeing their alleged works or deeds, they do so, according to Socrates, very differently from one another. The many gods indicate that we must rest satisfied with (fearing them upon) seeing their alleged works or deeds because, when they give us "the good things," which are evident to all, they themselves are invisible. With that, Socrates was only summing up the results of the conversation so far. For example, when Socrates asked the youth if heat comes from "the sun," he made no mention whatsoever of "the gods" (IV.3.8–9). For his first word about "the gods" was also, until his "natural theology" gave way to revealed theology at least, his last (IV.3.3). And even then, in that one case, Socrates merely asked Euthydemos if "the gods" provide us with light (IV.3.3) before going on to say in his own name that "the sun" is what does this (IV.3.4). If not for Euthydemos, who did not hesitate to mention gods—both individually (IV.3.3, IV.3.8) and collectively (IV.3.9, IV.3.12)—whom he did not hesitate to hold responsible for the sun (IV.3.3–4, IV.3.8–9), the gods would have been totally eclipsed by their alleged works or deeds as the conversation wore on for the simple reason that, while we do see the works or deeds from which the good things come, we do not see the gods who allegedly provide us with the works or deeds from which the good things come (compare I.4.8–9 with I.4.3–4). And Socrates went as far as the eye could see, but no farther. As for the one god, he indicates that we must rest satisfied with fearing the gods (upon seeing their alleged works or deeds) because, when the one god does the greatest things, his doing of which is evident to all, he does not appear to make any use whatsoever of the art of economics or household management on our behalf (IV.3.13, reading *tode* with the manuscripts). As far as we can see, there is no divine economy, that is, no divine providence. For this god, Socrates said, puts and keeps together the parts of the whole cosmos. And that term of art, *cosmos*, which the sophists used to refer to the nature of all things (IV.1.11), Socrates himself used to refer to the one god's doings here because, however much they may seem like "bad things" (IV.3.11) to gods and men, "all things" are noble and good to the god of Heraclitus and the other philosophers (Diels–Kranz 22B.102). That god always, as Socrates put it, provides us with "all things," "new, healthy, and ageless for our use," while they, in turn, serve innocently and thoughtlessly (*thatton de noēmatos hupēretounta anamartētōs*) (IV.3.13). Nothing meets this description, however, unless by "all things" Socrates meant all the classes or kinds of things: light, night, seasons, water, earth, plants, horses, lions, and so on. "The god," in that event, is nothing other than that which provides us with just such classes or kinds of things as are evidently given, if not evidently beneficial, to us. According to his conversation with Aristodemos, it was the natural motion internal to the bodies that did this; according to the conversation with Euthydemos, in keeping with the difference of emphasis in the two conversations,[28] the fiery rock named Helios does this (IV.7.6–8). But if, then, only evidently beneficial works can be said to be purposeful (I.4.4), the makeup of each class or kind of being is the work of chance. With that, too, Socrates was only summing up the results of the conversation so far. Among other things, which do not bear repeating, the sun leaves us in the dark and out in the cold.

That said, even if it were true that there is not a shred of evidence for the Olympian gods, "it is necessary to say not only the truth but also the cause of the error" (Aristotle, *Nicomachean Ethics* 1154a22–26). And it was with that necessity in mind that Socrates asked Euthydemos jokingly, and good natures seriously, to give thought, secondly, to the sun. That the sun is a contrivance of the gods, if it is not Helios himself, is evident to all according to generally accepted opinions (IV.3.14). But the truth, which runs contrary to generally accepted opinions, is that the sun does not permit human beings to see or contemplate its divinity without "shame" or "awe" (*anaidōs*)—that is, "precisely." Far from it, whoever tries to do so, like Anaxagoras (IV.7.6–7), will be deprived of his sight of the sun's divinity altogether (IV.3.14). Now as to this—namely, that whoever tries to contemplate precisely the works or deeds for which the gods are allegedly responsible will not find any evidence that they are, in fact, responsible for them—there is not all that much difference between the two things to which Socrates asked Euthydemos jokingly, good natures seriously, to give thought (IV.3.13 and IV.3.14). What the second thing really added to the first, however, was not only that the responsibility of the gods for the things we perceive is evident to all according to generally accepted opinions (I.4.15–16), but also that their responsibility for the things we perceive truly is evident, if not to all, at least to whoever does not try to contemplate "their" works or deeds precisely—that is, without shame or awe. Of this, as we saw, Euthydemos is living proof.

On account of not separating the things according to classes or kinds, the youth did not notice that the sun leaves us in the dark and out in the cold. Rather, standing in awe before its beauty, he was permitted to contemplate, albeit only very imprecisely, its divinity. And Socrates both concealed and revealed the cause of the error in the case of the sun by "praising" shame or awe as well as imprecision as a cause of extrasensory perception (I.4.13) of the sun's divinity, on one hand, and by "blaming" shamelessness or awelessness as well as precision as the cause of losing sight of it altogether, on the other. More than that, though, by bringing what he said of the sun to bear on lightning and winds, in the first place, and on the soul, in the second, he both concealed and revealed the cause of the error more generally. Not unlike the sun, lightning and winds are, according to generally accepted opinions, "ministers of the gods," while the soul, for its part, "participates in the divine." But contemplate them shamelessly or awelessly and precisely and, Socrates said to good natures, "you will find that they are also," as such, "invisible" (IV.3.14). Euthydemos did no such thing, of course, but on account of not separating things according to classes or kinds was he permitted extrasensory perception of their divinity? As the only instantly recognizable examples yet of harmful or bad things, lightning and winds (I.4.6), in the first place, stand out from the pack of good ones for which Socrates, by hook or by crook, made the gods out to be responsible. They would be completely out of place here, to say the very least, if not for the fact that the gods do bad things, too, according to generally accepted opinions—not least of all, when they punish evildoers (compare I.1.17–19 with I.4.19; *Oeconomicus* 7.31). And although Socrates noted in passing that there is no evidence to back this up (IV.3.14), lightning and winds are nevertheless, by almost all accounts, the instruments of Zeus's punitive justice par excellence. In the second place, when Socrates came to the soul, he said that it is clearly king not only "of," but also "in," the body (compare III.11.10). Of a soul separate and apart from the body, he noted, there is no evidence either. But nevertheless, according to generally accepted opinions, the destruction of the body does not necessarily entail the destruction of the soul (*Cyropaedia* VIII.7.17–22; consider *Symposium* 8.28–30, *Agesilaus* 11.8, *Memorabilia* II.2.33). Given what Socrates had said of the sun, was Euthydemos permitted to contemplate lightning and winds as instruments of divine, punitive justice on account of not separating the shameful things and the bad ones according to classes or kinds? And was he permitted to contemplate the soul as participating in some "divine" state of being (consider I.6.10), where "there shall be no more death," on account of not separating the noble (beautiful) things and the good ones? If so, Socrates was only picking up right where his elenctic teaching left off, "with a view to" both Euthydemos and, in a different way, good natures. With "lightning" and "winds," Homer says, Zeus destroyed Odysseus's comrades in retaliation for slaughtering the cattle of the Sun (*Odyssey* XII.399–419) shortly after Tiresias's "soul," separate and apart from the body (*Odyssey* XI.218–222), forewarned him about that in Hades (*Odyssey* XI.90ff.). And, however hard it may be for Euthydemos among others to be sure that Homer was speaking the truth about all this and more, the youth was not alone in thinking that the weak can save themselves from destruction at the hands of the stronger, if not also to destroy them, even though they are the stronger, so long as they are in the right. But the strong often destroy, enslave, or otherwise harm the weak (II.1.10–15; I.1.8, *Oeconomicus* 5.7, 5.13, contrast 5.12). And to hold out hope for the destruction of the doers and the salvation of the sufferers of injustice—up to and including destruction itself—is thus, just about, to have some perception of Zeus thundering out of heaven and life after death. In other words, while it was not so much his "knowledge" as his ignorance of the goodness of the beautiful or noble things that made divination necessary for Euthydemos, it was not so much his ignorance as his "knowledge" of their goodness that made it possible even for him, to whom the gods are not so friendly, to judge that Socrates was speaking the truth about his "*daimonion*" specifically, divination generally. It would not be entirely misleading to say that the gods were not "teaching" the diviners, and all other human beings through them, anything that Euthydemos among others did not already "know."

Good natures could not help noticing the distinction Socrates clearly, if tacitly, made between the *daimonion* and the gods of the city. Nor could they help noticing—while thoughtfully listening to Socrates teach, "with a view to" Euthydemos, the necessity and truth of divination—that the change from one opinion about the divine attributes to the other went unnoticed by Euthydemos, owing to the fact that he did not notice the distinction Socrates clearly, if tacitly, made between the noble or beautiful things and the good ones. Because he believed he knew that cities and nations, laws, and citizenship are not (only) beautiful or noble but (also) good, he believed he knew that the divine attributes include not (only) blind necessity but (also) the will, the intention to do justice. For their part, when good natures had given enough thought, first, to the truth and, secondly, to the cause of the error, they honored the *daimonion* by learning from the things that come to be that the gods are "envious," which is just another, more dolled up way of saying, powerless to do anything other than the things that actually come to be. And they went on to judge that Socrates was not being entirely serious or straightforward about his "*daimonion*," to say nothing of divination generally. Earlier, to put this differently, when Euthydemos said that he could scarcely know anything else, if he did not know himself (IV.2.24), he was righter than he knew. And in his long, roundabout way—by leaving them to think through for themselves what he told Euthydemos to believe and do (IV.2.40)—Socrates revealed to good natures how right he was. Without knowledge of oneself, there can be no knowledge of the natural world.

VIII

As for Euthydemos, he judged that Socrates was speaking the truth about his "*daimonion*" specifically, and divination generally, because, knowing what he knew or believed he knew of law, he was permitted to perceive, albeit only very imprecisely, the divine. And divination, in turn, gave its much-needed backing to the wisdom of the laws on account of which, the nobility of which, the envy of the gods escaped the youth's notice. In another stunning reversal, by persuading the youth of the truth of divination, Socrates clinched the argument for divine providence (if only by undermining it, in the very same breath, as an argument from facts evident to all human beings). Not in spite but because of this, however, Euthydemos became "depressed," for a second time. For how can we ever repay gods who do us so much good with the gratitude they deserve? The youth, full of gratitude, felt crushed by debt (IV.3.15). And so, to rally his spirits, Socrates pointed out that obedience to the law of the city is, according to the god at Delphi, pleasing to the gods. By obeying the law—Socrates took the liberty of adding the law concerning sacrifices or, let us say, "the ceremonial law"—maybe Euthydemos could repay the gods (IV.3.16). But does this, this way out of the youth's plight, not go in the opposite direction of everything Socrates had just revealed about law and the gods?

It was only when Socrates broached the subject of divination, not when he referred to political affairs, that the youth contradicted Socrates (IV.3.12). For the gods themselves did not teach Euthydemos, at least, what he should and should not do; yet he believed he knew what law is. And that means, since the gods did not teach Euthydemos what he believed he knew of law, either by themselves or by way of diviners, Socrates had revealed to good natures that the youth's extrasensory perception of the former was caused by what he believed he knew of the latter. Obedience to *laws* the nobility, goodness, or justice of which Euthydemos believed he knew something (without having to be taught by the gods) was, by that account, a cause of his extrasensory perception of gods pleased by obedience to the very same laws the nobility, goodness, or justice of which they believed they knew too. By this account (IV.3.16), however, the youth's extrasensory perception of gods pleased by obedience to them, *the gods*, is a cause of obedience to laws the nobility, goodness, or justice of which Euthydemos believed he knew nothing (without having to be taught by the gods). Just before he himself described Socrates's conversation with Euthydemos, Xenophon said that "others," present on other occasions, had already given descriptions of how Socrates tried to make other companions of his moderate toward gods (IV.3.2). And so, to reformulate Socrates's change of direction in language familiar to readers of the only other description of this sort of thing that has come down to us, Plato's *Euthyphro*, whereas Socrates revealed in the first place that the law is pleasing to the gods because it is the law, he revealed in the second place that the law is the law because it is pleasing to the gods. Like Euthyphro, Euthydemos believed that the law is not (only) noble, good, or just from the point of view of reason, but (also) the command of gods working in mysterious ways. The problem of the rationality of political affairs caused Euthydemos to flee into the arms of the gods. "Piety," which Socrates mentioned here for the first time in IV.3, is one of two solutions to that problem.[29]

In what followed (IV.3.17), Socrates asked Euthydemos not one but two apparently rhetorical questions with which he appeared to say that we could not possibly honor the gods more nobly and more piously than by doing as "they themselves" command (IV.3.16) and, in keeping with this, that we could not possibly please them more than by obeying them to the utmost (IV.3.17). And we do as they command, we obey them to the utmost, if we obey the law—not if we obey the law concerning one thing and not another, not if we obey the law sometimes, but if we obey the law, every law, always. At the same time, however, Socrates took the liberty of adding to the divine command, not only that one should obey the law *concerning sacrifices*, but also that one should obey the law (concerning sacrifices) *according to one's power*, which is as much as to say, he took the liberty of subtracting from the command as stated, not only the "every," but also the "always." The irony was not lost on good natures. Socrates was apparently saying that we should do what the gods themselves tell us to do while telling us himself, in almost the same breath, to do otherwise. In particular, by cutting the divine command down to size—by narrowing its scope, on one hand, and by making obedience to it conditional, on the other—Socrates was telling us himself neither to honor the gods most nobly and most piously nor to please them the most. The Socratic instruction and the divine command differ profoundly not only in their meanings, Socrates clearly indicated, but also in their intentions. *Either* we obey the divine command because it is immoderate to hope for the greatest good things ("no more death") otherwise than by pleasing the all-powerful gods, *or* we obey the Socratic instruction because, if we were not to please the gods by sacrificing as much as we can, it would be "visible, of course"—that is, visible to human beings—that we are not honoring the gods just then (IV.3.17). To drive the point home, Socrates had justified his deviation from the letter and the spirit of the divine command on the grounds that, "of course," it is law everywhere to please gods with sacrifices according to one's power (IV.3.16). He did not hide behind Hesiod; he spoke for himself (I.3.3). If truth be told, however, exactly nowhere was it the (written) law to sacrifice "according to one's power." But what Socrates meant by this becomes clear given the fact that, in the subsequent conversation reported by Xenophon, Socrates had recourse to such unwritten, "divine" laws as are everywhere automatically self-enforcing (IV.4.19ff.). The law against sacrificing less than we can is "divine," by that measure, insofar as those in breach of it are everywhere going to be punished by human beings for visibly doing unholy and shameful things. As should go without saying, even if Socrates brought Aristodemos around to the sane opinion that not to sacrifice "according to one's capacity" in public, if not in private, is against the "divine" law, that opinion, that reason for performing sacrifices, was itself against the merely human law (I.1.1, *Apology* 10–11). And Socrates concealed his thoughts from Euthydemos, who did not weigh his words, while he simultaneously revealed to good natures, who did, the profound difference between his own and Euthydemos's intentions toward the gods. In response to the youth's depression about the fact that he cannot ever repay the gods for all the good that they have done him, Socrates did not say anything to the effect that he can repay the gods by obeying them; instead, he appeared to Euthydemos to say that, if he obeys them, the gods will do him more good than any man can ever hope to do for himself (IV.3.17). Socrates thereby combined a debt so great that Euthydemos was powerless to repay it (by obeying the gods) (IV.3.15) with a hope so high that he was powerless to fulfill it (without obeying them). But of course, to repay a debt he can never repay, to get such goods as he can never get for himself, nothing he can do will ever be enough. In stark contrast to Socrates, Euthydemos can never obey the gods too much. Hesiod's verse, "according to one's power, offer sacrifices to the immortal gods," was mischievous: as if neither gratitude nor hope should be so great as to lead one to . . . sacrifice.[30] Euthydemos's intentions toward the gods were, if not altogether pure, lawful (compare IV.3.15ff. with IV.4.24, IV.4.17, and II.2.2–3). And the difficulty with this is not so much that Euthydemos's piety was going to lead him to waver between depression and hope—that can easily be chalked up to an imperfect, human being falling short of piety's perfection—the difficulty is more that the problem of the rationality of political affairs reappears on the level of the theological solution to the problem. For what, after all, is piety? According to Socrates, to tie everything together, piety is lawfulness or justice toward men that gives life to and nourishes an experience of gods toward whom justice is due also or instead. Therefore, in much the same way as fire is directly useful against darkness and cold, and indirectly useful against not a few other evils insofar as it is a sine qua non for the arts, the beauty of "the starry sky above" seems to be directly useful against darkness and cold, while the nobility of "the moral law within" seems to be indirectly useful against all other evils insofar as it is a sine qua non for piety.

CHAPTER 6

"Natural Law"

I

Xenophon's opening remarks may very well suggest (or confirm) that, whereas Socrates *did* conceal his thought concerning piety by saying and doing such things as made Euthydemos among others more pious and more moderate, he *did not* conceal his thought concerning the just "at any rate" (compare IV.4.1 with IV.3.18). And yet, if he did not conceal his thought concerning justice, too, he did not reveal it simply or straightforwardly either. To begin with, Xenophon said only that Socrates displayed it in deed; for he behaved both lawfully and beneficially in private, and lawfully, albeit not beneficially, in public (IV.4.1). Lawful deeds are not necessarily beneficial ones. But that means, Socrates's private deeds could not possibly reveal his thought concerning justice. For there would be no telling whether Socrates thought to do deeds that are both lawful and beneficial because they are lawful or because they are beneficial. Therefore, Xenophon gives three or four examples of Socrates doing lawful deeds in public, his ignorance of how beneficial or his knowledge of how harmful doing so may be (to himself and others) notwithstanding (IV.4.2–4). That said, whereas here Xenophon explains all of these public deeds in terms of Socrates's lawfulness—as if Socrates did them for no other reason than that they are lawful—elsewhere in the *Memorabilia* he gives alternative explanations of nearly all of them. And the real or (in one case) apparent contrast between what he says here and what he says elsewhere only leads us to doubt that Socrates thought to do lawful deeds simply because they are lawful.

First, Xenophon says here that when the demos wanted to put to death, in one fell swoop, the generals who had failed to retrieve their comrades after the battle of Arginusae, Socrates alone of the council members refused to go along with the demos contrary to the laws, even if that meant putting himself in harm's way (IV.4.2). But elsewhere, in the course of defending Socrates against the charge that he did not believe in the gods of the city, Xenophon says that this was all because of his piety rather than his lawfulness: Socrates refused to go along with the demos contrary to the laws, (merely) because he refused to break his sacred oath, as a council member, "to give counsel according to the laws." And he led us to believe that he refused to break his sacred oath, in turn, because he feared divine punishment or hoped for divine reward (I.1.17–19; I.4.19). Second, Xenophon says here that when the oligarchs commanded Socrates to do something contrary to the laws—when they forbade him from conversing with the youth, or when they commanded him to fetch Leon of Salamis to be put to death—he alone refused to go along with the oligarchs as well (IV.4.4). But elsewhere, in the course of defending Socrates against the charge that he corrupted the youth, Xenophon indicates that Socrates did indeed obey the law of the Thirty Tyrants forbidding him from conversing with the youth, or teaching them "an art of speeches," on pain of death (I.2.34). And if we only resist the temptation to put words into Xenophon's mouth, there is no contradiction between what Xenophon says here and there. For Xenophon never actually said, although he led not a few readers to believe he said,[1] that Socrates disobeyed the oligarchs when they made a law contrary to the laws forbidding him from conversing with the youth. That would be absurd: the rulers—whether the many or the few happen to be sovereign, it makes no difference—make the laws (I.2.40–46, IV.4.13). Therefore, Xenophon said no more than that Socrates disobeyed the oligarchs when they *commanded him to do something contrary to the laws*—namely, to go fetch Leon. When they *made a law*, and it was a law (I.2.31, I.2.33, I.2.34), *forbidding him from conversing with the youth*, which is something else entirely (IV.4.3), "he was obedient to the rulers in those things which the laws command" (IV.4.1).[2] Third, Xenophon says here that when Socrates was defending himself to the jury against the charges brought against him by Meletus, he refused to gratify, flatter, or beg them contrary to the laws, even if that meant certain death. But of course, so far from there being any law forbidding defendants from gratifying, flattering, or begging their juries, Xenophon notes that such things were customary, and many defendants frequently beat the rap by doing them. Indeed, had Socrates done such things even "moderately" or "in due measure," he would have beaten the rap "easily" (IV.4.4). To say that it was contrary to the laws for Socrates to mount an effective defense of himself and thus beat the rap is, then, just another way of saying that Socrates was guilty as charged.[3] Just as it was contrary to the laws for the demos to put the Arginusae generals to death, and for the oligarchs to put Leon of Salamis to death, it was contrary to the laws for the Athenians *not* to put Socrates to death. In that case, it is true, Socrates's lawfulness in accepting responsibility for his actions entailed the unlawfulness of the actions themselves. Maybe Socrates, in his old age, had a change of heart. But elsewhere, in the course of defending Socrates's behavior at his trial, Xenophon would seem to say that this was all because of his "*daimonion*": Socrates accepted responsibility for his actions because he, or his "*daimonion*," had reason to think that it was the best time for him to die.

Deeds alone will not do. Socrates obeyed the laws, to be sure, but *why* did he obey the laws? What were his reasons, his intentions in doing so? Contrasting what he says here with what he says elsewhere, there are three options. Either Socrates obeyed the laws, if and when he did so, because the gods make it beneficial to do so, or because the rulers make it beneficial to do so, or because the *daimonion* (IV.3.14, IV.3.11) makes it beneficial to do so. But which one is it? Seeing as how Socrates's deeds, even his public deeds, did not reveal his thought concerning justice, Xenophon leaves us no choice but to weigh his words. At no point, however, did he so much as try to say that Socrates revealed his thought concerning justice in the simplest and clearest manner. Instead, as with the conversation between Socrates and Aristodemos, Xenophon arranged for us to make up our own minds about what Socrates thought after considering a Socratic speech—Socrates's conversation with the sophist Hippias—for ourselves.

II

Hearing Socrates say that, while teachers of the arts are easy to come by, "there is no place" where teachers of justice can be found, Hippias joked that Socrates was still saying the same things that he himself had heard him say long ago, when Hippias was last in Athens. If, at that time, Socrates had refuted his opinions about justice as Xenophon seems to suggest, Hippias claimed to have learned, since then, to say something new (IV.4.5). "Now," at any rate, he believed himself to have something to say about justice against which neither Socrates nor anybody else would be able to speak (IV.4.7). And was Hippias, then, one of the very teachers of justice who are, according to Socrates at least, nowhere to be found? If so, Socrates said, Hippias had found a great good. Should he be willing to teach what justice is, in addition to being able to do so, the jurors will no longer be divided in their votes; the citizens will no longer contradict each other concerning the just things, or take one another to court, or overthrow their rulers; and the cities will no longer disagree concerning the just things and go to war with one another (IV.4.8).[4] Hippias was not willing to share so great a good (IV.3.12), however, not until Socrates revealed what he thinks justice is, first, at least. "For it is enough for you," he said to Socrates, "that you ridicule the others by questioning and refuting everyone, even though you yourself do not want to deliver a speech to anyone or to reveal your thought concerning anything" (IV.4.9, consider I.2.36). There is no escaping the fact that Hippias, a sophist who despised lawmaking and obedience to laws (IV.4.14),[5] believed he knew, but did not want to do, justice. For he did not want to teach the truth about justice and thus, by doing so, bring about peace both in and among the cities.

But where does that leave Socrates? However "terrible" this may be, he always says the same things about justice (IV.2.15 and IV.2.21), by his own account, because justice is something he knows. Justice is something he knows, on one hand, with no less certainty than he knows how many and which letters there are in his own name and, on the other hand, with no less certainty than he knows that twice five makes ten (IV.4.6). Did, then, Socrates know that justice has two parts of different kinds into which the whole is divisible and out of which it is made? And did he know that justice is somehow both conventional, like the name *Socrates*, and natural, like the number ten? However that may be for now, Socrates's knowledge of justice is such that he always says about it the same thing: teachers of justice are nowhere to be found. And if he were to be willing to teach that justice is unteachable, in addition to being able to do so, would he not bring about world peace? Citizens and cities come to blows, after all, because they disagree about the just things (IV.4.8); and they disagree about the just things because that (part of justice) which one citizen or city "knows" to be wholly just, another "knows" to be wholly unjust. Teach them their ignorance of justice, enlighten the people, and there will be peace on earth. This, by the way, should sound familiar. Today, people in the West claim that, "to recognize . . . the contingency of their own consciences . . . is the chief virtue of the members of a liberal society," ultimately because "absolutism" leads to intolerance, and intolerance leads to violence, whereas education, by which they mean, above all, the recognition of "the contingency of their own consciences," leads to tolerance, and tolerance finally to peace.[6] Since the recognition of "the contingency of their own," and other, "consciences" has no rational basis to which they can point, however, is it not going to have to be state-enforced? And since that recognition is itself just a part of another "absolutism," no less intolerant or violent in principle than the others, is it not going to have to be state-enforced self-contradiction? Recall that Rawls had no leg to stand on, except for the "cultural conditioning" of his friends, on one hand, and the extermination of his foes, "like war and disease," on the other. But Socrates, it should go without saying, was not thinking of that compulsory confusion, that antipolitical politics, which goes by the name of education today. Swearing, again, "by Hera," he was thinking of a future without manliness: universal liberal, liberating education giving rise to world peace without even state enforcement of the education needed to keep the peace. In any event, Socrates fell into his own trap. Precisely if Hippias can be blamed for not teaching justice, for not bringing about world peace by doing so, what is Socrates's defense?

Socrates was, to repeat, accused by Hippias of concealing his thought concerning not only justice but everything else (IV.4.9). But then, rather than reveal his thought concerning justice and prove Hippias wrong once and for all, he behaved in such a way as to make Hippias accuse him once more—this time, there can be no doubt, quite rightly—of concealing his thought concerning justice (IV.4.10–11).[7] At the same time, in the very act of concealing his thought, Socrates revealed (to someone even more perceptive than Hippias, to say nothing of Euthydemos) that he was concealing it. To walk through this slowly, when Hippias said that he would not reveal his thought until Socrates revealed his, Socrates replied that there was absolutely no need for him to do so. And there was absolutely no need for him to reveal his thought concerning justice, he insisted, because he displays which things are just in his opinion all the time, "if not in speech," at any rate, "in deed" (IV.4.10). Now Hippias himself readily agreed, under questioning, that actions speak louder than words—for, as it seemed to him, "many who say just things do unjust ones, but nobody who does just things would be unjust"—before going on, in the next place, to agree no less readily that he never saw Socrates doing anything unjust, such as making false accusations or sowing discord in or among cities (IV.4.10–11). And if only Hippias had agreed that refraining from unjust deeds is just, too, he would have had to agree that Socrates was just, notwithstanding his speech or the lack thereof. Instead, however, he accused Socrates of trying to conceal his thought concerning justice on the grounds that Socrates was not saying which things the just do, but which things they do not do (IV.4.11). Especially since Hippias had only just said that "nobody who does just things would be unjust," there was something to this. Socrates had indeed, to all appearances, lowered the bar considerably in allowing the doing of just deeds to be replaced by the refraining from unjust ones as the paradigm of (his) justice. But Hippias failed to notice that, if falsely accusing others and sowing discord in or among cities are unjust deeds according to Socrates, then truthfully accusing others and bringing about concord in and among cities are just deeds according to him. And so, on one hand, Socrates had all but said which things the just do—only he himself did not do them. For instance, when the demos sentenced the Arginusae generals to death, he did not accuse the demos, much less bring about concord between the demos and the generals; and when oligarchs sentenced Leon to death, he did not accuse the oligarchs, much less bring about concord between the oligarchs and Leon.[8] Socrates was no enlightener: he did not teach citizens and cities their ignorance of justice and thus, by doing so, bring about peace on earth. On the other hand, rather than open himself up to this objection by making it crystal clear that Hippias's accusation was groundless, at least as stated, Socrates responded to the accusation itself in such a way as to give grounds for it. For he believed, he said, that not wanting to do injustice is the paradigm of justice (IV.4.12). But who said anything about *wanting* to do, or not to do, anything? When Hippias said that "nobody who does just things would be unjust," he completely forgot about those who do just things unwillingly, without wanting to do them (consider *Oeconomicus* 1.23, 13.9, 14.9–10). Are they just? By Socrates's own admission, the fact that he refrained from unjust deeds does not prove anything. Again, what were his intentions?[9] More than that, though, if we put together the groundlessness of Hippias's accusation, as stated, with the ground that Socrates gave for it, we are forced to conclude that, according to Socrates, the paradigm of justice is wanting both to accuse others truthfully and to bring about concord in and among cities. And even if he himself wanted to do such things, even if he wanted to go for broke and make a good faith effort at teaching citizens and cities (their ignorance), he did not do so. The question is why. Perhaps, just as there are those who are forced to do just things unwillingly, Socrates did not accuse others truthfully of being ignorant and bring about concord in and among cities because he was forced not to. But still, in that case, forced by what exactly?

III

From there, naturally, the conversation turned to the law. Socrates claimed, in the next place, that the lawful is just (IV.4.12). But that is a deceptively simple thing to say. And Hippias, whose bewilderment should be a lesson to us all, did well to ask Socrates for clarification (IV.4.12–13).[10] For, by claiming that the lawful is just or rather, as Socrates also put it, that the lawful and the just are one and the same thing, he could have meant one of two things. *Either*, since laws are decrees of the ruling part of a city (IV.4.13, I.2.40–46), the just things are nothing but the arbitrary decrees of the ruling part of a city, *or* only those decrees of the ruling part of a city which are just, rather than arbitrary, are lawful too.[11] The second meaning is in perfect accord with generally accepted opinions the world over; the first, to put it mildly, is not. Yet Socrates clarified himself, in few words, as follows: if he who obeys the laws does just things, while he who disobeys them does unjust ones, and if he who does just things is just, while he who does unjust ones is unjust, then he who obeys the laws is just. And not only did Socrates make it clear that, by "the laws," he meant the decrees of the ruling part of a city—whether the demos or oligarchs happen to be sovereign, it makes no difference (contrast I.2.43 with IV.4.13)—but also, just after having indicated that Hippias completely forgot about those who do just things unwillingly when he said that "nobody who does just things would be unjust," Socrates leapt from *doing* just or unjust things, right over *wanting* to do them, to *being* just or unjust. Altogether, then, does the claim that the lawful is just mean, in Socrates's mouth, that doing whatever the rulers tell us to do, whether we want to or not, is just? Was this not, at bottom, what Socrates taught Alcibiades or what Alcibiades, while still a companion of Socrates, tried and failed to teach Pericles (I.2.40–46)? Perhaps, in that case, Hippias was not wrong to point to the fact that laws are frequently changed by the very people who make them as evidence that neither laws, laws so made and unmade, nor obedience to them are serious affairs (IV.4.14). But of course, if the just is nothing but the lawful, and if the lawful is nothing but the arbitrary decree of the rulers, who are above the law, the same goes for the just. And the claim that justice is the arbitrary decree of the rulers opens the door, if it does not lead the way willy-nilly, to the claim made famous by Thrasymachus in Book I of Plato's *Republic* that justice is the advantage of the stronger.[12] Now, to be sure, no sooner did Hippias make light of the laws than Socrates asked him whether (by disparaging those who obey the laws because they might be repealed) he thought he was doing anything other than finding fault with those who conduct themselves well in wars because peace might come to be, on one hand, or whether he finds fault with those who rush to the defense of their fatherland, on the other hand. And Hippias answered, "By Zeus, not I!" (IV.4.14) From this, though, it does not necessarily follow that, "however much of a wandering sophist he may be, Hippias cannot resist this appeal to his civic or patriotic feeling."[13] For Socrates had asked Hippias not one but two questions. And they were phrased in such a way that to answer one in the negative was to answer the other in the affirmative.

Did, then, Hippias emphatically not think he was doing anything other than finding fault with those who rush to the defense of their fatherland? Or did he emphatically not find fault with them? We cannot be sure; Xenophon made sure of that. But let us assume, precisely because Xenophon did so, that Hippias was not as hopelessly confused as our "legal positivists," whose strange brew of sophistication and naivete, "realism" and "idealism," leaves them blissfully unaware that the reduction of law to brute force, including the brute force of the demos, spells the end of respect for "the rule of law." For what else are we to make of the fact that the questions put to him by Socrates were tailor-made to let Hippias draw the ultimate implications of his denial that lawfulness is rational,[14] while letting him give the appearance, at the same time, of shying away from them? Either way, Socrates has not settled anything; he has only brought everything to a head. Doing whatever the rulers tell us to do, whether we want to or not—is that to our advantage, after all, or not?

With that question in mind, Socrates launched into a monologue on the benefits that cities and private persons derive from lawfulness (IV.4.15–17). First off, he went through the benefits that cities derive from lawfulness. And this Athenian called special attention to the fact that, by making it exceptionally obedient to the laws, Lycurgus made Sparta very different from, if not much better than, the other cities. Cities such as Sparta, in which the citizens are exceptionally obedient to the laws, are best in war and peace (IV.4.15).[15] "However" *(alla mēn)*, Socrates hastened to add, concord is the greatest of goods also in the opinion of all those other cities, like Athens, which are much less lawful than Sparta, for the citizens are very frequently exhorted to live in concord, at any rate, and all over Greece there is a law according to which the citizens are to take an oath to live in concord. And concord—not wisdom (IV.5.6, contrast also II.4.2)—is the greatest of goods in their opinion too, according to Socrates's not so subtle indications, because only citizens who live in concord decide in favor of, praise, choose, or take pleasure in the *same* laws and, for this reason, obey them. If, then, citizens all over Greece do not as a matter of fact live in concord, as Xenophon clearly indicates here in more ways than one, even though they take an oath to do so, this is because they disagree about which things should and should not be laws—that is, about who among them should rule, and who should obey (IV.4.16).[16] More exactly, citizens all over Greece do not live in concord because they are not exceptionally obedient to the laws. They are not exceptionally obedient to the laws because they cannot agree about which laws are just, on one hand, even as they can and do agree, each of them, that all should agree—agree *with them*—about which laws are just, on the other

(IV.4.8). How Lycurgus did a better job of making citizens agree about this than anyone else, we shall soon see. For now, however, there is agreement the world over that only those decrees of the ruling part of a city which are just, rather than arbitrary, are lawful. Citizens and cities come to blows, as we saw, because they disagree about the just things. That law which one citizen or city "knows" to be wholly just, another "knows" to be wholly unjust. And Socrates has not said a single word about which laws are just, which unjust, much less about what it is that makes them just or unjust. He said only that cities are at their best or strongest and happiest when the citizens all agree that the laws—the laws of their city, that is—are just (IV.4.15–16). In other words, instead of saying which decrees of the ruling part of a city are just, rather than arbitrary, and hence lawful, Socrates said only that it is a "great," albeit not a "very great" or the "greatest," good (contrast IV.4.8 with IV.4.16) when the citizens all agree that the decrees of the ruling part of their city are just, rather than arbitrary, and hence lawful. Secondly, from the benefits that cities derive from lawfulness (IV.4.15–16), Socrates turned to the benefits that private persons derive from it (IV.4.17). But this time, instead of speaking in his own name, Socrates asked Hippias twelve carefully worded and no less carefully arranged questions. Suffice it to say, to make a long story short, that they can be evenly divided into two parts, both of which go to show, each in its own way, how lawfulness is beneficial to private persons. And the division into two parts finds expression in the fact that Socrates began by asking Hippias whether the lawful are "least" punished by their city and ended by asking him whether the lawful, if only they have in their fellow citizens an army of friends and allies, are "least likely" to be attacked by other cities. Even those with the least to fear from their own and other cities, however, have something to fear from them.[17] At the same time, seeing as how Socrates put each of the benefits derived from lawfulness in the form of a question, there was nothing to prevent Hippias from answering that at times the lawless, by force or fraud, have less to fear from their own and other cities than the lawful.[18] Nor was there anything to prevent Socrates, shortly thereafter, from admitting as much himself, as indeed he did (IV.4.21). Lawfulness is not necessarily beneficial (as the fate of Leon and the six Arginusae generals who, in obedience to the law, returned to Athens to face the Council goes to show), and lawlessness not necessarily harmful (as the fate of the two generals who disobeyed the law goes to show).[19] Hence, whereas Socrates had said of *cities* not a moment ago that they are at their best or strongest and happiest when the citizens are lawful, he gave no indication whatsoever that *citizens*, when they are lawful, are at their best or strongest and happiest (IV.4.16)—after all, dialecticians are happiest (IV.5.12) even when their city is not (*Apology* 18), and lawful citizens are not necessarily dialecticians.[20] Lawfulness is, to be sure, a small price to pay for a reasonable expectation of safety from human beings at home and abroad. But still, the fact remains, it is one thing for private persons to obey the laws, unwillingly, for safety's sake—because, without abiding by the arbitrary decrees of the ruling part of their own cities, they run the risk of punishment and because, without cities to call their own, they are completely at the mercy of other cities. It is another thing entirely for citizens to obey the laws of their city because they agree that they are just—their ignorance of how beneficial or their knowledge of how harmful doing so may be to themselves notwithstanding. Whether it is the private person looking to benefit or the citizen who is least likely to conduct himself well in wars should go without saying.

Socrates displayed, in this way, that the lawful and the just are one and the same thing. And he asked Hippias, if he thinks otherwise, to teach that they are not. To this, Hippias replied that he does not think otherwise: according to him, too, the lawful and the just are one and the same thing (IV.4.18). And yet, lest we be too quick to declare Socrates the victor, what does that even mean, that the lawful and the just are one and the same thing? As we saw, it means either that the just things are nothing but the arbitrary decrees of the ruling part of a city or that only those decrees of the ruling part of a city which are just, rather than arbitrary, are lawful. And Hippias never denied that the lawful is just; he denied only that laws and obedience to them are serious affairs. But then, if Hippias took Socrates to be saying that the just things are nothing but the arbitrary decrees of the ruling part of a city, perhaps he affirmed that the lawful is just and denied, at the same time, that laws and obedience to them are serious affairs. And how else was Hippias, who was no slouch, to take what Socrates said? After all, instead of saying anything about which decrees of the ruling part of a city are just, rather than arbitrary, and hence lawful, Socrates said only that it is beneficial for a *community*, not necessarily for the *individuals*, when the individuals obey the decrees of the ruling part of their city in the belief that they are just, rather than arbitrary, and hence lawful.[21] In accord with this, just as if he had not achieved victory over Hippias, Socrates followed up his monologue on the benefits that derive from lawfulness with a dialogue in the course of which he tried to make the case that laws and obedience to laws are serious affairs, in another way, again (IV.4.19ff.). Again, Socrates found a way to let the sophist speak his mind, while letting him give the appearance, at the same time, of changing it.

Socrates did not obey the laws because the rulers make every effort, at least, to make it beneficial to do so. For they are bound to fail. But if, then, (merely human) laws and obedience to them cannot be taken seriously, where once there were three, now there are two remaining options: either the gods make it beneficial for Socrates, among others, to obey the laws or the *daimonion* does so. In other words, the problem of the rationality of political affairs would seem to have either a theological or a philosophic solution. And Socrates, in the dialogue to follow, would seem to offer a theological solution to that problem.

IV

From the laws of (the ruling part of) a city, Socrates turned to "unwritten laws."[22] According to Hippias, unwritten laws are held, as laws, in every country (IV.4.19). For all the disagreement in and among cities about which things should and should not be laws, there remains, then, some area of agreement. Everywhere, there are laws commanding reverence for gods (IV.4.19) and honor for parents (IV.4.20). And such generally accepted laws can only be made by gods, Hippias all but said, not by men (IV.4.19). "All but said," on one hand, because Hippias never actually said that human beings cannot make the unwritten laws; he only asked how we can do so if we cannot all come together or speak the same language (IV.4.19). But of course human beings the world over, who can neither come together nor speak the same language, say the same things about the same things all the time. And who is to say that our knowledge of law is nothing like our knowledge that, say, twice five makes ten? Our knowledge of law does not have to be like our "knowledge" of a name. On the other hand, even if Hippias professed to believe that gods make the unwritten laws for us, he only did so, as he himself put it, because all human beings hold the command to revere gods, "first," as law (IV.4.19). And how does that follow? Just because all human beings hold the command to revere gods as law does not mean that gods make the unwritten laws, including that one, for us. What Hippias said makes no sense whatsoever, unless his point was that by professing to believe that gods make the unwritten laws for us, he was obeying the unwritten law commanding reverence for gods, albeit not such and such reverence for such and such gods with these or those names, for fear of human beings. In sum, especially since human beings in different countries say different things in different languages about which gods are to be revered in which way, perhaps human beings and not gods make laws commanding such and such reverence for such and such gods with these or those names.[23] And perhaps, for all the disagreement about which gods are to be revered in which way, the unwritten law commanding reverence for gods is nothing more than a synopsis of the remaining area of agreement. In that case, to put this more generally, even if human beings make the unwritten laws (IV.3.12), they are something more than the completely arbitrary decrees of the ruling part of a city; they are, insofar as they are generally accepted, the minimum requirements that must be met for individuals to come together to form communities.[24] Falling somewhere in between names (*Socrates*) and numbers (ten), they are quasi-natural. As for Hippias, fully in keeping with the fact that he had only all but said that laws commanding reverence for gods and honor for parents are divine because they are generally accepted, he went on to say that laws forbidding parent-child incest and commanding gratitude are not divine despite the fact that they are generally accepted. And they are not divine by his account, despite the fact that they are generally accepted, because they can be disobeyed with impunity (IV.4.20–21, IV.4.24). For a law to be divine, Hippias thought, it is not enough to be generally accepted; the law must be automatically self-enforcing too, so that it is necessarily beneficial to follow the law, necessarily harmful to break it (IV.4.24). Now about this, too, Socrates and Hippias were in full agreement. For, instead of trying to prove to him that laws forbidding incest and commanding gratitude are divine despite the fact that they are not self-enforcing, Socrates took it for granted that non-self-enforcing laws are merely human, however generally accepted they may be (IV.4.21), before making as if to prove to Hippias that laws forbidding incest and commanding gratitude are automatically self-enforcing too (IV.4.21–23, IV.4.24). And so, in the end, the question is whether the unwritten laws, which are nothing more or less than the basic requirements of political life (IV.4.13), are divine or merely human. Or rather, since to be divine is to be held by human beings the world over (*Oeconomicus* 17.1–3) as good or beneficial, while to be merely human is to be nothing but brute force, if generally accepted, the question is whether political life is rational or not.

Now, according to Hippias, the unwritten laws forbidding parent-child incest and commanding gratitude, if not also those commanding reverence for gods and honor for parents, are irrational. For, despite the fact that they are held in every country, as laws, they are not automatically self-enforcing. Socrates made as if to prove Hippias wrong. Of the four unwritten laws under discussion,[25] only one is a prohibition not a command, only one is handled dialogically, and only one so much as appears to be enforced not by human beings, but rather, let us say, *by nature*: the law forbidding incest. So, to begin there, it is true that if we give no thought to the way in which, it seems, "Socrates convinces Hippias that the unwritten law against incest is divine," we will be led to conclude that, according to Socrates, "the unwritten law against incest is divine because incest is always punished by poor offspring."[26] But for a child to have sexual intercourse (*mignusthai*) with his or her parent, or for a parent to do so with his or her child—if *that* is parent-child incest, then Socrates spoke of incest once, when he first asked Hippias if the prohibition against it is a divine law, and then *never again* (IV.4.20). Completely absent from his proof of incest's harmfulness was, then, any mention whatsoever of . . . incest. While making as if to prove to Hippias that parent-child incest is automatically punished (IV.4.21), Socrates did not so much as try to prove more than this: that the children of parent-child incest are, for reasons having nothing to do with the crime of incest, badly conceived (IV.4.22). And even if we, too, were to make the gratuitous assumption that to conceive badly means to produce "poor offspring," then, since couples frequently have sexual intercourse without conceiving a child, and without wanting to conceive one (I.4.12, II.2.4), parent-child incest frequently goes unpunished. But the comedy does not end there; it is only just beginning. For when Hippias said that nothing prevents an incestuous couple from conceiving a child well, if both of them are "good," Socrates readily agreed that a child who has sexual intercourse with his or her parent and a parent who does so with his or her child are, perhaps, "good," notwithstanding the fact that they flout the unwritten law (IV.4.23). His one and only reservation was that the seeds of those in the prime of life are not the same as the seeds of those before or past their prime: the seeds of those in their prime are better (for being energetic) and, although they can still perform their function, the seeds of those before or past their prime are worse for not being energetic (*ou spoudaia*) (IV.4.23). By this account, however, the children of parent-child incest are conceived no worse than the children of a nonincestuous couple, one of whom is in the prime of life, the other of whom is past it. And the children of incest are conceived no worse, and perhaps even better than, the children of a nonincestuous couple, both of whom are before their prime, on one hand; and no worse, and perhaps even better than, the children of a nonincestuous couple, both of whom are past their prime, on the other. Last but not least, why must we assume that "to conceive badly" meant, to either Socrates or Hippias, to produce "poor offspring"? That would be gratuitous. Not once, after all, did Socrates say that the *children* of those before or past their prime are bad; yet he belabored the point that their *seeds* (*spermata*) are worse for not being energetic. And the first chapter of Xenophon's *Regime of the Lacedaemonians*, the end of which is highly relevant here, leaves no room for doubt: those past their prime "conceive badly" insofar as their "fruitfulness," their "fertility" (*eugonia*), is low (*Regime of the Lacedaemonians* 1.6–8). When all is said and done, while making as if to prove to Hippias that parent-child incest is automatically punished, Socrates proved only that, owing to their low fertility, those before or past their prime will have a harder time conceiving a child than those in the prime of life. And will incestuous couples who only want to have sexual intercourse, not children, not derive benefit from this state of affairs? In any case, by failing in truly spectacular fashion to make the case that incest is automatically punished, Socrates revealed to those who did not pass up the opportunity to think through what he said that the unwritten law forbidding incest, however generally accepted it may be, is contrary to nature. And Hippias agreed with this, what Socrates said about incest, "too" (IV.4.23). For the sophist's earlier agreement that the lawful and the just are one and the same thing did not mean what it seemed to the thoughtless to mean; and his agreement with what Socrates said about incest—which meant one thing to someone even less perceptive than Hippias, and another thing entirely to someone at least as perceptive as him—was no different. According to Hippias, although those before or past their prime will have a harder time conceiving a child than those in the prime of life, those who commit incest are, perhaps, "good." And so too, perhaps, are their children. The law forbidding incest is not automatically self-enforcing. Yet again, Socrates—who, together with his much younger wife, conceived children when he was well past his prime—found a way to let the sophist speak his mind, while letting him give the appearance, at the same time, of changing it.

To come now to the law commanding gratitude, Socrates made as if to prove that it, too, is automatically self-enforcing (IV.4.24). In discussing the benefits that private persons derive from lawfulness, however, only just a moment ago, Socrates asked two questions—the only ones linked by the disjunction *ē*—about gratitude. Namely, is lawfulness the reason for gratitude? "Or," seeing as how human beings are more likely to do good to those from whom they believe they will receive good in return, is contriving (ways to benefit) the reason for it (IV.4.17)? And all Socrates did here, as if this proved anything at all, was ask Hippias whether ingratitude is punished insofar as there are those with whom it is beneficial to be friends who, because they are lawful, hate ingratitude. For does ingratitude to such people not put you under the necessity of pursuing them, like a hunter, not least of all by showing them that much more gratitude? The punishment for ingratitude, in that case, is gratitude. In some cases, to spell this out a bit more fully, ingratitude puts you under the necessity of showing more gratitude to those who know that ingratitude is not automatically punished, yet hate it all the same, than would otherwise be necessary. And for the same reason that Socrates did not go so far as to say that—he only asked whether—ingratitude is thus punished, he put each of the benefits derived from lawfulness in the form of a question. Namely, just as the benefits of lawfulness are not natural consequences of lawfulness, the punishments for ingratitude are not natural consequences of ingratitude (compare IV.4.24 with IV.4.17). Such things are due entirely to human action, whereas those before or past their prime will have a harder time conceiving a child, to give *the* counterexample, by nature. There are, to be sure, those with whom it is beneficial to be friends who, so far from being "good friends," hate you for not harming yourself for their benefit. And to be friends with the madmen with whom it is wise to be friends without doing more than is necessary, then, it is necessary to obey the law commanding gratitude. But this is not to affirm, this is to deny, that the law commanding gratitude is automatically self-enforcing.

Now, that said, Socrates never even made as if to prove that the laws commanding reverence for gods and honor for parents are automatically self-enforcing. Nor did he have to. Reverence for gods and honor for parents are, after all, forms of gratitude (IV.3.15–17, I.4.18; II.2).[27] Ingratitude generally differs from ingratitude to gods or parents in particular, it is true, in that ingratitude to gods or parents (II.2.13) is typically punished by cities (*Cyropaedia* I.2.7). But that only means the law commanding gratitude is divine insofar as those in breach of it are everywhere going to be "punished," so to speak, if only by the hatred of the bad friends to whom they are visibly ungrateful, whereas the laws commanding reverence for gods and honor for parents are divine insofar as those visibly in breach of them are everywhere going to be punished by cities.[28] "All these things befit gods," Hippias said, not insofar as those in breach of the unwritten laws are automatically punished—just as those before or past their prime are punished with low fertility—but only, rather, insofar as those caught breaking them are automatically punished by human beings, who are not necessarily good themselves, in every country (IV.4.24, reading *theois* with the manuscripts). Accordingly, when Socrates asked him in next place whether the gods legislate (enforce) the just things or things other than the just ones, Hippias professed to believe that they do not legislate things other than the just ones; yet he only did so, as he himself put it, because hardly anyone else would legislate the just things—surely no demos or oligarchs, for example—if not a god. And how does that—that belief, which flies in the face of everything Socrates has just said about incest and gratitude—follow? Socrates, for his part, saw the sophist's non sequitur exactly for what it was: bearing in mind that it "pleases" (*areskei*) Hippias that the lawful and the just are one and the same thing (IV.4.12), he drew the conclusion that it "pleases" (*areskei*) the gods "too," that the lawful and the just are one and the same thing (IV.4.25). What he, either Socrates or Hippias, meant by that should go without saying. Socrates thus found a way to say what he thought, while giving the appearance, at the same time, of changing the sophist's mind.

Although they do not legislate the just things, the gods legislate that human beings in every country make every effort, at least, to do so. That human beings hold the basic requirements of political life to be laws is only natural. The laws themselves, however, are merely human. Even the unwritten laws, much less the written ones, have to be distinguished from those things, those natural things, which the gods legislate—and not only legislate for us but also do for themselves: for, when speaking of the prohibition against incest, Socrates swore, "by Zeus," twice, something he had not done since his private conversation with Euthydemos (IV.2.11, IV.2.32, IV.2.35) and something he will do only once more before the end the *Memorabilia* (IV.8.5); he did so here of all places, when speaking of the prohibition against incest, because Zeus was the ("good," surely) child of parent-child incest who, among other things, did not revere gods, did not honor his parents, and was under no necessity of showing anyone gratitude.[29] And with that distinction, the distinction between nature and convention, there arises the problem of the rationality of political affairs. According to the philosophic solution to that problem, obedience to the unwritten laws is almost perfectly in keeping with obedience to "natural law," if that way of putting it is not an oxymoron, despite the distinction between the two. To flout openly the basic requirements of political life is, after all, to poke a sleeping bear with a stick. Punishment will be automatic. Still, the fact remains, the unwritten laws are not natural. And obedience to "natural law," which is just another way of saying obedience to the *daimonion*, however closely it may track with the unwritten laws, is therefore not obedience to the unwritten laws. Xenophon's Socrates was one of those to whom Marsilius of Padua refers, "who call natural law the dictate of right reason" (*The Defender of the Peace* II 12, 8). But there would seem to be another solution, besides the philosophic one, to the problem of the rationality of political affairs. As we saw, Lycurgus did a better job of making citizens obedient to the laws than anyone else (IV.4.15), but why? Hippias had said that "hardly anyone else" would legislate the just things if not a god, as we also saw, but why (IV.4.25)? Both questions have the same answer: Lycurgus, "legislator of the Lacedaemonians," was said to be likened to a god by

Apollo himself (*Apology* 15). His laws were held to be divine or divinely sanctioned, and disobedience to them was accounted, therefore, "not only lawless, but also unholy" (*Regime of the Lacedaemonians* 8.5). Hippias had also said that in every country human beings hold the command to revere gods, "first," as law (IV.4.19, IV.3.2, IV.6.2; I.4.16; consider *Cyropaedia* VIII.8.2). And now we know why; after all, if or since nature does not make it beneficial to obey the laws, respect for the rule of law (as something other than brute force) is irrational without either divine or divinely sanctioned legislators. Finally, seeing as how not even Sparta's divine or divinely sanctioned laws are automatically self-enforcing, did those who said that justice is, like colt breaking, a matter of training or habit rather than learning (compare IV.4.5 with I.2.19–23; IV.1.3–5) have in mind, not only merely human laws, but also divine or divinely sanctioned laws? Not even Lycurgus, one of the very best rulers, was a teacher of justice (*Regime of the Lacedaemonians* 10.4–7). However that may be, the philosophic appreciation for the political necessity of theology, to say nothing of belief in the theological foundations of politics itself, is bound to give rise to the objection that just about the first thing held as law today, at least in every "enlightened" country, is that there shall be no law respecting an establishment of religion. But this, while true, does not alter the fact that that people in the West would not be so quick to forget the problem if not for the "sword and a hundred appetites" hanging over them (Nietzsche, *Thus Spoke Zarathustra*, Part 1, Chapter 11, "On the New Idol"). In any event, although or because he was no enlightener, Socrates displayed his thought exactly as Xenophon said (IV.4.1)—or he displayed which things are just in his opinion all the time, exactly as he himself said (IV.4.10)—namely, "in deed." By not truthfully accusing others of being ignorant and bringing about concord in and among cities, by obeying the law forbidding the teaching of "an art of speeches," in particular, Socrates expressed his doubts that political life is, in the last analysis, the life for man (consider *Cyropaedia* V.1.27).

V

"The best men," according to Socrates, very frequently exhort citizens to live in concord, which is to say, they exhort citizens to obey the laws (IV.4.16). And not only are they "most fit to lead"—most fit to lead others, that is, to lawfulness or justice—but they are also "happiest" themselves (IV.5.12). Now Socrates was one of "the best men." As Xenophon put it, not only did Socrates lead others to gentlemanship—if not all the way toward it—but he was also blessed himself (I.6.14). And his conversation with the sophist Hippias, like his conversation with the sophist Antiphon, was an example of this. Euthydemos was surely present for the conversation with Hippias (consider IV.4.25); yet Socrates conversed with Hippias, not with Euthydemos, for this reason: because Hippias, not Euthydemos, was the interlocutor best suited to bring out that Socrates was most fit to lead others and happiest himself. For recall, in the first place, that in their conversation about piety Euthydemos contradicted Socrates only when he broached the subject of divination, not when he referred to political affairs (IV.3.12). Euthydemos took laws and obedience to them seriously already. And that means, unless Socrates were to begin by calling the seriousness of laws and obedience to them into question, there was no way for him to make the case to Euthydemos that they are indeed serious affairs. Nor perhaps was there any way, even if he did begin by calling the seriousness of laws and obedience to them into question, for Socrates to make the case that their seriousness is beyond question. But his apparent victory over the sophist Hippias, which he achieved in the presence of Euthydemos, "established it in Euthydemos's mind forever."[30] In the second place, not only did Socrates lead Euthydemos to be more just or lawful than he already was by conversing with Hippias, but Hippias also, simultaneously, gave Socrates a way to reveal his own happiness to good natures, like Xenophon, who were thoughtfully listening in. For Hippias was the sophist who, although he was a sophist, nevertheless accused Socrates of concealing his thought. Or he was a "modern," rather than an "ancient," sophist (Plato, *Greater Hippias* 281c3ff.).[31] And thus, by revealing the foolishness of the "modern" sophist's accusation against him, Socrates revealed his own happiness.

CHAPTER 7

The Foundation of Wisdom

I

The time has come to try to say for the first time how the nonelenctic teaching of Socrates is ordered. We cannot avoid the subject entirely. Since this is just the sort of thing that should go without saying, however, we can at least mention only the essential points. *Memorabilia* IV.3–4 is devoted to moderation: IV.3 to moderation concerning gods or piety; IV.4 to moderation concerning men or justice. While moderation in either sense of the term consists in obedience to the laws of the city, which tell us what (not) to do, say, and think, *Memorabilia* IV.5 is devoted to the art of action, IV.6 to the art of speech, and IV.7–8.3 to the art of contriving—none of which consists in obedience to the laws of the city. So far (IV.3–4), the nonelenctic teaching has made no mention whatsoever of wisdom. Going forward, wisdom will appear at every turn (IV.5.6; IV.6.7, IV.6.13; IV.7.10). The distinction between moderation or obedience to the laws, on one hand, and wisdom or the art of speech, action, and contriving, on the other, is the Xenophontic equivalent of the Platonic distinction between political or vulgar virtue, on one hand, and genuine, philosophic virtue, on the other (Plato, *Phaedo* 68b2–69c3, 82a11ff., *Republic* 518d9–e3, 430c3–5).[1] In the aftermath of the refutation, Xenophon said that before making his companions skilled in speech, action, and contriving, Socrates tried to make those of his companions who were not already somewhat moderate, at least, moderate (consider, however, I.2.19–23). He tried to do so, Xenophon said, because he believed that making youths without any moderation whatsoever skilled in speech, action, and contriving would only make them even more unjust and more capable of evildoing than they already were (IV.3.1–2). In *Memorabilia* IV.3, Socrates tried to make those of his companions who were not already somewhat pious, at least, pious. For this reason, while Xenophon drew special attention to the fact that he was present for the conversation between Socrates and Euthydemos, he was careful not to say that Euthydemos was the companion whom Socrates tried to make pious (IV.3.2). To be clear, "he tried" (IV.3.2). And he succeeded marvelously in making those of his companions who were already somewhat pious more pious (IV.3.18).[2] Likewise, all Socrates succeeded in doing in IV.4 was making those of his companions who were already somewhat just more just (IV.4.25). Loosely speaking, even if any of his freshly refuted companions were already somewhat impious and unjust, there was nothing for Socrates to do but try to undo the damage he had caused, if for no other reason than to make absolutely certain that they had no one to blame but themselves for being even more willing and able to do injustice in the event that he failed to make them moderate. That was according to nature and correct. On the other hand, even though or precisely because there was nothing for Socrates to do but try to make the case for moderation, the conversations reported in IV.3–4 were not simply miserable failures. To say nothing of the likes of Euthydemos, who was made even more moderate than he already was, the conversations made refuted good natures skilled in action and in speech or conversation, if not in contriving, too. For IV.5 is devoted to how Socrates made those of his companions who were already somewhat skilled in action more skilled in action (IV.5.1). And IV.6 is devoted to how—Xenophon only "tries" to say how, by the way; he does not necessarily say how—Socrates made those of his companions who were already somewhat skilled in speech or conversation more skilled in speech or conversation (IV.6.1). The conversations reported in IV.5–6 only made those of his companions who were already made somewhat skilled in action and somewhat skilled in speech or conversation by the conversations reported in IV.3–4 more skilled in action and more skilled in speech or conversation. So close is the connection between moderation and wisdom that here, as elsewhere, Socrates found success even, or precisely, in failure (consider I.2.8).

As for Euthydemos, even though or precisely because the conversations reported in IV.3–4 made him more pious and more just, they did not make him skilled in speech, action, or contriving. Nor did the conversations or speeches reported in IV.5–8.3 make him more skilled in speech, action, or contriving. As Book IV ascends, Xenophon drops the ruse that Socrates desired the youth's education. To the conversation reported in IV.5, Xenophon appends a number of suggestions of the utmost importance that Socrates saw no need to make in the presence of Euthydemos (IV.5.12). And not one, but two, trans-Euthydemean appendices follow the conversation reported in IV.6 (IV.6.12, IV.6.13–15). By the time Xenophon gets to IV.7, Euthydemos is out of the picture completely. Slowly but surely, the youth fades from view. His education was over even before it began. But we already knew that—if not from the ridiculous figure Euthydemos cut throughout the protreptic teaching, then from the fact that the elenctic and, thus the nonelenctic, teaching of Socrates was so far over his head. Still, the fact remains, Euthydemos was forever changed by Socrates. Once the youth had been refuted by him, he turned toward Socrates as a "teacher" who leads by example, along the lines spelled out in his third exhortatory or protreptic speech: to become "worthy of mention" Euthydemos tried to do, alongside Socrates, some of the things that Socrates himself did (compare IV.2.40 with IV.2.6).[3] In particular, seeing as how Socrates did not engage in political affairs (I.6.15), the youth gave up his political ambitions and joined the ranks of Socrates's gentlemanly associates (I.2.48, contrast I.2.47). Giving up political ambitions was, in such cases, just one side of the coin, the other side of which was more piety. On one hand, the elenctic teaching left the rationality of political affairs in at least some doubt, and the only way to bury away, if not put to rest, lingering, reasonable doubts about the rationality of political affairs was with more piety, on the other. Under Socrates's influence, Euthydemos went from being (not so much a citizen of the heavenly kingdom as) a citizen of the earthly kingdom to being (not so much a citizen of the earthly kingdom as) a citizen of the heavenly kingdom.[4] But of course, whereas Euthydemos needed Socrates or his "*daimonion*" to tell him what to believe and do (IV.2.40), Socrates did not need anyone else to tell him what to believe and do (IV.8.11).[5]

II

As—*not after*—Socrates tried to make his already somewhat immoderate companions moderate, he made them skilled in action. In the next place, Xenophon says how Socrates made them more skilled in action, in the art of action, than they already were (IV.5.1). Not once does Socrates use the term *skilled in action* (*praktikos*), however. And Xenophon, after having used the term only just this once, never uses it again. Instead, to say how Socrates made those of his companions who were already somewhat skilled in action more skilled in action, Xenophon reports a conversation between Socrates and Euthydemos about continence (IV.5.1–2). "First" (contrast IV.5.1 with IV.3.2) and "always," because Socrates held continence to be "good" for one intending to do anything noble, he made it clear to his companions that he was more continent than anyone else in deed (contrast IV.3.18 and IV.4.25), and he urged or exhorted them to continence more than anything else, including even moderation, in speech (IV.5.1–2).[6] Since piety (IV.6.2, IV.3.16) and justice (IV.6.5; IV.1.2, IV.2.11, IV.5.10) are noble things, Socrates held continence to be good for one intending to do pious and just or moderate things. Good in what way? Skipping to the end of his conversation with Euthydemos, Socrates concluded that continence makes it possible to contemplate the strongest of the things of concern to us (*ta kratista tōn pragmatōn*). Only such contemplation—in or through which the continent at any rate separate the (good and bad or most pleasant) things, by speech and by deed, according to classes or kinds—makes one choose the "more fundamental," good things rather than the bad or most pleasant ones (IV.5.11). And what is that, that which makes one choose the good things rather than the bad or most pleasant ones, if not the art of action? Socrates finally came to the conclusion, therefore, that, by making it possible to contemplate the strongest of the things of concern to us—the good things—continence makes it possible for the moderate, who intend to do noble things, to become skilled in action also or instead. He did so, however, in his long, roundabout way. That is, given that Socrates told Euthydemos in the simplest and clearest manner only what he believed *Euthydemos* should believe and do (compare IV.2.40 with IV.7), Xenophon appends to the conversation a number of suggestions about genuine, philosophic virtue that Socrates saw no need to make in the presence of Euthydemos (IV.5.12). And he suggested among other things that only "in this way," by making it possible to contemplate and choose the good things, does continence make it possible to become most capable of conversing or most skilled in conversation. As for that—namely, dialectic—Socrates suggested that the word for "conversing" (*to dialegesthai*) is etymologically derived from the word for "separating" (*to dialegein*), the reason being that to converse is to deliberate in common by separating the things according to classes or kinds. The etymology is patently absurd, not only because it is attested to nowhere else in Greek literature,[7] but also, and above all, because it would mean that there were once upon a time people conversing with one another who had no word for conversing, only separating. Socrates suggested, in other words, that the plain meaning of the word comes after the highly technical meaning that he gives to it, whereas just the reverse must be true. What did such people think they were doing? The highly technical meaning of the word that he gives to it must come after, not before, its plain meaning. And so, at the same time as the joking etymology made the serious point that, technically speaking, conversing is separating the things according to classes or kinds, it made the equally serious point that there are always people conversing with one another who, even though they have a word for conversing, have no idea what conversing should be. But then, in IV.5, Socrates urged or exhorted Euthydemos to continence. And Xenophon lays special emphasis on the fact that he did so, as usual (IV.2.8, IV.3.2, IV.4.5), in a "conversation" with the youth (IV.5.1–2). And what stands out about their conversation is the dizzying array of things by reference to which continence is defined in its first half. Continence would seem at first glance to be defined at unnecessary length and in excruciating detail by reference to "the best things" and "the beneficial (or good) things," "the noblest things" and "the fitting things," or "the most excellent things," on one hand, and by reference to "wisdom" and "moderation," which is to say, "learning" and "caring about" any and all such things, on the other (IV.5.3–8). Considering the fact that continence is only "useful" for virtue (IV.5.2) or the "foundation" of virtue (I.5.4) and yet, for the simple reason that it can be used either for good or for ill (I.5.3, II.6.1), training or learning (I.5.5, II.1.20, IV.5.10), not itself (a) virtue,[8] Socrates was apparently laying it on pretty thick.[9] More to the point, though, just because a noncontradictor like Euthydemos, who was completely ignorant of dialectic or the art of conversation, did not separate any of these things according to classes or kinds does not mean that there are not distinctions to be made, for example, between wisdom and moderation. By now, on the contrary, refuted good natures knew perfectly well that (Euthydemos did not at all know that) there are. To see how continence makes it possible to be skilled in action by making it possible to contemplate the good things, they need look no further than Euthydemos. The youth has not been able to follow any of his conversations with Socrates so far. Only this time, if Euthydemos should be unable to follow the conversation about continence, too, his inability to do so—the cause of his inability to follow his conversations with Socrates—would be the subject matter of the conversation itself. For, in that case, Euthydemos would be unable to follow a conversation about continence that traces the inability to follow such a conversation—the inability to separate the things according to classes or kinds—to incontinence! As for refuted good natures who were already somewhat skilled in action and in conversation, while thoughtfully listening to Socrates jokingly urge or exhort Euthydemos to continence, would they not have the opportunity to see for themselves how incontinence makes it impossible for the moderate Euthydemos to contemplate and choose, much less to converse about, the good things? And would they not be made more skilled in action by seeing how incontinence in the form of softness of soul lies at the bottom of his self-ignorance and bad choices?

In any event, to begin with the first half (IV.5.3–5) of the first part (IV.5.3–8) of the conversation, when Socrates asked Euthydemos whether one so ruled by the bodily pleasures as to be unable to do "the best things" (*ta beltista*) is free, the youth answered that such a one is, in his opinion, "least" free. To be least free is not to be wholly unfree. However, by putting words in his mouth, Socrates got Euthydemos to agree with him quite reluctantly and much to his own surprise that, "in all likelihood, by Zeus," insofar as they are prevented from doing "the best things," the incontinent are "wholly" unfree (IV.5.3–4). But then, as if he were not changing the subject, Socrates asked the youth whether the incontinent are not only prevented from doing "the most noble things" (*ta kallista*), in his opinion, but also compelled to do "the most shameful things" (*ta aiskhista*). With that, though, he turned from "the best things" to "the noblest things," and from "the worse" (*to kheiron*) (IV.5.6) to "the most shameful things," in the first place, and he made it explicit that the latter are compulsory for the incontinent, in the second. Euthydemos noticed the second, minor alteration, but not the first, major one. The distinction between "the worse" and "the most shameful things" was just as completely lost on him as the distinction between "the best things" and "the noblest things." So here we have two very different kinds of incontinence, defined by reference to two very different kinds or classes of things: one according to which the incontinent are prevented from doing "the best things" and compelled to do "the worse"—which is only less than, by no means the opposite of, the "best" (IV.5.3)—and another according to which they are prevented from doing "the noblest things" and compelled to do "the most shameful things" (IV.5.4). However, in consideration of the fact that Euthydemos did not separate the things in question according to classes or kinds, Socrates turned from "the best things" and "the noblest things" to "the most excellent things" (*ta arista*), and he turned from "the worse" and "the most shameful things" to "the worst things" (*ta kakista*); and he defined continence and incontinence, for a third and final time, by reference to "the most excellent things" and "the most shameful things." "The most excellent things" and "the most shameful things" better represent the youth's view of the matter in its entirety because, in the class of "the most excellent things," both "the best things" and "the noblest things" come together as one, while in the class of "the worst things" (*ta kakista*), both "the worse" (*to kheiron*) and "the shameful things" (*ta aiskhista*) do so. Accordingly, whereas Socrates got Euthydemos to agree with him, only by sleight of hand, that one prevented from doing "the best things" is wholly unfree—in his opinion, such a one is least free, to repeat, not wholly unfree (IV.5.3–4)—he had no trouble at all getting him to agree that one prevented from doing "the most excellent things" and compelled to do "the worst things" is enslaved to the "worst" (*kakistoi*) masters in the "worst" (*kakistē*) slavery (IV.5.5). The youth was reluctant to agree with Socrates that the incontinent, in the precise, Socratic sense of the term, are wholly unfree for the simple reason that to be prevented from doing "the best things" is not to be compelled to do the opposite of the "best." For example, nothing prevents such a one from doing the second-best things. And surely Euthydemos had in mind, in that case, one prevented by bodily pleasures from doing the most excellent things yet not compelled, for all that, to do the worst, which is as much as to say, he had in mind, he thought, most of us. But who, then, did Socrates have in mind? The youth was not at all reluctant to agree that the incontinent, in the loose, Euthydemean sense of the term, are wholly unfree. That said, if to be incontinent is indeed to be enslaved to the "worst" masters in the "worst" slavery, what is continence? Continence and incontinence, in all likelihood, cause opposite effects (IV.5.8). To be continent is, therefore, to be enslaved to the "most excellent" masters in the "most excellent" slavery; to be prevented from doing "the worst things" and compelled to do "the most excellent things." Did Socrates make a point of getting Euthydemos to agree with him, contrary to the youth's own view of the matter, that one prevented from doing "the best things" is wholly unfree because Socrates had in mind, paradoxically, one compelled to do "the most excellent things," at least insofar as they are "the noblest things"? If so, to put this differently, the continent in the loose, Euthydemean sense of the term are incontinent in the precise, Socratic sense of the term.

Incontinence prevents wisdom, according to what Socrates said in the second half (IV.5.6–8) of the first part of the conversation (IV.5.3–8), and compels the opposite of wisdom. So, on one hand, because they are ruled by the pleasures, incontinent "(ordinary) human beings" (*anthrōpoi*) are prevented from taking heed of "the beneficial things" and from learning them. On the other hand, because they are ruled by the pleasures, they are compelled to choose "the worse instead of the better" (*to kheiron anti tou beltionos*), despite perceiving "both the good things and the bad things" (IV.5.6). The opposite of wisdom is therefore ignorance, madness, or both. But then, in exactly the same way as he turned from "the best things" to "the noblest things," Socrates turned from wisdom, which has to do with the good or beneficial things, to moderation (IV.5.7). And he got Euthydemos to agree, to begin with, that moderation "least" belongs to the incontinent on the grounds that the works or deeds of moderation and incontinence are opposite; yet, even or precisely if moderation least belongs to the incontinent, moderation belongs to the incontinent. How, then, can the works or deeds of moderation and incontinence possibly be opposite? After that, Socrates got Euthydemos to agree that nothing prevents one from caring about the things fitting to care about more than incontinence; but again, to say that nothing prevents that caring more than incontinence is by no means to say that incontinence prevents that caring. So, to be sure, moderation differs from wisdom as learning and choosing the best or beneficial things differs from caring about and doing the noblest or fitting ones.[10] More than that, though, incontinence does not prevent moderation, much less compel the opposite of moderation. The incontinent are prevented from wisdom and compelled to be ignorant or mad; yet they are only least moderate or most prevented from caring about the things fitting to care about, which is as much as to say, they are not wholly immoderate. And perhaps then, although the distinction between wisdom and moderation was completely lost on Euthydemos, the ignorant or mad are at least somewhat moderate. Socrates did not leave it at that, however. In consideration of the fact that Euthydemos did not separate (the opposite of) wisdom from (the opposite of) moderation, he turned from wisdom and moderation to continence as something "most excellent" (*ariston*) in exactly the same way as he turned from "the best things" and "the noblest things" to "the most excellent things" (*ta arista*), and he turned from ignorance or madness and immoderation to incontinence as something "worse" (*kakion*) than anything in exactly the same way as he turned from "the worse" (*to kheiron*) and "the most shameful things" (*ta aiskhista*) to "the worst things" (*ta kakista*). And he defined continence and incontinence, or so it seemed, by reference to what is "most excellent" (*ariston*) and "worst" (*kakiston*). To better represent the youth's view of the matter in its entirety, to spell this out, Socrates seemed to say that ignorance or madness and immoderation come together as one in incontinence, while wisdom and moderation come together as one in continence. For what could be "worse" (*kakion*) for an (ordinary) human being, he asked Euthydemos, than that which both makes one choose and care about the worse or harmful things and compels one to do immoderate or shameful things (IV.5.7)? Since Euthydemos did not think that there was anything "worse" (*kakion*) for an (ordinary) human being than this (incontinence?), Socrates had no trouble at all getting him to agree that continence is "most excellent" on the basis of his prior agreement that continence and incontinence cause opposite effects. This time, however, it was Socrates's turn to agree reluctantly, indeed, to disagree, with Euthydemos. Continence and incontinence are only "likely" to cause opposite effects in (ordinary) human beings, as he put it, and continence is only "likely" to be "most excellent" for them (IV.5.8). For Socrates merely seemed to say that ignorance or madness and immoderation come together as one in incontinence—in fact, to that unhappy marriage of ignorance or madness and immoderation which both makes one choose and care about the worse or harmful things and compels one to do immoderate or shameful things, he never actually gave the name *incontinence*. And he did not do so because, according to what he had only just said of incontinence worthy of the name, while incontinent (ordinary) human beings are indeed compelled to be ignorant or mad, they are *not* compelled to do immoderate or shameful things. Far from it, they are at least somewhat moderate. Although this escaped his notice, then, Euthydemos was in a jam. Continence and incontinence are only "likely" to cause opposite effects in (ordinary) human beings because, while it is true that the former causes wisdom, and the latter ignorance or madness, continence causes not only moderation but also immoderation, even as incontinence causes not only immoderation but also moderation. And continence is only "likely" to be "most excellent" for (ordinary) human beings because, just as the incontinent are not wholly immoderate, the continent are not wholly moderate. Finally, those pleasures which prevent the incontinent from learning (the good or beneficial things), on one hand, and compel them to choose the worse or harmful things, despite "knowing better," on the other, are not necessarily bodily pleasures (contrast IV.5.6 and IV.5.10 with IV.5.3). Paradoxically, then, are the continent not wholly moderate insofar as they stand firm against the pleasures of the soul, too, that prevent wisdom and compel ignorance or madness? If so, to repeat, the continent in the precise, Socratic sense of the term are incontinent in the loose, Euthydemean sense of the term. To be enslaved to the "most excellent" masters in the "most excellent" slavery would seem to be "most excellent" for "(ordinary) human beings" (*anthrōpoi*). Only for "a real man" (*anēr*)—who, being like a city, is not "a real man" in the usual sense of the term (I.5.5)—is freedom worth having (IV.5.2).[11]

So then, in the first part of the conversation (IV.5.3–8), the two halves of which mirror one another (IV.5.3–5 and IV.5.6–8), Socrates gave refuted good natures the opportunity to see just how unable Euthydemos was to follow the conversation about continence, which is to say, to separate the things by reference to which continence was defined according to classes or kinds. According to Socrates, by contrast, one compelled to do the works or deeds of moderation is wholly unfree and incontinent, on one hand, while the continent are perhaps wise, albeit not wholly moderate, on the other. Then, in the second part of the conversation (IV.5.9–11), he gave refuted good natures the opportunity to see that he thought in all seriousness that incontinence, albeit incontinence vis-à-vis specific nonbodily pleasures, is the cause of the youth's inability to follow the conversation.

Socrates starts small. By his account, contrary to popular belief, according to which the continent rise above the bodily pleasures, only the continent experience bodily pleasures worthy of recollection. Put simply, "hunger is the best sauce" (I.3.5, *Cyropaedia* I.5.12). Unless the desires for food, drink, sex, rest or sleep have grown quite strong, that is, we do not take the most pleasure in them; hence, the very same thing that makes us stand firm against the desires for food, drink, sex, rest or sleep—the very same thing that makes the desires for them grow accordingly—makes us take the most pleasure in them too (IV.5.9). But then, when Socrates brought the point about continence vis-à-vis the bodily pleasures to bear upon continence vis-à-vis the "noble and good" things (IV.5.10), Euthydemos took him to be saying that no virtue whatsoever belongs to a real man (*anēr*) whose bodily pleasures get the better of him (IV.5.11). More specifically, he took Socrates to be saying that whereas the virtuous are not, the vicious are so ruled by the "nearest," bodily pleasures as to lose out completely on "very great" or even the "greatest," nonbodily pleasures: the pleasures of doing noble things. Now, to be sure, Socrates did give some indication that those ruled by the "nearest," bodily pleasures lose out most of all, albeit not completely, on the "greatest," nonbodily pleasures, but that was just the tip of the iceberg (IV.5.10). For the latter, however much more continent they may seem to be than the former, are incontinent in the precise, Socratic sense of the term. Suffice it to say that whereas the incontinent, in the precise sense of the term, do not reap the benefits of doing noble things, the continent, in the precise sense of the term, do. And they do so, according to Socrates, because they stand firm against the aforementioned "greatest" pleasures, if or since they are not beneficial (or good), whereas the continent, in the loose sense of the term, do not (IV.5.10). Moreover, since Socrates brought the point about continence vis-à-vis the bodily pleasures (IV.5.9) to bear upon continence vis-à-vis the noble and good things (IV.5.10), and since the continent and the incontinent vis-à-vis the bodily pleasures have one and the same end in mind—namely, the most pleasure—with the difference that only the continent have the means to it, do the continent and the incontinent vis-à-vis the noble and good things have the one and the same end in mind, too, with the difference that only the continent have the means to it? The end is the good, in this case, not the most pleasure. And the aforementioned "greatest" pleasures—that is, "the most pleasant things" (IV.5.11)—are therefore also, or instead, the pleasures of hoping for the "greatest" good things (IV.3.17), up to and including a state of being where, there being perfect happiness, "there shall be no more death." In other words, while those ruled by the "nearest," bodily pleasures lose out almost completely on the "greatest," nonbodily pleasures, those ruled by the "greatest," nonbodily pleasures—by their *hopes*—lose out on the good things. Contrary to popular belief, according to which the continent rise above the good things, only the continent reap the benefits of doing noble things. For only they can contemplate the strongest (*ta kratista*) of the things of concern to us, the things by reference to which continence (*enkrateia*) is defined, at the cost of losing out on the "greatest" pleasures or "the most pleasant things" (IV.5.11). And only they can act accordingly, or be "skilled in action."

CHAPTER 8

The (Rhetorical Treatment of the) Dialectical Method

I

Xenophon will now try to say how Socrates made those of his companions who were already somewhat skilled in conversation more skilled in conversation. According to his introductory remarks, Socrates himself never ceased examining with his companions, in conversation with his companions, what each of the beings is. Seeing as how this unceasing examination of his was a conversational one, to say how Socrates made his companions more skilled in conversation is to say how he prepared them to examine, for themselves, what each of the beings is (IV.6.1, reading *sun* with most editors).[1] And Xenophon will only "try" to say how Socrates prepared his companions—some, if not "all," of them (contrast IV.5.2)—to examine what each of the beings is in conversation with others because, when it comes to this, he was treading on dangerous ground. Socrates conversed about the nature of "all things" differently than the other, "pre-Socratic" philosophers did. For he was always conversing about "the human things," for example, by examining the pious, the noble, the just, wisdom, and courage (I.1.16);[2] yet somehow, by doing so, he conversed about the nature of all things—he examined what both he and the sophists called the "cosmos"—all the same. (I.1.11). He was always conversing about the human things, that is, "and about the other (nonhuman) things" (*kai peri tōn allōn*) (I.1.16). And it would not be safe—nor, as should go without saying, would it be according to nature and correct—for Xenophon to say in the simplest and clearest manner how Socrates conversed about the nature of all things by conversing about the human things, much less how he prepared some of his companions to follow in his footsteps. Remember, while just about all of the Athenians were persuaded that he did not believe in the gods in whom the city believed, only some of them were persuaded that he corrupted the youth (compare I.1.20 with I.2.1). As Strauss put it, "Xenophon cannot well present the results of these considerations without defeating the purpose of the *Memorabilia*. He will therefore give only as many specimens as in his opinion will make manifest the manner," the method, "of Socrates' inquiry."[3] In IV.6, to spell this out a bit more fully, Xenophon reports six conversations between Socrates and Euthydemos—about such human things as the pious (IV.6.2–4), the just (IV.6.5–6), wisdom (IV.6.7), the good (IV.6.8), the noble (IV.6.9), and courage (IV.6.10–11)—before leaving us to put everything together in such a way as to make manifest the Socratic method, if not also how he defined (the nature of) "all things" as a result, with only a few brief words of introduction (IV.6.1) and a brief appendix or two in conclusion to guide us (IV.6.12, IV.6.13–15). We have our work cut out for us. *Memorabilia* IV.6 is a jigsaw puzzle. The six conversations are the puzzle pieces. Xenophon's introductory remarks, along with the two appendices with which he concludes IV.6, give us the guidance we need to put the pieces together. And our first order of business, even before we take a long, hard look at the puzzle pieces themselves, is to let ourselves be guided by Xenophon's introductory remarks.

Socrates did not examine what each of the beings is, without cease, by himself; he never ceased examining what each of the beings is in conversation with his companions, but why? What did he need them for? According to Xenophon's introductory remarks, Socrates thought that those who know what each of the beings is should be able "to explain" this to "the others"—the others, that is, who do not know. And he thought at the same time that the others, who do not know what each of the beings is, are both baffled themselves and leave others baffled. "On account of these things," both of them, Socrates examined what each of the beings is in conversation with his companions (IV.6.1).—Not a few readers will be unable to resist the temptation to jump to the conclusion that Socrates examined what each of the beings is in conversation with his companions, by this account, because he himself knew what each of the beings is and thus, in order to free those of his companions who did not know from their bafflement, he explained this to them. On that view, however, Socrates himself would not be examining anything whatsoever in conversation with his companions, much less examining what each of the beings is without cease; he would be presenting his companions with the results of his examinations: the knowledge, the possession of which would render further examination pointless, of what each of the beings is. Besides, not to dwell on this any longer than we have to, why did Socrates think that those nonknowers who are baffled themselves leave others baffled? Are those whom they leave baffled knowers or not? If they are knowers, how can nonknowers leave them baffled? For they should be able to explain what each of the beings is to the nonknowers and thus, on this view, free *them* from their bafflement. And if they are nonknowers, they are, on this view, baffled themselves already. Either way, it is hard to fathom how the baffled can leave others baffled.—Recall, in this connection, that the elenctic teaching, the Socratic refutation of Euthydemos's opinions about justice, started with Socrates asking the youth if he would be able "to explain" (*ekhoien an exēgēsasthai*), to him, the works or deeds of justice (IV.2.12). By the end of the refutation, it turned out that Euthydemos was unable to explain to Socrates even whether they are, or are not, good. (About the good, similarly, he told Euthydemos "to explain" [*exēgēsai*] it to him [IV.2.31]). Now Socrates, too, was "perplexed," "at a loss," or ignorant about such things, as we saw, with the difference that he knew this, whereas Euthydemos did not. The Socratic refutation left the youth only for the moment, only somewhat "perplexed" or "at a loss." Did, then, Socrates examine what each of the beings is in conversation with his companions, both good and bad natures, because he himself did not know them in some way, shape, or form, while they believed they did, and thus, being baffled himself, set out to baffle them, too, by asking them if they would be able "to explain" (*an exēgeisthai dunasthai*) themselves to him? In other words, did his conversational examinations with his companions take the form of refutations of them?[4]

It was the sophist Hippias—and not Hermogenes, say, to whom Xenophon entrusts the bulk of the *Apology*—who said that Socrates would rather question and "refute" everyone than deliver a speech to anyone or reveal his thought concerning anything (IV.4.9). There are some things to which only the least reputable man can safely give the most pointed expression (consider also I.2.31–38). But Hippias's was not a lone voice in the wilderness. Xenophon says in passing that by asking questions—according to Charicles, questions the answers to which he himself already knew (I.2.36)—Socrates "refuted" those who believed they knew everything (I.4.1). Aristippus undertook to "refute" Socrates, just as Socrates had, on some other occasion, "refuted" Aristippus (III.8.1). Socrates had refuted Aristippus, on that occasion, *just as he had refuted Euthydemos* (compare III.8.2 with IV.2.31–36).[5] There is reason to believe that he refuted Hippias, too, when he was last in Athens (compare IV.4.6–7 with IV.4.9). In keeping with this, while still a companion of Socrates, Alcibiades had asked Pericles the question "What is law?" before going on to refute the great statesman.

And everything, the question, the refutation, and even the answer, bore the mark of Socrates (I.2.40–46). Also in passing, Xenophon says that Socrates "refuted" Alcibiades, when he was not so much a companion of his as a statesman himself (I.2.47), perhaps not much differently from the way Alcibiades, while still one of his companions, had refuted Pericles. In the eulogy of Socrates with which Xenophon concludes the *Memorabilia*, when praising Socrates for his piety first, his justice second, then for his continence and his prudence (contriving), he deviates only ever so slightly from the order of the nonelenctic teaching: finally, when the time comes to praise Socrates for his speech, Xenophon does not let so important a moment pass by without expressing his admiration for Socrates's ability to test others (compare IV.2.26) and "refute" them (IV.8.11).[6] Was that, rather than his continence, not what drew youths better than Euthydemos to Socrates in the first place (I.2.14–15)? Now, to repeat, Xenophon says that Socrates was "always," without cease (IV.6.1), conversing about the human (and other) things by asking "what is" questions (I.1.16). And yet there are no more than three examples of Socrates doing this sort of thing to be found in the whole entire *Memorabilia* (III.9, IV.2, IV.6). If his conversational examinations with his companions took the form of refutations of them, and indeed they did, there is really only a single, solitary example of Socrates doing this sort of thing. In the one and only private Socratic conversation found in Xenophon's writings, Socrates—who, it turns out, was not always visible (I.1.10)—refuted someone, Euthydemos, for the one and only time in Xenophon's writings (IV.2.8ff.). But again, seconding Hippias, Xenophon tells us that so far from being a one-off, Socrates refuted quite a few others much as he refuted Euthydemos (IV.2.40).[7] What was front and center for Socrates, what Plato's *Apology* represented as his "Delphic mission," Xenophon allows to recede into the background of his Socratic writings. We know, *because he himself tells us*, that the peak is all but missing from the *Memorabilia* as a whole, just as the peak of the all but missing peak is all but missing from *Memorabilia* IV.2.[8]

But I digress. To return to IV.6, there would seem to be no Socratic refutation in sight. There are, instead, six conversations between Socrates and Euthydemos, about such human things as the pious, the just, wisdom, the good, the noble, and courage, that would seem, at any rate, to be anything but. Socrates asked the youth a total of fifty-four, leading questions, brief and to the point, in rapid-fire succession, to which the youth's answers were always (with two or three hardly noticeable, albeit notable, exceptions) the same. In a word, "yes." All of the questions or answers seem to be so obvious in themselves and so hard to tell apart from one another that the conversations have a soporific effect.

This is a far cry from a refutation. That said, so long as we manage to stay awake, we cannot help noticing that Socrates started by asking the youth whether he is "able to say" what something is (IV.6.2, consider IV.6.9), which is not a little reminiscent of how the refutation of the youth's opinions about justice and the good started (IV.2.12, IV.2.31), on one hand, and of how Socrates thought about those who know what each of the beings is, according to Xenophon's introductory remarks, on the other (IV.6.1, consider I.2.52). And what if it should turn out that Euthydemos was not, in fact, "able to say" anything clear (IV.6.13)? What if Socrates got the youth to agree to quite a few things that were—so far from being obvious in themselves and hard to tell apart from other things that Socrates got the youth to agree to—highly paradoxical in themselves and in contradiction with other things that Socrates got the youth to agree to? Here we have, in that case, an exact parody or caricature of a refutation, in which agreement after agreement to highly paradoxical and self-contradictory things does not sow confusion but "perfect clarity," because the agreements would seem, at any rate, to be obvious and all of a piece.[9] Or rather, to put this more generally, do we have here the "safe" (*asphalēs*), Odyssean or rhetorical treatment of the dialectical method by means of which Socrates, "being baffled" himself (*to sphallesthai*), set out "to baffle" others (*sphallein*) (compare IV.6.15 with IV.6.1)? Now it is entirely possible, of course, to lay the groundwork for a refutation, to establish the possibility or necessity of one, without actually going through with it. To do so, you need only get your interlocutor to agree to *P*, on one hand, and to *Q*, on the other, where *P* and *Q* contradict one another. Then, rather than disturb your interlocutor by rubbing his nose in the mess he made of things, a painful ordeal that Socrates had no wish to repeat in the case of Euthydemos (IV.2.40), you might just leave matters at that. It is entirely possible, therefore, that should it turn out to be the case that we do indeed have here an exact caricature of a refutation, the groundwork for the real thing would be laid here too.[10]

II

The six conversations that follow are so densely populated with questions and answers that, for the sake of clarity, parenthetical references will be to each question and answer—that is, to both Socrates's question and Euthydemos's answer. So the conversations about the pious, the just, wisdom, the good, the noble, and courage will be referred to by the letters *P*, *J*, *W*, *G*, *N*, and *C*, respectively.

Then, since there are ten sets of questions and answers in the conversation about piety, they will, each of them, be referred to as P1, P2, P3, . . . P10. Since there are fourteen in the conversation about justice, they will be referred to as J1, J2, J3, . . . J14. Since there seven in the conversation about wisdom, they will be referred to as W1, W2, W3, . . . W7. And so on for the conversations about the good, in which there are five sets of questions and answers; the noble, in which there are four; and courage, in which there are fourteen. Again, the six conversations are pieces of a puzzle. After taking a long, hard look at each of them, one by one, we will be in a better position turn to the two appendices for guidance. And only then, after having done that, too, will we be in a position to put them together in such a way as to make manifest the Socratic method.

First, when it came to piety, Socrates asked Euthydemos ten leading questions. All of them, to repeat, seem to Euthydemos to be obvious. However, while Euthydemos began by saying that *to do* the gods honor is *to be* pious (P2), he ended up agreeing that *to know* the laws concerning the gods is *to be* pious (P10). And insofar as it is entirely possible to know the laws and yet not do as they say (II.1.5), to be pious according to the first definition is quite possibly to be impious according to the last. So far from being obvious the last definition of piety is far from obvious according to the first definition, which is to say, according to generally accepted opinions. They don't call it the Socratic paradox for nothing. But Socrates was able to lure Euthydemos away from the first definition of piety to the last one, without the youth so much as batting an eye, by getting him to agree that *to know* the laws (concerning the gods) is necessarily *to do* as they say (P7). He did so, with marvelous sleight of hand, by getting Euthydemos to agree that *to know* the way in which one should (*dei*) do the gods honor is *to believe* one should do the gods honor in that way (P5) and that *to believe* one should do (the) gods honor in that way is, in turn, necessarily *to do* them honor in that way (P6).[11] So far, so good. At the same time, however, just before getting Euthydemos to agree for this reason that *to know* the way in which one should do the gods honor is necessarily *to do* them honor in that way, Socrates got Euthydemos to agree that to know the laws (concerning the gods) is to know the way in which one should do the gods honor (P4). That agreement is the major premise while the agreement that *to know* the way in which one should do the gods honor is necessarily *to do* them honor in that way is the minor promise of a syllogism whose conclusion is that *to know* the laws (concerning the gods) is necessarily *to do* the gods honor in accord with the laws (P7). And it was smooth sailing from there. Taking that conclusion (P7) as the major premise of a new syllogism, Socrates did not have to do much more (compare P8 with P3) than remind Euthydemos of the premise from which the youth began (compare P9 with P2) to get him to agree, in conclusion, that *to know* the laws concerning the gods is *to be* pious (P10). Having said that, the major premise (P7) of the second syllogism was only as good as the minor premise of the first. And Socrates got Euthydemos to agree that to know the laws (concerning the gods) is to know the way in which one should do the gods honor only because the youth took it for granted that to know the laws "concerning the gods" is to know the laws "in accord with which one should do the gods honor" (P3–4). Socrates for his part never spoke of the laws as anything but the laws—that is, the laws of the city—"concerning the gods" (P7, P10). After all, did he himself not believe that, instead of honoring "the gods" by obeying the laws concerning them, one should honor "gods" (contrast P6 with P2–5, P7, P10) by learning the nature of all things (IV.3.14)? However that may be, if to know the laws concerning the gods is *not* (believed to be) to know the laws in accord with which one should do the gods honor, then to know the laws concerning the gods is *not* necessarily to believe one should do the gods honor in accord with the laws (P5). Nor is knowing the laws concerning the gods, in that case, to do the gods honor in accord with the laws. That is not only entirely possible—Aristodemos, for example, knew the law concerning sacrifices—but also, according to Socrates's indications, bound to happen. For the laws concerning the gods were only just defined in opposition to doing the gods honor in whatever way one wants (P3). Doing whatever one wants, to gods or to men (J1), is not permitted by the laws. And so, then, to know the laws concerning the gods is not necessarily to (believe one should) do the gods honor in accord with them for the simple reason that to know the laws is not necessarily to want to obey them. Euthydemos understood the Socratic paradox in the way in which it was vulgarly understood, which is to say, misunderstood (consider I.2.19).[12]

Next, when it came to justice, Socrates did not change tack. He asked Euthydemos fourteen leading questions. Only this time, having only just been lured to state the view that to know the laws concerning the gods is to be pious, Euthydemos not only *ended up* but also, pretty much, *began* by stating the paradoxical view that virtue is knowledge. Specifically, when Socrates asked Euthydemos whether it is permitted to make use of human beings in whatever way one wants, the youth began by saying "no," on the grounds that *to know* what is lawful—as he put it, to know the laws in accord with which we should make use of one another—is *to be* lawful (compare P10 with J1 and contrast P2). Since knowing what is lawful and making use of others in whatever way one wants are not mutually exclusive, however, what Euthydemos said betrayed his misunderstanding of the Socratic paradox. That was not at all unexpected of course. Nor was it unexpected that, instead of letting what Euthydemos said be the end of it, Socrates steered the conversation around in a circle: from the first definition, according to which *to know* what is lawful is pretty much *to be* lawful or just (J1), he lured the youth to another, according to which *to do* what is just is *to be* just (J8), before luring him back around to the first definition (J14). And all, just about, without the youth batting an eye. For, by steering the conversation around in a circle, to and from the Socratic paradox, Socrates was enlarging upon the misunderstanding of the paradox. He did so, at the risk of repeating ourselves (consider IV.4.6), as follows. Putting it more bluntly than he did in the conversation about piety (P5–6), Socrates got Euthydemos to agree that to know what one should do is *not* to believe one should not do what, one knows, one should (J10), and that to believe one should do something is, in turn, necessarily to do it (J11). At the same time, just before getting Euthydemos to agree for this reason that to know what one should do is necessarily to do it, Socrates got Euthydemos to agree that to do what is lawful is to do both what is just and what one should (J7; J5, J2). That agreement is the major premise, while the agreement that to know what one should do is necessarily to do it is the minor premise, of a syllogism or enthymeme whose conclusion is that to know what is lawful concerning human beings is necessarily to do what is lawful or just (J12). Finally, taking that conclusion (J12) as the major premise of a new syllogism, Socrates did not have to do more than remind Euthydemos of the premise granted by the youth already (J8) to get him to agree, for pretty much a second time (J1), that to know what is lawful concerning human beings is to be lawful or just (J14). But of course, as before, the major premise of the second syllogism (J12) was only as good as the minor premise of the first (J7). And Socrates took up the sleight of hand that went into the minor premise of the first syllogism in greater detail here, in the conversation about justice, than he did in the conversion on piety. To begin with, he got Euthydemos to agree that to do what is lawful is to make use of other human beings as one should (J2) and that to make use of other human beings as one should is, in turn, to make use of other human beings nobly (J3). That went off without a hitch. But then, when Socrates tried to get Euthydemos to agree that to make use of other human beings nobly is to take part in or manage human affairs nobly—that is, to rule nobly—the youth only agreed with reluctance (J4). "It is likely, at least," he said. And his unprecedented reluctance stemmed from his dim awareness of the fact to which the conversation between Socrates and Hippias already drew attention (IV.4.15–16)—to say nothing of the conversation between Alcibiades and Pericles

(I.2.40–46)—that to be ruled or to obey the laws is one thing, but to rule or to make the laws is another thing entirely. In other words, lawfulness was defined from the first in opposition to doing whatever one wants (J1). And the rulers, if or when they make the laws, do whatever they want. However reluctant Euthydemos may have been to agree that doing what is lawful (equals making use of other human beings as one should equals making use of other human beings nobly) equals ruling or doing whatever one wants nobly, he readily agreed that doing what is lawful (equals making use of other human beings as one should equals making use of other human beings nobly) equals doing what is just (J5). But doing what is just would mean doing what the rulers want you to do, in that case, whether you want to or not. With that possibility in mind, Socrates got Euthydemos to agree that what the laws command is "called," *merely* "called," just (J6) before going on to ask him if doing what the laws command is *both* just *and* what one should do; and the youth agreed, without a moment's hesitation, that what the laws command is both—that is, both just and what one should do (J7). And yet, insofar as doing what the laws command means doing what the rulers want you to do, whether you want to or not, would it not be truer to say that what the laws command is both "called" just and *not* what one should do? If so, that would bring a whole new meaning to the agreement that to know what one should do is necessarily to do it (J10–11). Again, whereas Euthydemos took it for granted that to know the laws (concerning human beings) is to know the laws "in accord with which one should make use of other human beings" (J1), Socrates never spoke of the laws as anything but the laws "concerning human beings" (J12, J14). Not only is it entirely possible to know the laws concerning human beings and not make use of other human beings in accord with them, but also, if we do not (believe we should) do anything we do not want to do, that is bound to happen (consider II.1.5).

Turning from piety and justice or moderation, on one hand, to wisdom, on the other, Socrates began by asking Euthydemos whether, in his opinion, the wise are wise in what they know or, also, in what they do not know—genuinely know.[13] And Euthydemos, hard-pressed to imagine how anyone could be wise in what he does not know, answered that the wise are wise only in what they know (W1). Since he was just as hard-pressed to imagine how anyone could be wise if not by knowing (W2)—if not by knowing, that is, what they know (W1)—and since he readily agreed that the wise are wise by wisdom (W3), Socrates led Euthydemos to conclude that knowledge is wisdom (W4). In the youth's opinion, the wise are wise both *in* what they know *by* knowing what they know. But complications begin to emerge, in the next place, when Socrates asked Euthydemos whether it is possible for a human being to know all the beings. For Euthydemos answered that it is impossible for a human being to know even the least part of all the beings (W5). But then, taking it for granted that knowledge is wisdom (in what is known, by knowing it), he declared it to be impossible for a human being to be wise, not only in everything, but even in anything (W6). And Socrates left off with this: that what a human being knows, in this he is wise too (W7, reading with manuscript B). Now that means, to state the obvious, no human being is wise, or "human wisdom" is not wisdom worthy of the name, at least according to Euthydemos. According to Socrates, however, what a human being knows, in this he is wise, "too," as if wisdom were somehow, contra Euthydemos, something other than knowledge. Bearing this in mind, note that Socrates began the conversation about wisdom by doing something he had never done before, something he would do only once more. Instead of asking Euthydemos a leading question, he gave the youth a choice: the wise are wise *either* in what they know *or*, also, in what they do not know (W1, compare N1). And although Euthydemos was hard-pressed to imagine how, subsequent events have shown that someone could be wise in what he does not know. To make use of the otherwise inexplicable distinction that Socrates made between that *in* which (W1) and that *by* which the wise are wise (W2), a human being could be wise in what he does not know by knowing that it is impossible for a human being, for any human being, to know it. For example, a human being could be wise in all the beings by knowing that it is impossible for a human being, for any human being, to know all the beings. In any event, wisdom is perhaps knowledge of ignorance.[14]

"At the beginning of the next inquiry," the inquiry regarding the good, "Socrates addresses Euthydemos by name, something he had not done in this chapter except at the beginning of the inquiry regarding piety and which he will only do once more in the chapter,"[15] at the beginning of the inquiry regarding courage. Can the conversations be divided, along these lines, into three main parts?

* * *

About the good, Socrates got Euthydemos to agree that nothing is good except insofar as it is beneficial to the man to whom it is beneficial (G4–5). But then, since the same thing is not beneficial to all men (G2), or since the same thing is sometimes beneficial to one man and harmful to another (G3), the same thing can be both good (insofar as it is beneficial to one man) and bad (insofar as it is harmful to another) at once. Sometimes, there is no common good. Not at all unexpectedly then, the good is one thing, the noble another, but not at all for the reason one might expect. Socrates began the conversation about the noble by giving Euthydemos, one last time, a choice. As he put it, can "we" speak of the noble any differently than "we" had just spoken of the good—in which case, in the same way as there was nothing always good for all men at once, there is nothing always noble for all things—*or* do "you," Euthydemos, know something always noble for all things (N1)? Now Euthydemos, for his part, did not know anything of the sort. But Socrates led him to conclude that to use each thing for whatever it may be useful for is noble (N2) and thus, since each thing is noble only for whatever it may be noble to use it for (N3), each thing is noble only insofar as it is noble to use it for whatever it may be useful for (N4). And that means, precisely if each thing is noble only insofar as it is noble to use it for whatever it may be useful for, *the* question is: For what is it "noble," for what is it useful, to use each thing (for whatever it may be useful for)? For example, to put this in plain language, while a horse is noble insofar as it is noble to use it for riding, for what is it "noble," or useful, to ride the horse? From what is it "noble" to flee, to what is it "noble" to go in pursuit of, on horseback (consider IV.3.10; contrast *Oeconomicus* 5.6 with 11.17)? Socrates reduced the noble to the useful, to spell this out a bit more fully, but the useful is always useful *for something*. And for what, then, is that "something" useful? For something useful, in turn, for something else? Since this cannot meaningfully go on forever, is not the useful finally useful for the good, that is, the beneficial? In that case, contra Euthydemos, knowledge of the good or beneficial—knowledge of that for which it is useful to use each thing for whatever it may be useful for, if not knowledge of whatever each thing may be useful for—would be useful for all things. Sometimes, however, there is no common good. And the laws, since they speak with one voice to many men in common, are therefore sometimes noble in the non-Socratic sense of the term (consider *Cyropaedia* I.3.16–18, IV.3.15–22). To know the laws is not to know the good things. As we are about to see, to know the laws is not to know the bad or terrible things either.

* * *

Courage or manliness, according to Euthydemos, is most noble (C1). But that means, if or since the noble is the useful, courage is most useful in his opinion. Accordingly, in his opinion, courage is useful for the greatest things (C2). And Socrates tried to get Euthydemos to agree on this basis that those who are ignorant of the terrible and dangerous things cannot possibly be courageous (C3). After all, so far from being most useful, those who are ignorant of the terrible and dangerous things will flee non-terrible and undangerous things in the mistaken belief that they are terrible and dangerous, on one hand, and go in pursuit of terrible and dangerous things in the mistaken belief that they are non-terrible and undangerous, on the other. The youth agreed, sort of, on other grounds. He agreed that those who do not fear the terrible things in the mistaken belief that they are non-terrible are not necessarily courageous, at least, on the grounds that in that case many madmen and cowards would have to be counted among the courageous (C4), before he went on to agree that those who fear even the non-terrible things in the mistaken belief that they are terrible are *still less courageous* than those who do not fear the terrible things in the mistaken belief that they are non-terrible (C5). On one hand, that is to say, those who do not fear the terrible things in the mistaken belief that they are not terrible are only not necessarily courageous, according to Euthydemos; they are not necessarily cowards. However ignorant of the terrible things they may be, they do not necessarily fear such things as they believe to be terrible. And those, on the other hand, who fear even the non-terrible things in the mistaken belief that they are terrible are still less courageous than them, according to Euthydemos, because they do necessarily fear such things as they believe to be terrible. Therefore, while Socrates tried to get Euthydemos to agree that there cannot possibly be courage without knowledge on the grounds that courage is most useful for fleeing the terrible things, on one hand, and for going in pursuit of the good or beneficial things, on the other—in which case, to be clear, those who fear even the non-terrible things in the mistaken belief that they are terrible are *no less (or more) courageous* than those who do not fear the terrible things in the mistaken belief that they are non-terrible—Euthydemos "agreed," albeit only in such a way as to betray how much he disagreed with Socrates. According to the youth, courage is most noble for having no fear of such things as are, and are believed to be, terrible. On that view, however, courage is not knowledge. For those who fear and indeed flee the terrible things in the knowledge that they are terrible are, at least on that view, cowardly rather than courageous. But Socrates steered the conversation in the direction of his eponymous paradox, that virtue is knowledge, properly understood. From the view that to fear or flee the terrible things in the knowledge that they are terrible is cowardly, Socrates lured Euthydemos to the view that this is courageous—indeed, wise (C14). He did so, almost without Euthydemos batting an eye, less by sleight of hand than by brute force. Specifically, with six of the fourteen leading questions about courage down and eight to go, Socrates got the youth to agree that only those who know how one should make use of the terrible things are able to make use of them ("nobly") (C11). Nor can they, who know how to make use of the terrible things, make use of them "badly"—even if they were to try to do so (consider III.9.5)—for they do not mistakenly believe that the terrible things are not terrible, and that the non-terrible things are terrible (C12). Therefore, on the basis of the youth's prior agreements that to make use of the terrible things "nobly" is to be "good" as regards them (C7), while to be "good" as regards the terrible things is to be courageous (C6), he had no choice but to agree that those who know, genuinely know, how one should make use of the terrible things are courageous (C14). For they make use of the terrible things as they believe, or know, they should (C9). At the same time, Socrates got Euthydemos to agree that those who do not know how one should make use of the terrible things are unable to make use of them "nobly" (C10). And they make use of the terrible things "badly," those who do not know how one should make use of them, for they mistakenly believe that the terrible things are not terrible, and that the non-terrible things are terrible (C13). Therefore, on the basis of the youth's prior agreements that to make use of the terrible things "badly" is to be "bad" as regards them (C8), while to be "bad" as regards the terrible things is to be cowardly (C6), he had no choice but to agree that those who mistakenly believe they know how one should make use of the terrible things are cowardly (C12). For they, too, make use of the terrible things as they believe they should (C9). For all that, of course, the agreement between Socrates and Euthydemos was more apparent than real. To the question of whether those who do not know how one should make use of the terrible things are unable to make use of them "nobly," the youth replied, "Perhaps not, at least" (C10). Likewise, to the question of whether those who do not know how one should make use of the terrible things make use of them "badly," simply because they mistakenly believe that the terrible things are not terrible and that the non-terrible things are terrible, he replied, "It is likely, at least" (C13). And his almost unprecedented reluctance was only to be expected, if not natural, given that those who behave in cowardly fashion do not do so, according to (his) generally accepted opinions, on account of being ignorant of the terrible and dangerous things. Socrates would have Euthydemos believe that the cowardly are none other than those who use the terrible things "badly" in the mistaken belief that non-terrible things (either being destroyed or enslaved for rushing to the defense of the fatherland or running and hiding from the enemies on the field of battle) are to be feared. And he would have Euthydemos believe that the courageous are none other than those who, being "good" or beneficial for themselves, use the terrible things "nobly" in the knowledge that terrible things (either running and hiding from the enemies on the field of battle or being destroyed or enslaved for rushing to the defense of the fatherland) are to be feared. In that case, however, the cowardly and the courageous would have the same intention, to flee from danger, with the sole difference between them being that the latter know, while the former wrongly believe they know, where danger lies! Socrates flipped the script on Euthydemos. To the old, familiar terms, *courage* and *cowardice*, he has given entirely new meaning. The opposite of courage in the precise, Socratic sense of the term is madness, not cowardice. For those who use the terrible things "badly"—those who put themselves in harm's way, in the mistaken belief that the terrible things are not terrible and that the non-terrible things are terrible—are mad (IV.6.10, I.1.14). Moreover, if the courageous, in the loose, Euthydemean sense of the term, have no fear of the terrible things, this is simply because they mistakenly believe that the terrible things are not terrible, and that the non-terrible things are terrible. They are, therefore, mad. And the conversation was as much about madness, the opposite of wisdom (III.9.6–7), as it was about courage.

Finally, if the conversations can be divided into three main parts, just as the last was as much about madness as it was about courage, was the first as much about wisdom, the opposite of madness, as it was about moderation (piety and justice), while the second was about the good and the noble?

III

The groundwork for a refutation of Euthydemos, for yet another refutation of Euthydemos, was thus laid. For now, though, turning to the second appendix—or, rather, returning to it after all this time—Xenophon says that if someone contradicted Socrates about something without being able to say anything clear himself, then Socrates led the speech up toward the assumption or hypothesis on which it was based (IV.6.13). To illustrate the point, Xenophon gives the following, admittedly not literally true, example. If Socrates were to praise someone for statesmanship, and if someone were to contradict him on the grounds that someone else is a better statesman, Socrates would propose that they examine, "first," what the work or deed of a good citizen is. For, as we saw, good citizenship is the core of great statesmanship. Xenophon then lets us watch Socrates work—at least, for a moment. Socrates, by asking the contradictor four leading questions, gets him to agree that it is the work of a good citizen, first, to enrich the city; second, to make the city superior to its adversaries in war; third, to provide the city with friends in place of enemies in embassies on its behalf; and, fourth, to bring about concord in the city in public speeches. But then, all of a sudden, Xenophon breaks off. All of a sudden, he draws the conclusion that once the speeches were led up in this way (toward the assumption or hypothesis on which they were based) "the truth" became clear also to the contradictors themselves, leaving us with more questions than answers (IV.6.14). For who did Socrates praise for statesmanship? Who did the contradictor praise? If this is the sort of thing that Socrates proposed to do "first," what did he do second? Or, at any rate, up toward what fundamental assumption or hypothesis did Socrates lead the speech? And what truth became clear? Why Xenophon's example was admittedly not literally true, why it was only going to illustrate his point "somehow" (*pōs*)—that is the only question to which we get a quick answer. *The* example of how Socrates, when someone contradicted something he said, led the speech up toward the assumption or hypothesis on which it was based, and therewith toward the truth, left everything out of account: what Socrates said to begin with, what his interlocutor said against what he said to begin with, the hypothesis toward which Socrates then led the speech, and the truth. How, then, does the example work as advertised? All we get are the four aforementioned, leading questions. Note, however, that the contradictor's answers to Socrates's questions were always essentially the same: "yes," with one hardly noticeable, albeit notable, exception. When Socrates asked if it is the work of a good citizen to provide the city with friends in place of enemies, the contradictor answered with unprecedented reluctance, "It is likely, at least." To see the reason for this, only recall that justice is among other things the will, the intention to harm enemies in war, even if they are stronger (IV.2.15ff., IV.4.14). Perhaps then, even or precisely if the choice is between a shameful peace and a noble military campaign almost certain to end in disaster, destruction or slavery, it is not the work of a good citizen to sue for peace. The whole episode bears a striking resemblance to a previously reported conversation between Nichomachides, a veteran soldier, and Socrates. There, to cut a long story too short, when Socrates praised a wealthy man named Antisthenes for generalship, Nichomachides contradicted him on the grounds that he himself is a better general (III.4). Nichomachides was especially surprised to hear Socrates seem to say that good household managers are good generals, and even great statesmen. So Socrates proposed that they inquire into the works or deeds of each (III.4.7ff., compare IV.6.13–14). And the sticking point, for Nichomachides, was that generals fight—courageously, to the death (contrast III.4.11)—whereas household managers do not (III.4.10). The reduction of the city (politics) to the household (economics)—that is, the reduction of the great statesman to the skilled household manager to which Socrates steered his conversation with Nichomachides (III.4.12)—is just another way of putting his paradox that virtue is knowledge.[16] And the assumption or hypothesis on which that paradox is based was, as we saw from the Socratic refutation of Euthydemos itself, the equally paradoxical reduction of the noble to that which is useful or beneficial (consider III.8). Thus, to return to Xenophon's illustration of a Socratic refutation, did Socrates praise some skilled household manager or other for statesmanship, well aware of how such paradoxical praise would be received, and did someone contradict him on the very same grounds that Nichomachides contradicted Socrates when he praised Antisthenes for generalship? The fact that the contradictor answered with unprecedented reluctance when Socrates asked if it is the work of a good citizen to bring about concord *among* the cities, despite the fact that he was not the least bit reluctant to agree that it is the work of a good citizen to bring about concord *in* the city (IV.4.8, IV.4.11), indicates as much. But if that is indeed the case, then, did Socrates lead the speech up toward the fundamental assumption or hypothesis that the noble is useful or good in much same way as he did already once before, with Euthydemos?

The main takeaway from this is that even though Xenophon promised to take us to see how Socrates refuted a contradictor, we came late to the party and were made to leave early;[17] yet the short time we spent there was enough for us, who have already attended one much like it, to figure out for ourselves how it began and came to an end. For Xenophon said in the very beginning that Socrates would be contradicted not only if he were to praise someone for statesmanship, but also, for instance, if he were to praise someone for wisdom or courage (IV.6.13). And while Socrates went on to speak of statesmanship or good citizenship (IV.6.14) rather than wisdom or courage, it just so happens that wisdom (IV.6.7) and courage (IV.6.10–11) were questions, if not *the* questions, taken up before, in the six conversations to which all of this is merely an appendix. Now, of course, Euthydemos did not contradict Socrates. But he too answered, twice, "It is likely, at least." And the fact of the matter is that he should have contradicted Socrates. Xenophon left us to figure out for ourselves from the second appendix both the contradiction that set in motion a refutation about good citizenship and the fundamental hypothesis up toward which Socrates led the speech, to say nothing of the truth. In much the same way, did he leave us to figure out for ourselves, from the conversations between Socrates and Euthydemos, both the contradictions that would have set in motion refutations about wisdom and courage and the fundamental hypotheses up toward which Socrates would have led the speeches? In the first place, to spell this out, had the reader contradicted Socrates when Socrates said that to know the laws concerning gods and men is to be pious and just—as well he should have, for it is entirely possible to know the laws and yet not do as they say—Socrates would have led the speech up toward the assumption or hypothesis on which it was based. Piety was said to be noble (P1). So, too, was justice (J3–4). For what, then, are the laws concerning gods and men useful (IV.6.9)? The assumption or hypothesis on which the speech was based, on which the Socratic paradox vulgarly understood was based,[18] was that the noble is useful for the good of one's own life. With the speech led up in this way toward the assumption or hypothesis on which it was based, the truth became clear. Wisdom is knowledge of ignorance, specifically, of the "nobility" of the laws concerning gods and men. In the second place, had the reader contradicted Socrates when Socrates said that to fear or flee the terrible things in the knowledge that they are terrible is to be courageous—as well he should have, for that is cowardice—Socrates would have led the speech up toward the assumption or hypothesis on which it was based. Not only the pious and the just, but also, it turns out, courage was said to be noble (C1). And the assumption or hypothesis on which the speech was based, on which the Socratic paradox properly understood was based, was that the noble is useful for the good of one's own life. With the speech led up in this way toward the assumption or hypothesis on which it was based, the truth became clear. Courage, courage in the loose sense of the term, is the opposite of wisdom.[19]

The six conversations can indeed, then, be divided into three main parts. With Euthydemos in tow, Socrates ascended from the vulgar understanding of the Socratic paradox to the assumption or hypothesis on which it is based, and then descended from that assumption or hypothesis to the proper understanding of the Socratic paradox. As for Euthydemos, who did not separate the written laws from "natural law," he did not know what he believed he knew about law—that is, about what law is. Nor, therefore, did he know what he believed he knew about piety and justice. Even or precisely if he was unwise, however, he was courageous.

IV

Somehow, by refuting his companions about the human things, Socrates conversed about the nature of all things; he examined the cosmos. Somehow, yes, but how? With that question in mind, we turn at long last to the first appendix (IV.6.12). There, all of a sudden, Xenophon stops to say a few words about what Socrates "held" or "believed," specifically, about what rule over human beings is and what is a fit ruler (compare I.1.16). But what does this have to do with anything? *Memorabilia* IV.6 is the rhetorical treatment of the dialectical method. And this report of what Socrates believed about various kinds of rule, aside from the fact that it, too, has a soporific effect, seems wildly out of place here. According to Xenophon, Socrates believed that kingship and tyranny, although they have in common with one another that they are both kinds of rule, nevertheless differ from one another in that kingship is rule—rule of a fit ruler—over willing human beings and according to laws of the cities, whereas tyranny is rule over unwilling human beings and not according to laws. Socrates therefore differentiated kingship from tyranny in such a way that a "mixed regime," falling in between kingship and tyranny, was conspicuously absent from Xenophon's report. If kingship is rule over willing human beings and according to laws of the cities, and if tyranny is rule over unwilling human beings and not according to laws, what is rule over willing human beings not according to laws or, to put this the other way around, rule over unwilling human beings according to laws? We are led to believe that there is no such thing; that human beings are always willing to be lawful. And yet, even as Socrates had banished this very thought from Euthydemos's mind in their conversations about the pious and the just, the laws concerning gods and men were defined *in opposition* to doing whatever one wants (P3, J1; compare *Cyropaedia* I.2.2)![20] Looking back on it now, moreover, while the willingness of human beings to be unlawful or their unwillingness to be lawful was conspicuously absent from Xenophon's report of his teacher's beliefs, such a thing was inconspicuously present too. For Xenophon said that Socrates believed that rule over unwilling human beings and not according to laws, "but in whatever way the ruler wants," is tyranny (compare *Cyropaedia* I.3.18). So human beings are not always willing to be lawful, after all. And Xenophon concludes the first appendix by saying that Socrates believed that where the rulers are drawn from those who complete or perfect the lawful (compare *Cyropaedia* I.2.15), the regime is aristocratic; where they are drawn from the rich, the regime is plutocratic; and where they are drawn from all of the above, the regime is democratic. The point is that the rulers in plutocratic and democratic regimes do whatever they want, even or precisely if they make laws, yet the rulers in aristocratic regimes, those who complete the lawful, do not do whatever they want. For they are willing to be lawful (against their will). But that means, since kingship is rule over willing human beings and according to laws of the cities, the written laws rather than "natural law," the rulers in aristocratic regimes are themselves ruled, if not by human beings, by a king. They are citizens of the heavenly city. Or, at any rate, so they think. Insofar as those who complete the lawful believe they know what law is, just as Euthydemos showed himself to do in his conversations with Socrates about the pious and the just, they believe they know just about everything (consider I.4.1). For this reason, even as Euthydemos declared it to be impossible for a human being to know and hence to be wise even in the least part of all the beings, he betrayed that he believed himself to know and hence to be wise in the greatest being of them all when he swore twice, in the very same breath, "by Zeus" (W5–6; consider C4–5). According to Euthydemos, in effect, "fear of the Lord, that is wisdom; and to depart from evil is understanding" (Job 28:20–28; see also Proverbs 3:7). According to Socrates, however, wisdom is knowledge of ignorance—knowledge of ignorance, finally, of not the least of all the beings (contrast Thomas Aquinas, *Summa Theologica* I, q.1a.5, with Aristotle, *Parts of Animals* 644b22–645a5). And perhaps he never ceased examining what each of the beings is in conversation with his companions because he never ceased learning that it was impossible for a human being, for any human being, to know more than he did.

CHAPTER 9

Human Wisdom and Divine Providence

I

Hippias had accused Socrates of questioning and refuting everyone yet never delivering a speech of his own to anyone or revealing his thought concerning anything (IV.4.9, IV.4.11). And the Socratic, nonelenctic teaching (IV.3–6) was Xenophon's partial defense of Socrates against this accusation.[1] For even if Socrates did not deliver speeches of his own, to Xenophon at least, it is clear from all that has been said hitherto that by revealing his thought "with a view to" someone—by concealing his thought, for example, concerning piety and justice—Socrates simultaneously revealed his thought to someone else (compare IV.7.1 with IV.4.1). And now, now that Xenophon has said enough to make clear that, in addition to questioning and refuting everyone, Socrates revealed his thought about everything in his long, roundabout way, he will say that Socrates took care "also," in or by doing so, to make his companions self-sufficient in the activities befitting them (IV.7.1). Such self-sufficiency, according to Xenophon's eulogy of Socrates, is prudence; and to be prudent is to have no need of anyone else, not even a god, to know the better and the worse (IV.8.11). By now, as we saw, Euthydemos is out of the picture completely. And *Memorabilia* IV.7 is trans-Euthydemean, for one thing, because the youth was never going to become self-sufficient—from Socrates or his "*daimonion*." Socrates did not need anyone else (IV.8.11, IV.7.1), to repeat, whereas Euthydemos needed Socrates or his "*daimonion*" to tell him in the simplest and clearest manner what he should believe—as IV.7 itself goes to show—and do (IV.2.40).[2] But then, when Socrates took care to make his companions self-sufficient, was he taking care to free them from their dependence not only on him but also, what is more, on his "*daimonion*" specifically, and divination generally?

Xenophon, it is true, concludes IV.7 with a deceptively simple statement about human wisdom, the thrust of which is that someone may well be—and, to get a bit ahead of ourselves, may well be right to be—resigned to the lack of a better guide than human wisdom (IV.7.10). And he goes on from there to conclude the *Memorabilia* as a whole with another no less deceptively simple statement about someone who may well think—and, once again, may well be right to think—that Socrates was lying about his "*daimonion*" (IV.8.1). However that may be for now, though, ever since the start of the nonelenctic teaching, we have been led to believe that IV.7 would be devoted to the art of contriving (IV.3.1). Judging from the one and only use of the term since then, contriving means reasoning about the things we perceive in order to benefit from the good things and save ourselves from the bad ones (IV.3.11; consider III.1.6). Contriving is the opposite of trusting to chance (III.11.6), then, just as "doing well" is the opposite of "good luck" (III.9.14). However, the only contriving that shows up here, in IV.7, is the contriving of the god or gods: the way in which the god or gods contrive each of the heavenly things (IV.7.6). As for what that contriving, which Socrates believed to be impossible for any human being to discover (IV.7.6, I.1.13), has to do with *human* contriving, an answer is ready to hand. For it is easy to see that (human) contriving is just another way of saying prudence, self-sufficiency, or human wisdom (IV.7.10). And to say that Socrates took care to make his companions skilled in contriving, prudent, self-sufficient, or resigned to human wisdom is, in that case, as much as to say that he took care to make them aware that human beings are, all of them, ignorant of the contrivances of the god or gods; reason, in other words, "is [our] only Star and compass."

Self-sufficiency in the fitting activities, what that is, is clear enough. Far less clear, however, is the fact that Xenophon explained the care that Socrates took to make his companions self-sufficient in terms of the care that Socrates, more than anyone else, took to know whatever his companions genuinely knew (IV.7.1). And when Xenophon adds to this already very mysterious explanation the further remark that Socrates taught his companions most readily whatever he himself knew of the things fitting for a gentleman to know, in the first place, while he led them to others who, he thought, genuinely knew whatever he himself did not know of the things fitting for a gentleman to know, in the second, the mystery deepens. For, that means, Socrates did not teach his companions everything that is fitting for a gentleman to know for the simple reason that he himself did not know everything that is fitting for a gentleman to know.[3] And while he led his companions to others who, he thought, genuinely knew at least some of the things (fitting for a gentleman to know) that he himself did not know, the possibility remains that there are other things fitting for a gentleman to know that *neither* he himself *nor* anyone else, so far as he was aware, genuinely knew. As we saw, there are such things; they are not the least of all things. So, when Xenophon said that Socrates took more care than anyone else to know whatever his companions genuinely knew, did he mean that Socrates stood out for caring to know, specifically, whether those of his companions who presumed to have genuine knowledge of such things did, in fact, have genuine knowledge of them? Now why Socrates, in order to know whatever they genuinely knew of at least some of the things fitting for a gentleman to know, took so much care to make his companions skilled in contriving, which is as much as to say, why he desired the education of the youth, is one of the deepest mysteries of the Socratic education. By the end of IV.7, Xenophon gives us a final clue to the mystery's solution. For the time being, though, did Socrates take care to make his companions aware that reason "is [our] only Star and compass" in order to know whether they had genuine knowledge to the contrary? And if so, to begin with, why?

II

Whatever Socrates himself knew of the things fitting for a gentleman to know he taught most readily (IV.7.1). Therefore, since it is fitting for a gentleman to know that it is fitting for a gentleman to know some things and not others, Socrates taught this, which things a gentleman should and should not know, most readily (IV.7.2). For example, he urged his companions to learn only as much geometry (IV.7.2) and astrology (IV.7.4) as would be useful for those who required considerable wealth to maintain their high standard of living (*Oeconomicus* 11.1–20) to know. More than that, however, Socrates discouraged them from learning—even though, Xenophon tells us, he himself knew more. And that means, while teaching his companions not to waste their time seeking knowledge unless it was absolutely necessary to maintain their high standard of living, Socrates himself lived in poverty seeking knowledge, of geometry and astronomy, for its own sake (contrast I.1.15).[4] Now, according to Xenophon's indications, Socrates discouraged his companions from learning astronomy more "strongly" than he discouraged them from learning the higher branches of geometry for the reason that the former is harder, hence, a greater hindrance to learning or doing useful things than the latter. To learn astrology is easy if and only if you have a teacher (IV.7.4), according to Socrates, whereas to learn basic geometry is easy even without one (IV.7.2). So no wonder that Socrates, whose nickname was "the thinker" (*Symposium* 6.6–8, 7.2ff.), "completely" discouraged his companions from becoming "thinkers" about how the god contrives each of the heavenly things—that is, even more strongly than he discouraged them from learning astronomy proper. For he believed it to be impossible for a human being, for any human being, to discover how the one god contrives each of the heavenly things. And he believed that investigating those things which the many gods did not want to make clear—including especially whether they are, in fact, responsible for the contrivances for which they are allegedly responsible—would not be pleasing or gratifying to gods, at any rate, if they existed (IV.7.6). To discover how the god or gods contrive each of the heavenly things is thus impossible, not just hard; hence, to try is impious, not just a hindrance to learning or doing useful things. But then, in much the same way as Socrates more or less strongly discouraged his companions from learning as much geometry and astronomy as he himself knew on the grounds that it was not useful to do so, did he not completely discourage his companions from learning as much about how the god or gods contrive each of the heavenly things as he himself knew on the grounds that it was not pious to do so? After all, how else did Socrates come to believe it to be impossible for any human being to discover how the god or gods contrive each of the heavenly things if not by trying to discover as much himself?[5]

There was indeed a time, as we saw in the Introduction, Section II, when a young, "pre-Socratic" Socrates tried, and failed. And Xenophon lets us catch a glimpse of this here.[6] Having already told us that Socrates knew more geometry and astronomy than he taught his companions it was useful to learn (IV.7.3, IV.7.5), here Xenophon shows us—*merely* (given popular prejudice against the philosophers) shows us—that Socrates knew more about discovering how the god contrives each of the heavenly things than he taught them it was sane to learn. For what he said to discourage his companions from trying to explain away the contrivances of the gods was that he who tries to do this sort of thing runs the risk, at least, of going out of his mind no less than Anaxagoras went out of his mind (IV.7.6). Even besides the fact that there is no guarantee by this account that such a man will suffer the same fate as Anaxagoras, however, Socrates stopped short of saying how much, if at all, Anaxagoras went out of his mind.[7] How far gone, then, was Anaxagoras really? Xenophon lets us make up our own minds, just as Socrates let his companions make up theirs. Socrates took Anaxagoras to task, first of all, for claiming that fire and sun are the same thing (IV.7.7). Now fire, as we may recall, picks up the sun's slack by providing us with light and heat, too. So, given their similarities, Anaxagoras was perhaps barking up the right tree; yet when he made the claim that fire and sun are the same thing, Socrates said, he was ignorant of their differences. To wit, we look upon fire with ease, yet we cannot look straight at the sun; sunlight tans our skin, yet fire does no such thing; plants depend on the light of the sun if they are going to grow, yet the heat of fire destroys them. Now, to be sure, if Anaxagoras really were ignorant of such things, he would be very far gone indeed (consider III.9.6). That he was not ignorant of them, at least not in any simple sense of the word, follows from another claim of his for which, it seems, Socrates also took him to task (IV.7.7). For Anaxagoras claimed not only that sun and fire are the same thing, but also, or instead, that the sun is a fiery rock. And a fiery rock (Diels–Kranz 59A.1) is not the same thing as fire. The other, "pre-Socratic" philosophers assumed or tried to discover that, so far from being the divine contrivances that they are alleged to be, the heavenly things are, in fact, the works of "causes," which is to say, "necessities" (compare IV.7.5 with I.1.11 and I.1.15). According to what Xenophon shows us here, however, in the course of trying to discover the causes or the necessities responsible for their coming into being they lost sight of the very things, the heavenly things, whose causes or necessities they were trying to discover. They only had eyes for the necessary causes: earth, water, "and each of the other great beings," or elementary bodies (I.4.8, I.4.17). That said, since they could scarcely deny that the things whose necessary causes they were trying to discover were things in their own right, too, they became confused. That is to say, just as Anaxagoras claimed that fire and sun are the same thing, on one hand, and are not the same thing, on the other, they reduced the things (whose necessary causes they were trying to discover) to their necessary (material) causes, on one hand, and they did no such thing, on the other. Anaxagoras and the other, "pre-Socratic" philosophers were confused, to put this simply, as to whether being is one or many (consider I.1.13–14).[8]

On the other side of the coin, had we not understood a word of what Socrates said to Euthydemos about piety (IV.3), we would be positively shocked to hear Xenophon say that Socrates believed it to be impossible for any human being to discover how the god or gods contrive each of the heavenly things. No less shocking, had we not understood a word of what Socrates said there, would be the closely related fact that when Socrates took Anaxagoras to task for claiming that the sun is a fiery rock, he did not launch into yet another "argument from design" for the view that the sun is a contrivance of the god or gods. Rather, he said that Anaxagoras was ignorant of the fact that the sun differs from a rock in fire, at least, insofar as a rock in fire neither shines bright nor lasts a long time, yet the sun lasts for all time while shining more brightly than anything (IV.7.7). As before, if Anaxagoras really were ignorant of this, he would be quite mad; however, he never claimed that the sun is "a rock in fire," he claimed that the sun is "a fiery rock." And by this, no doubt, he meant that the sun is a fiery rock that lasts for all time while shining so much more brightly than anything that we cannot look straight at it; that our skin is tanned by it; that the plants, which depend on it (Diels–Kranz 59A.117), would be destroyed on account of its heat if it were to come any closer (compare IV.3.8–9). Socrates did not really take Anaxagoras to task for claiming that the sun is a fiery rock; he deliberately made the very same mistake that he was accusing Anaxagoras of making involuntarily: he confused one thing with another, different thing. And thus, while none of the rocks here below shine bright or last for long in fire, there remains the distinct possibility—no more to be wondered at than the fact that water, being wet, puts out fire while oil, despite being wet, too, feeds it (*Symposium* 7.4)—that the sun is a rock that feeds a fire.[9] Quite possibly, that means, there was nothing divine about the sun. To us, however, none of this comes as a shock. For Socrates tried and failed to discover not only how the one god contrives each of the heavenly things but also, as we saw, whether the many gods are or are, in fact, responsible for the contrivances for which they are allegedly responsible. In the next place, therefore, Xenophon goes on to speak of the fact that Socrates urged his companions to learn "calculations" (*logismous*) by which he can only mean "reasoning"—that is, reasoning about the things we perceive (compare IV.7.8 with IV.3.11). Now, as was roughly true of geometry and astrology or astronomy, Socrates urged his companions to guard against foolishly occupying themselves with reasoning about the things we perceive. In this case, however, instead of discouraging some of his companions from *learning*, Socrates thereby urged other companions of his to "guard against" *teaching*, more than was useful: instead of telling us that Socrates himself knew more about all things than was useful in this case too, Xenophon tells us that Socrates himself both "examined" (*suneskopei*) and "went through" (*sundiexēei*) all things with his companions insofar as it was useful for his way of life to do so (IV.7.8).[10] It should be needless to repeat: "To examine" (*episkeptesthai*) is one thing (IV.6.14); "to go through" (*diexienai*) something in speech is another thing entirely (IV.6.15). And Xenophon not only tells us but also shows us that Socrates did both at once, for example, when conversing with Euthydemos about piety or when taking Anaxagoras to task for his claims about the sun. That is, by going through "all things" with some of his companions in such a way as to remain safely within the confines of their own, generally accepted opinions, Socrates examined "all things," simultaneously, with other companions of his. For the (self-contradictory) rhetorical recapitulation of generally accepted opinions was—for a good nature, at any rate—an opportunity to reach the truth by thinking the opinions through. Bad natures, merely listening to Socrates go through all things in one way or another (I.4, IV.3, IV.7.7), were thus given additional reason to believe that divine contriving, economy, or providence is so evident to all that to claim that the sun is a fiery rock is not even sane.[11] At the same time, good natures reached the truth that the sun, contemplated shamelessly or awelessly and precisely, is just a fiery rock. There is not a shred of evidence, at any rate, to the contrary.

So far, under the pretext of telling us which things a gentleman should and should not know according to Socrates, Xenophon has been widening the gulf separating Socrates, the philosopher, from the gentleman. Only one of them can be "correctly educated" (IV.7.2). According to Socrates, to recap, the gentleman should be innocent of natural philosophy. But he should nod his head enthusiastically in agreement while listening, merely listening, to Socrates among others make "likely arguments [from design]." And therefore, instead of seeking knowledge for its own sake, a ridiculous thing to do if the gods are, in fact, responsible for the contrivances for which they are allegedly responsible, the gentleman should learn just enough to accumulate the wealth required, above all, to honor the gods, help friends, and adorn the city (*Oeconomicus* 11.9, 2.4). By contrast, despite the impiety of doing so, Socrates tried his hand at natural philosophy only to discover before long that it must end in failure. Moreover, however displeasing to the gods it may be (to investigate whether they are, in fact, responsible for the contrivances for which they are allegedly responsible), by examining "all things," while at the same time making "likely arguments [from design]," he discovered that "natural theology," too, ends in failure. And therefore, instead of accumulating the wealth required to perform many and great sacrifices, Socrates lived in poverty seeking knowledge for its own sake. There is just one problem. The gentleman, no less than Anaxagoras, believed he knew more than it was possible, according to Socrates, for any human being to know. How then, to repeat the question that has been under consideration ever since the start of the nonelenctic teaching, could Socrates be sure that he did not know as much as he believed he did? For Socrates had discovered that natural philosophy ends in failure. But Anaxagoras went out of his mind, if at all, only insofar as that was deemed to be necessary to preserve his sanity. And now that he knew Anaxagoras and the other, "pre-Socratic" philosophers had no leg to stand on when they assumed, merely assumed, that necessary causes are responsible for the coming into being of the cosmos, how did Socrates preserve his? He had no choice but to face the fact that there are perhaps human beings who know, genuinely know, more than he thought possible. In this situation, Socrates took care to make his companions self-sufficient.

III

Socrates did not just urge, he "forcefully" urged his companions to learn as much as possible from doctors (IV.7.9). Only in the case of medicine did Socrates make it absolutely clear to his companions that you can never know too much. And there is no end to the search for knowledge of medicine because of the need to look after yourself, your good (IV.2.31ff.). Because even the best doctor can only do so much for his patients, however, there are those for whom medicine is not enough. As Xenophon puts it, they want to be benefited by more than human wisdom (IV.7.10, consider *Cyropaedia* I.6.23). Now of this, human wisdom, medicine is just the best example. There is reason, on one hand, and revelation, on the other. And yet, whereas Socrates forcefully recommended human wisdom to his companions—and even urged them to learn some geometry, for example—he did not urge them to use divination at all (contrast IV.7.10 with IV.7.9). Nor, of course, did he discourage them from doing so (consider I.3.1). But if and only if someone already wanted to be benefited by superhuman wisdom, that is, if and only if someone was already in a state that Socrates did not urge upon him at all, much less forcefully urge upon him, Socrates gave him this bit of advice: care about divination. That he did not "teach" "the outcome" himself, despite his "*daimonion*," should go without saying. For this, Xenophon suggests, was not something that he knew (compare IV.7.10 with IV.7.1). But he did not "lead" this companion of his to diviners either, Xenophon also suggests, because they were ignorant of this, so far as Socrates was aware, too (compare IV.7.10 with IV.7.1). And some indication of the reason for this, for this stance toward superhuman wisdom, is given here. Xenophon has Socrates explain the (human) advice he gives anyone who wants to be benefited by superhuman wisdom, by saying that he who knows the things through which the gods give signs to human beings about their affairs would never be bereft of the advice of gods (IV.7.10). For, if I may add, he who knows such things, having exercised care about the truth of divination, would never want to be benefited by superhuman wisdom.

Socrates took his own advice. The nonelenctic teaching of Socrates was devoted, first, to moderation (IV.3–4), and second, to wisdom (IV.5–7). Because we cannot entirely avoid having to say something about how the rest of the teaching is ordered, the essential points are these. In *Memorabilia* IV.5, Socrates offered refuted good natures roughly the same explanation that Xenophon offered the reader in IV.2, through the Socratic monologue concerning self-knowledge, of the effect of the elenctic teaching. Here, however, Socrates comes at it from another angle. The effect of speaking precisely about the human things was, according to IV.2, depression. According to IV.5, incontinence vis-à-vis specific, very great pleasures of the soul lies at the bottom of the inability to converse, without self-contradiction, about the human things. Claims to knowledge that all things are ruled by Zeus the king were subsequently traced, in IV.6, to the inability to converse about such things. And it was perhaps, to put IV.5 together with the rest of IV.6, in order to confirm his suspicion that such claims can and must be traced, in the end, to incontinence vis-à-vis specific, very great pleasures of the soul, and not to genuine knowledge of the contrivances of the gods, that Socrates refuted his companions about the human things. In other words, by taking care to make his companions self-sufficient in the activities fitting for them, which is to say, by teaching good natures in his long, roundabout way the (human) things through which the gods give signs to human beings about their affairs, Socrates was learning from them (IV.7.1) whether he was right to say that he who knows such things would never be bereft of the advice of gods.

* * *

The beginning of *Memorabilia* IV.8, "and if someone" (*ei de tis*), reads like a continuation of IV.7 (compare IV.8.1 with IV.7.10). However, whereas the end of IV.7 directed attention to someone who wanted to be benefited by superhuman wisdom generally, by Socrates's "*daimonion*" specifically, the beginning of IV.8 directs attention to someone who, even, or precisely, after everything Xenophon has said, thinks that Socrates was lying about his "*daimonion*." And Xenophon, by way of concluding *Memorabilia* IV, would seem to say that Socrates was not lying (IV.8.1–3). With that, then, the *Memorabilia* circles back to the beginning. For it would seem that the *Memorabilia* all but began, too, with Xenophon saying that Socrates was not lying about his "*daimonion*" (I.1.5). Not once, however, does Xenophon actually say that Socrates was not lying, or that he was telling the truth, about his "*daimonion*." In the beginning, instead, Xenophon says that if it ever became clear that Socrates was lying about his "*daimonion*," his reputation among his companions would have suffered; yet Socrates was concerned with his reputation among them, was he not? From this, however, it only follows that Socrates was not saying anything on the authority of his "*daimonion*" in the truth of which he did not have confidence. But then, if his confidence sprang from his human wisdom, Socrates *was* lying about his "*daimonion*," maybe even out of concern for his reputation (for piety) among his companions, after all.[12] And Xenophon, for his part, does not say that his confidence did not spring from his human wisdom. He asks, he *merely* asks, "who would have confidence, when it comes to such things, in anyone other than a god?" (I.1.5) Suddenly fleeing, he lets us make up our own minds (recall I.4.1). Now, according to Xenophon, Socrates told his "companions" (*sunontōn*) to do such and such a thing on the authority of his "*daimonion*" (I.1.4). And to this Xenophon adds, shortly thereafter, that Socrates told his "friends" (*epitēdeious*), "too," to do as *he himself* thought best concerning such things as are "necessary," which is to say, such things as have clear outcomes (I.1.6). Did, then, Socrates tell his "companions" to do such things on the authority of his "*daimonion*" as he told his "friends" to do on the grounds that they are necessary, their outcomes clear?[13] Not to repeat the observations made already about *Memorabilia* I.1.7–8, in the first place, and I.1.9, in the second, the conclusion of *Memorabilia* IV leaves no room for doubt.

Recall that neither Palamedes nor Daedalus, for all their wisdom, knew with absolute certainty which pursuits will produce good, and which will produce bad outcomes (IV.2.33). Their wisdom was, then, human wisdom. And if Socrates—who, elsewhere, likens himself to Palamedes (*Apology* 26)—was just another wise man whose wisdom let him down,[14] his wisdom, his "*daimonion*," was really only human wisdom, too. In keeping with this, the beginning of IV.8 directs attention to someone who thinks that Socrates was lying about his "*daimonion*," specifically, for the reason that the Athenians put him to death. Did he, or his "*daimonion*," not see that coming? To someone who thinks, for this reason, that Socrates was lying about his "*daimonion*," Xenophon replies by saying that it should be considered, at any rate, that Socrates was so old by the time the Athenians finally put him to death that death was better for him, just then, than clinging to life. And so perhaps, if Socrates knew that his death was fast approaching, and if he knew that his health and his mental powers were going to decline in the short time that he had left, his "*daimonion*" did not let him down after all (IV.8.1).[15] Did he, though?

According to what Socrates only just said, there are those for whom medicine, human wisdom, is not enough because even the best doctor can only do so much for his patients. And even the best doctor can only do so much for his patients, looking back on it now, partly because even he can only know so much about what his patients should and should not do for their health. When Socrates forcefully urged his companions to learn as much medicine as possible, he spoke so highly of looking to oneself that he came awfully close to saying that doctors, knowers of *the* human body, are unnecessary if only you know *your* body (IV.7.9). The universal, the class or kind, is one thing; the particular is another, somewhat different thing. So, for example, to know when the human body naturally declines and dies is not to know when exactly your body will decline and die. And did Socrates know, with superhuman wisdom, that his death and decline was not only inevitable but also imminent? Or was his "*daimonion*," to repeat, really only human wisdom? Socrates himself says that his decline was "perhaps" imminent—"perhaps" imminent, what is more, "if" his death were not (IV.8.8; contrast *Apology* 6–7). Maybe there was a hard-to-find doctor who knew Socrates's body better than Socrates himself did (IV.7.9). And so, in effect, to someone who thinks that Socrates was lying about having superhuman wisdom, since the Athenians put him to death, Xenophon replies by saying that Socrates knew, on the grounds of his human wisdom alone, that death was better for him, just then, than clinging to life.[16]

The fact that Socrates was not being entirely serious or straightforward about his "*daimonion*" should, by now, come as no surprise. Nor should it come as a surprise that the Socratic education ends on that note. For, through the Socratic education, Socrates revealed to good natures the truth about his "*daimonion*," which is to say, his thought. And Socrates thought that it was particularly important to learn that, after having gained self-knowledge as a result of his elenctic teaching, some youths judged his "*daimonion*" one way, whereas others, who did not, judged it another way. Reading what Xenophon wrote about his recollections of Socrates is no substitute, as we saw, for being together with Socrates. All the same, by writing down his recollections, Xenophon gave readers across the centuries, who could not be together with Socrates, a window of opportunity, however small, to judge his "*daimonion*" for themselves.

NOTES

INTRODUCTION

1. "The Idea of Public Reason Revisited," in *Political Liberalism: Expanded Edition* (New York: Columbia University Press, 2005), 485.

2. "Public Reason," 460, 490, 458–59; *Political Liberalism: Expanded Edition* (New York: Columbia University Press, 2005), xxxvii–xxxviii.

3. "Public Reason," 489; see also 488, 447, 438. Rawls was not always so clear. Just a few pages earlier, he said, "*While no one is expected to put his religious or nonreligious doctrine in danger*, we must each give up forever the hope of changing the constitution so as to establish our religion's hegemony, or of qualifying our obligations so as to ensure its influence and success" (460; emphasis added), which makes no sense, since there are not a few people whose religious doctrines prevent them from giving up for a moment the hope to which Rawls referred. See also *Collected Papers*, ed. Samuel Freeman (Cambridge, MA: Harvard University Press, 1999), 619–20. "In a democracy," Rawls wanted to believe, "[the] culture is not, of course, guided by any one central idea or principle" ("Public Reason," 443). As he conceded here, in the passage quoted above, and elsewhere, though, "If a comprehensive conception of the good is unable to endure in a society securing the familiar equal basic liberties and mutual toleration, there is no way to preserve it consistent with democratic values" (*Political Liberalism*, 198). "A just liberal society can never be without loss," without exclusion of people who feel no allegiance to "democratic values" or the society's "central idea or principle." For, "in the realm of values, as opposed to the world of fact, not all truths can fit into one social world" (197n32; *Justice as Fairness: A Restatement* [Cambridge, MA: Harvard University Press, 2001], 36n26; "Public Reason," 483, 485). Rawls was not always so clear about the secular presuppositions or implications of his position because he was never entirely clear about the fact that the supreme law of the land appears to contradict itself. See Ronald Beiner, *Civil Religion: A Dialogue in the History of Political Philosophy* (Cambridge: Cambridge University Press, 2011), 297: "Political liberalism does not exist—it is a phantom of the Rawlsian imagination." But what is the "Rawlsian imagination," phantoms and all, if not a human imagination under the influence of our law?

4. *The Law of Peoples* (Cambridge, MA: Harvard University Press, 1999), 126.

5. *Political Liberalism*, xvi–xvii, 126, 143–44; *A Theory of Justice: Revised Edition* (Cambridge, MA: Harvard University Press, 1999), 485–86; consider *Law of Peoples*, 21–22.

6. *Law of Peoples*, 62.

7. See *Lectures on the History of Political Philosophy* (Cambridge, MA: Harvard University Press, 2007), 2.

8. *Political Liberalism*, 4; "Public Reason," 483.

9. *Justice as Fairness*, 184; *Political Liberalism*, 153. Rawls's "method of avoidance" has severe limitations. To the charge that "the avoidance of general and comprehensive doctrines implies indifference or skepticism as to whether a political conception of justice is true," or to the charge that "this avoidance may appear to suggest that such a conception might be the most reasonable one for us even when it is known not to be true, as if truth were simply beside the point," Rawls replied, "*it would be fatal to the point of a political conception to see it as skeptical about, or indifferent to, truth, much less as in conflict with it*" (*Political Liberalism*, 150; emphasis added). Rawls cannot do without truth. For this reason, "in following the method of avoidance, as we may call it, we try, *so far as we can*, neither to assert nor to deny any religious, philosophical accounts of truth and the status of values" (*Collected Papers*, 434, 394, 395, 429, 621–22; emphasis added). In other words, because Rawls cannot do without truth, he cannot avoid asserting or denying "religious, philosophical accounts of truth and the status of values" either. As for where the rubber hits the road, "political liberalism abstains from assertions about the domain of comprehensive views *except as necessary* when these views are unreasonable and reject all variations of the basic essentials of a democratic regime" ("Reply to Habermas," in *Political Liberalism: Expanded Edition* [New York: Columbia University Press, 2005], 375; emphasis added). Or, better,

> in affirming a political conception of justice we may eventually have to assert at least certain aspects of our own comprehensive (by no means necessarily fully comprehensive) religious or philosophical doctrine. This happens whenever someone insists, for example, that certain questions are so fundamental that to ensure their being rightly settled justifies civil strife. The religious salvation of those holding a particular religion, or indeed the salvation of a whole people, may be said to depend on it. *At this point we may have no alternative but to deny this, and to assert the kind of thing we had hoped to avoid.* (*Political Liberalism*, 152; emphasis added)

Rawls cannot "leave philosophy as it is," he cannot "stay on the surface, philosophically speaking," after all ("Habermas," 375; *Collected Papers*, 395). For he cannot hope to avoid denying the truth of "*transcendent* values such as salvation and eternal life" if or when they override "worldly values" ("Public Reason," 483). When it comes to the limitations of the "method of avoidance," Rawls repeatedly contradicts himself. See, for example, "Habermas," 395; *Political Liberalism*, 63; "Public Reason," 484n89; *Collected Papers*, 306–7. He was confused about the fact that sooner or later the rubber hits the road, and his confusion led him to avoid philosophy even when philosophy was, by his own admission, absolutely necessary. For further discussion, see Judd Owen, *Religion and the Demise of Liberal Rationalism: The Foundational Crisis of the Separation of Church and State* (Chicago: University of Chicago Press, 2001), 97–128.

10. "Public Reason," 459.

11. "Public Reason," 442, 488. See also *Theory of Justice*, 182: "the duty to religious and divine law being absolute, no understanding among persons of different faiths is permissible from a religious point of view. Certainly men have often acted as if they held this doctrine. *It is unnecessary, however, to argue against it*" (emphasis added). Contrast, however, *Justice as Fairness*, 183: "If it is said that outside the church there is no salvation, and hence a constitutional regime cannot be accepted, *we must make some reply*" (emphasis added). Now the "reply" given there, which Rawls made in the space of a single sentence, is neither a reply nor coherent (contrast 183 with 184); yet, by betraying some inkling of the need to make a reply, Rawls also betrayed some inkling that his "theory" always had feet of clay.

12. *Theory of Justice*, 433, 405–16, and consider 192–93; *Justice as Fairness*, 194–98; *Law of Peoples*, 7; *Political Liberalism*, 163.

13. *Political Liberalism*, 196–97.

14. See *Collected Papers*, 264.

15. *Political Liberalism*, 64n19, 61, xvi–xvii; emphasis added.

16. See *Law of Peoples*, 123.

17. See *Collected Papers*, 394–95.

18. *Justice as Fairness*, 25. See also *Political Liberalism*, 8, 60–61, 150–53; *Theory of Justice*, 17; *Lectures on the History of Political Philosophy*, 309.

19. "Tyranny and Wisdom," in *On Tyranny*, by Leo Strauss, ed. Victor Gourevitch and Michael Roth (Chicago: University of Chicago Press, 2000), 167–68. Just before exhorting his friends to take up "the practical task of containing [his foes]—like war and disease," Rawls said, "That there are doctrines that reject one or more democratic freedoms is itself a permanent fact of life, *or seems so*" (*Political Liberalism*, 64n19; emphasis added). Elsewhere, Rawls said, "There is, *or need be*, no war between religion and democracy" ("Public Reason," 486; emphasis added). There *need be* no war between religion and democracy, according to Rawls, because "doctrines that reject one or more democratic freedoms" merely *seem to be* a permanent fact of life. Rawls, to repeat, looked forward to a time when such doctrines, or the people who affirm them, would "cease to exist."

20. *Theory of Justice*, 34. See "Habermas," 379n8: According to Rawls, the statement "every event has a cause" is "metaphysical." Moreover, "to deny certain metaphysical doctrines is to assert another such doctrine." The statement "every event has a cause," if true, means that the world is eternal. To assert that the world was created in time is to deny that "every event has a cause." Seeing as how Rawls cannot hope to "leave philosophy as it is," for example, whenever "the religious salvation of those holding a particular religion, or indeed the salvation of a whole people, [is] said to depend on [civil strife]"—see note 9 in this introduction—Rawls cannot hope to avoid asserting the eternity of the world and denying the creation of the world in time. But again, although he admits the absolute necessity of *not* avoiding philosophy's longstanding problems whenever that happens, Rawls avoided them.

21. See *Political Liberalism*, 198n33.

22. *Law of Peoples*, 123; see also *Justice as Fairness*, 36n26; *Political Liberalism*, 197n32.

23. *Theory of Justice*, 193; emphasis added.

24. Katrina Forrester, *In the Shadow of Justice: Postwar Liberalism and the Remaking of Political Philosophy* (Princeton, NJ: Princeton University Press, 2019), xv.

25. *Between Naturalism and Religion: Philosophical Essays* (Malden, MA: Polity, 2008), 1.

26. *Between Naturalism and Religion*, 211.

27. See Allan Bloom, "Justice: John Rawls Vs. The Tradition of Political Philosophy," *American Political Science Review* 69, no. 2 (1975): 648: "[*A Theory of Justice's*] vogue results from two facts: It is the most ambitious political project undertaken by a member of the school currently dominant in academic philosophy; and it offers not only a defense of, but also a new foundation for, a radical egalitarian interpretation of liberal democracy."

28. See Jürgen Habermas, "Pre-Political Foundations of the Democratic Constitutional State?" in *The Dialectics of Secularization: On Reason and Religion* (San Francisco: Ignatius Press, 2006), 40–42: "The starting point for the philosophical reflection about reason and revelation is . . . that when reason reflects on its deepest foundations, it discovers that it owes its origin to something else," hence, "without initially having any theological intention, the reason that becomes aware of its limitations thus transcends itself in the direction of something else." Note, however, "secular

discourse" cannot *rightly* claim "to be accessible to all men" if, like "religious discourse that is dependent on the truth of revelation," "it owes its origin to something else," other than reason.

29. "On My Religion," in *A Brief Inquiry into the Meaning of Sin and Faith*, ed. Thomas Nagel (Cambridge, MA: Harvard University Press, 2009), 261.

30. "On My Religion," 262–64.

31. *Tusculan Disputations* 5.10; *Brutus* 31; *Academica* 1.15–16; *On the Orator* 1.42.

32. Dustin Sebell, *The Socratic Turn: Knowledge of Good and Evil in an Age of Science* (Philadelphia: University of Pennsylvania Press, 2016).

33. *Xenophon's Socrates* (Ithaca, NY: Cornell University Press, 1972), 94; *Persecution and the Art of Writing* (Chicago: University of Chicago Press, 1952), 11n6. See also E. C. Marchant, *Xenophon: Memorabilia, Oeconomicus, Symposium, Apology* (Cambridge, MA: Harvard University Press, 1923), xviii: "we are introduced to something like a complete system of Socratic education."

34. Christopher Moore, "Xenophon's Socratic Education in *Memorabilia* Book 4," in *Socrates and the Socratic Dialogue*, ed. Alessandro Stavru and Christopher Moore (Leiden: Brill, 2018), 501.

35. *A History of Western Philosophy* (New York: Simon and Schuster, 1945), 82–83.

36. *Platon: The Apology of Socrates, the Crito, and Part of the Phaedo: With Notes from Stallbaum, Schleiermacher's Introductions, and His Essay on the Worth of Socrates as a Philosopher*, ed. William Smith, 8th ed. (London: John Murray, 1890), 10.

37. W. W. Baker, "An Apologetic for Xenophon's *Memorabilia*," *Classical Journal* 12, no. 5 (1917): 293–94.

38. Review of *Xenophon's Socrates*, by Leo Strauss, *Philosophical Review* 83, no. 3 (1974): 410. See also W. K. C. Guthrie, *Socrates* (Cambridge: Cambridge University Press, 1971), 14–15.

39. Thomas Brickhouse and Nicholas Smith, *The Philosophy of Socrates* (Boulder, CO: Westview Press, 2000), 38, 40. See also J. K. Anderson, *Xenophon* (London: Duckworth, 1974), 2; Charles Kahn, *Plato and the Socratic Dialogue: The Philosophical Use of a Literary Form* (Cambridge: Cambridge University Press, 1996), 400, 87; A. R. Lacey, "Our Knowledge of Socrates," in *The Philosophy of Socrates: A Collection of Critical Essays*, ed. Gregory Vlastos (New York: Palgrave Macmillan, 1971), 32–33.

40. Georg Wilhelm Friedrich Hegel, *Lectures on the History of Philosophy: Greek Philosophy to Plato*, trans. Frederick Beiser (Lincoln: University of Nebraska Press, 1995), 414.

41. Michel de Montaigne, *Essays*, trans. Donald Frame (Stanford, CA: Stanford University Press), I:6.

42. See Christopher Nadon, *Xenophon's Prince: Republic and Empire in the Cyropaedia* (Berkeley: University of California Press, 2001), 3; Christopher Tuplin, *The Failings of Empire: A Reading of Xenophon Hellenica 2.3.11–7.5.27* (Stuttgart: Franz Steiner Verlag, 1993), 21–28.

43. Friedrich Nietzsche, posthumous fragment 18 [47] 1876, trans. Thomas Pangle, quoted in Pangle, *The Socratic Way of Life: Xenophon's "Memorabilia"* (Chicago: University of Chicago Press, 2018), vii.

44. John Beversluis, *Cross-Examining Socrates: A Defense of the Interlocutors in Plato's Early Dialogues* (Cambridge: Cambridge University Press, 2000), 79–80.

45. *Works of John Adams*, 10 vols., ed. Charles Francis Adams (Boston: Little, Brown, 1856), 1:45–46.

46. *Works of John Adams*, 3:433.

47. J. R. R. Tolkien, *Sir Gawain and the Green Knight* (Boston: Houghton Mifflin, 1975), 17. See also Anderson, *Xenophon*, 2; David Johnson, "From Generals to Gluttony: *Memorabilia* Book 3," in Stavru and Moore, *Socrates and the Socratic Dialogue*, 481.

48. Gerasimos Santas, *Socrates: The Arguments of the Philosophers* (New York: Routledge, 1979), 4.

49. See Gregory Vlastos, "The Paradox of Socrates," in Vlastos, *Philosophy of Socrates*. Vlastos takes issue with Xenophon's Socrates because, he thinks,

> his Socrates could not have attracted men like Critias and Alcibiades, haughty aristocrats both of them, and as brilliant intellectually as they were morally unprincipled. Xenophon's Socrates, pious reciter of moral commonplaces, would have elicited nothing but a sneer from Critias and a yawn from Alcibiades, while Plato's Socrates is just the man who could have gotten under their skin. . . . Plato, and he alone, gives us a Socrates who could have plausibly been indicted for subversion of faith and morals. Xenophon's account of Socrates, apologetic from beginning to end, refutes itself: had the facts been as he tells them, the indictment would not have been made in the first place. (2–3)

See also Vlastos, "Socratic Piety," in *Reason and Religion in Socratic Philosophy*, ed. Nicholas Smith and Paul Woodruff (Oxford: Oxford University Press, 2000), 69n39. For this reason, Vlastos felt that Plato's Socrates is "incomparably more interesting" than Xenophon's ("Paradox of Socrates," 2). "One of the many things for which we may be grateful to Plato is that, as [James] Boswell said of his own treatment [Samuel] Johnson, he 'did not make a cat out of his tiger.' Unlike Xenophon's cat, Plato's tiger stands for the savage doctrine"—too savage for Vlastos: see note 4 in Chapter 3—"that if you cannot pass the stiff Socratic tests for knowledge you cannot be a good man" (6). But of course, in the end, Vlastos did not think for a moment that Plato's Socrates was any more guilty than Xenophon's of "subversion of faith and morals." On the contrary, "no saint has ever claimed more for the power of faith over the passions than does Socrates for the power of knowledge." After all, "if you do have this kind of knowledge," which is not so much knowledge as "religious faith" (16, 21), "you cannot fail to *be* good and *act* as a good man should, in the face of any emotional stress or strain" (6). The secret to the success of Plato's Socrates in recent years, at least relative to Xenophon's, is that Plato's Socrates would seem, at a glance, to be a cat crossbred with a tiger, hence, neither a cat nor a tiger. See also Lacey, "Our Knowledge of Socrates." Lacey takes issue with Xenophon's Socrates because he is "dreary and moralizing" (33, 39). And yet, while the "dull didacticism" of Xenophon's Socrates is "perhaps to be explained as [Xenophon] putting into explicit form what he took to be the natural implications of Socrates' teaching," the fact remains: according to Lacey, Xenophon was not wrong. For all his scorn for the "moralizing" of Xenophon's Socrates, "we can assume," he says, "that Socrates made it plain enough that he was 'against sin'" (40). See note 62 later in this introduction.

50. *The Autobiography and Other Writings on Politics, Economics, and Virtue*, ed. Alan Houston (Cambridge: Cambridge University Press, 2004), 13–14.

51. Gregory Vlastos, *Socrates: Ironist and Moral Philosopher* (Cambridge: Cambridge University Press, 1991), 105. See also Deborah Levine Gera, *Xenophon's "Cyropaedia": Style, Genre, and Literary Technique* (Oxford: Oxford University Press, 1993), 34; Lacey, "Our Knowledge of Socrates," 39. Contrast Tad Brennan, "Socrates and Epictetus," in *A Companion to Socrates*, ed. Sara Ahbel-Rappe and Rachana Kamtekar (Malden, MA: Blackwell, 2006), 292.

52. Guthrie, *Socrates*, 27–28.

53. Taylor, *Socrates* (London: Thomas Nelson and Sons, 1939), 14.

54. Guthrie, *Socrates*, 28n1.

55. See Sebell, *Socratic Turn*, 158–59n8, 164n37, and 180–81n13. For further discussion of the historical context in which Xenophon wrote, see Richard Janko, "Socrates the Freethinker," in Ahbel-Rappe and Kamtekar, *A Companion to Socrates*, 57; E. R. Dodds, *The Greeks and the Irrational* (Berkeley: University of California Press, 1951), 189ff.

56. Johann Wolfgang von Goethe, Letter to Passow, October 20, 1811, in *Goethes Briefe unde Briefe an Goethe*, ed. Karl Mandelkow (Munich: Beck, 1988), 3:168.

57. See Louis-André Dorion, "The Straussian Exegesis of Xenophon: The Paradigmatic Case of *Memorabilia* IV 4," in *Oxford Readings in Classical Studies: Xenophon*, ed. Vivienne Gray (Oxford: Oxford University Press, 2010), 283: there are "two main reasons for "the renewal of interest in Xenophon's Socratic writings," namely, "Strauss's works and the impossibility of resolving the Socratic question." See also Dorion, "Fundamental Parallels Between Socrates' and Ischomachus' Positions in the *Oeconomicus*," in Stavru and Moore, *Socrates and the Socratic Dialogue*, 522: "[Strauss's interpretation of the *Oeconomicus*] brought about a veritable paradigm shift," "[it] enjoys fairly wide acceptance today and is even adopted . . . by commentators who do not openly claim to follow Strauss." Now, it is true, for as long as Strauss lived, classicists were no less hostile to his efforts to rehabilitate Xenophon than they were to Xenophon himself. But, eventually, Strauss's efforts paid off. Xenophon *was*, to a considerable extent, rehabilitated. "'Xenophon is a subtle writer' became a regular description of this 'rehabilitation'" (Vivienne Gray, "Introduction," in Gray, *Oxford Readings*, 5). And, on the whole, "scholarship on Xenophon has shifted considerably in the ironic direction since Strauss's day, with many a conventional scholar noting tensions, if not necessarily contradictions or disguise, in these works" (David Johnson, "Strauss on Xenophon," in *Xenophon: Ethical Principles and Historical Enquiry*, ed. Fiona Hobden and Christopher Tuplin [Leiden: Brill, 2012], 131). According to Marina Tamiolaki, "Leo Strauss' approach . . . has greatly contributed to a deeper understanding of Xenophon . . . the various reactions to it have led to a categorization of scholars, who tend to be divided into those who offer ironical readings and those who prefer to take Xenophon more at face value" ("Virtue and Leadership in Xenophon: Ideal Leaders or Ideal Losers?" in Hobden and Tuplin, *Xenophon*, 565). Or, to quote the latest OCD, "a (perhaps *the*) central question, which divides [Xenophon's] modern readers into two camps, is how far style and content are really *faux-naïf* and informed by humour and irony" (Christopher Tuplin, "Xenophon," in *The Oxford Classical Dictionary*, ed. Simon Hornblower, Antony Spawforth, and Esther Eidinow, 4th ed. [Oxford: Oxford University Press, 2012], 1581).

Nevertheless, although it was Strauss who almost single-handedly rehabilitated Xenophon over the streneuous objections of the classicists, and who put the now "central question" of Xenophon's irony on the map, hostility to Strauss himself has grown unabated, at least among classicists. See Michel Narcy, "Xenophon, Socrates, and Strauss," review of *The Socratic Way of Life*, by Thomas Pangle, *Classical Review* 69, no. 1 (2019): 48–49: "As a result of [Strauss's] way of reading, Xenophon is no longer the writer indulging in platitudes he was taken for in the mid-twentieth century, nor is his Socrates the conformist bourgeois he looks like in some sketches of *Memorabilia*. Instead, the latter appears as upsetting and thought-provoking as the *atopos* Platonic Socrates. Thus, thanks to Strauss, prejudices about Xenophon and his Socrates were dispelled. . . . Quite ironically, *nowadays it is Strauss's turn to be the subject of prejudice*" (emphasis added). For example, when, in a testament to Xenophon's rising fortunes, Oxford University Press finally got around to publishing a handbook to Xenophon, the volume's editor frankly acknowledged that Strauss is "highly influential" (Vivienne Gray, "Introduction," in Gray, *Oxford Readings*, 4). One indication of this is that she herself felt "ambushed," when writing her own book, by the need to critique "'ironical' or 'subversive' or 'darker' readings" (Vivienne Gray, *Xenophon's Mirror of Princes: Reading the Reflections* [Cambridge: Cambridge University Press, 2011], 177). However, while not a single "Straussian" was asked to contribute to the volume, an entire essay—the volume's single longest contribution—was set aside for the sole purpose of an attack on the "Straussian" exegesis of Xenophon. This is par for the course. See also, for additional examples, Stavru and Moore, *Socrates and the Socratic Dialogue*; *The Cambridge Companion to Xenophon*, ed. Michael Flower (Cambridge: Cambridge University Press, 2017).

There is no need to dwell on the fact that by attacking the "Straussian" exegesis of Xenophon now dominant among political theorists, while shutting out anyone who would offer a sympathetic reading, much less a defense, classicists do not inspire confidence in their good faith. But the fact that Strauss has exerted an "immense influence" on classicists (Dorion, "Straussian Exegesis," 285), despite their hostility to him, should give us pause. By making the case that "Xenophon is a subtle writer" over the strenuous objections of previous generations of classicists, who were not willing or able to change their minds about anything, much less everything, Strauss rehabilitated Xenophon for a new generation of classicists, who were. And yet, while siding with Strauss against previous generations of classicists, the new generation of classicists still maintains the hostility to Strauss of the previous generations! Paradigm shifts normally involve a changing of the guard, with the conservative defenders of the status quo ceding authority to the revolutionaries and progressives; but not here. Strauss has exerted an "immense influence" on classicists, as we saw—but even so, they avoid, "in many cases, expressly admitting as much" (321), and what is more, "'reading between the lines' [remains] a phrase requiring scare quotes and raised eyebrows" (Johnson, "Strauss on Xenophon," 124; but see, for example, note 18 in Chapter 8). And it is hard not to draw the conclusion that Strauss got something so right that even those unalterably opposed to him—at least partly because they styled themselves authorities on the ancient philosophers, and Strauss questioned their authority—were simply unable to resist the power of his observations for long. That is to say, despite their hostility to Strauss, and despite their best efforts to prevent him, by hook or by crook, from changing any minds, his evidence was so compelling that eventually he changed even their own minds, if not about everything, about quite a few things.

Note, finally, that it is therefore scarcely meaningful to speak loosely, as I have allowed myself to do, of "Straussians." Insofar as "scholarship on Xenophon has shifted considerably in the ironic direction," we are all, or almost all, "Straussians" now, at least to some extent—even critics of Strauss. Moreover, admirers of Strauss do not necessarily agree about much or anything of importance. Because Strauss remains shrouded in mystery, expressing admiration for Strauss cannot possibly make one a "Straussian" exegete of Xenophon. For example, although Thomas Pangle and I would appear to agree with Strauss that Xenophon was an exoteric writer, our agreement is merely verbal—in fact, we profoundly disagree about how Xenophon wrote (or how Strauss read him). For the most important discussion of the "Straussian" exegesis of Xenophon in the strict sense of Strauss's own exegesis of Xenophon, see Christopher Bruell, "Strauss on Xenophon's Socrates," *Political Science Reviewer* 14 (1984): 262–318.

58. See Montaigne, *Essays*, 2:12, 3:9; Francis Bacon, *The Advancement of Learning*, ed. G. W. Kitchin (Philadelphia: Paul Dry, 2001), 404–5; Pierre Bayle, *Dictionnaire historique et critique*, 5th ed., 4 vols. (Amsterdam: P. Brunel, 1740), 1:328–29; Jean-Jacques Rousseau, *Collected Works*, 13 vols., ed. Roger Masters and Christopher Kelly (Hanover, NH: University Press of New England, 1992), 2:45–46n; Chaninah Maschler, "Lessing's Ernst and Falk, Dialogues for Freemasons: A Translation with Notes," *Interpretation* 14, no. 1 (1986), 8; Friedrich Nietzsche, *Beyond Good and Evil*, trans. Walter Kaufmann (New York: Random House,

1966), §30. For further discussion of these and many other passages, see Arthur Melzer, *Philosophy Between the Lines: The Lost History of Esoteric Writing* (Chicago: University of Chicago Press, 2014).

59. Gottfried Wilhelm Leibniz, *New Essays on Human Understanding*, trans. Peter Remnant and Jonathan Bennett (Cambridge: Cambridge University Press, 1996), II.xxix.12.

60. For "perverse," see Owen Goldin, review of *Aristotle as Teacher: His Introduction to a Philosophic Science*, by Christopher Bruell, *Journal of the History of Philosophy* 54, no. 1 (2016): 155; Gray, *Xenophon's Mirror*, 177; David Johnson, "Xenophon's Intertextual Socrates," in *Plato and Xenophon: Comparative Studies*, ed. Gabriel Danzig, David Johnson, and Donald Morrison (Leiden: Brill, 2018), 91; Goerge Sabine, review of *Persecution and the Art of Writing*, by Leo Strauss, *Ethics* 63, no. 3 (1953): 220; J. W. Yolton, "Locke on the Law of Nature," *Philosophical Review* 67 (1958): 490. For "twisted," see Jonathan Lear, "The Socratic Method and Psychoanalysis," in Ahbel-Rappe and Kamtekar, *A Companion to Socrates*, 460, 448.

61. For a small sampling of which, see Sebell, *Socratic Turn*, 160–161n21. Again, for much more, see Melzer, *Philosophy Between the Lines*.

62. See John Burnet, *Greek Philosophy: Thales to Plato* (London: Macmillan, 1914). On what did Burnet's judgment that "it is really impossible to preserve Xenophon's Sokrates, even if he were worth preserving" (150), ultimately rest? According to him, "Xenophon wished to prove that Sokrates was unjustly accused of being irreligious." So Burnet set out to find "admissions in any degree inconsistent with that [purpose]." Now, "one of the chief arguments for the soundness of his religious attitude is that he refused to busy himself with natural science." And yet, Burnet keenly observed, "[Xenophon] gives his point away completely by adding twice over: 'Yet he himself was not unversed in these subjects'—subjects of which he gives a list, and which correspond exactly to the most highly developed mathematics and astronomy of the time. Further, he knew that what Aristophanes burlesqued as the *Phrontisterion* was a reality; for he makes Sokrates [say] that he does in fact study the writings of the older philosophers with his friends." When Burnet said, "it would be possible to find a good many more admissions of this sort in Xenophon," he did not know the half of it (148). For he never seriously considered the possibility that Xenophon did not simply wish to prove that Socrates was unjustly accused. Instead, completely forgetting the holes that Xenophon had poked in his own case, Burnet concluded, "in fact, Xenophon's defence of Sokrates is too successful. He would never have been put to death if he had been like that" (149). Burnet's judgment of Xenophon's Socrates, later echoed almost verbatim by one classicist after another (Taylor, *Socrates*, 12–14; Brickhouse and Smith, *Philosophy of Socrates*, 42, 44; Santas, *Socrates*, 5; Vlastos, "Paradox of Socrates," 2–3; *Socrates*, 166n41), therefore ultimately rested on the fact that he himself was, on one hand, too sophisticated for such an innocent Socrates. On the other hand, however, he was too naïve even to entertain the possibility of a guilty one. See also John Burnet, *Plato's Phaedo* (Oxford: Clarendon Press, 1911), xi–xii. See note 49 in this introduction. The question of Socrates's stance toward religion and natural philosophy, like the question of his exhortatory and his methodical treatments of morality or politics—not to mention, last but by no means least, the question of the relationship between his treatments of the latter and his stance toward the former—is, in this way, lost on us today.

63. For this take on exoteric writing, which is all too common, see Michael Flower, "Introduction," in Flower, *Companion to Xenophon*, 7: "'ironic' reading [is] reading according to the principle that what Xenophon says is consistently the opposite of what he means." But it is chiefly,

as we will see, if not exclusively, the classicists who read Xenophon according to this—I agree, frankly absurd—principle.

CHAPTER 1

1. I have relied mainly on Michele Bandini and Louis-André Dorion's edition of the text, *Xenophon, Mémorables I–III.* Paris: Budé, 2010–11. Translations are my own, although I have frequently consulted Amy Bonnette's *Memorabilia* (Ithaca, NY: Cornell University Press, 1994).

2. See Gray, *Xenophon's Mirror,* 8; Paul Vander Waerdt, "Socratic Justice and Self-Sufficiency: The Story of the Delphic Oracle in Xenophon's *Apology of Socrates,*" *Oxford Studies in Ancient Philosophy* 11 (1993): 44n120.

3. See Leo Strauss, *Xenophon's Socratic Discourse* (Ithaca, NY: Cornell University Press, 1970), 84–86. According to Narcy, "Strauss maintained a systematic organisation of Xenophon's Socratic writings. This view was grounded merely in one phrase of the *Memorabilia* and an alleged parallel in the *Anabasis* (*Xenophon's Socratic Discourse,* p. 86 n. 7)" ("Xenophon, Socrates, and Strauss," 49). Now, if it were really true that this view of the "classification of Xenophon's Socratic writings" was grounded merely on *Memorabilia* I.1.19 and *Anabasis* V.6.28, Strauss would indeed be guilty of "over-interpretation," as Narcy puts it. But this is not true. At least, if the plain meaning of his words is any indication, Strauss put this view in provisional terms ("seems to underlie") because the proof is in the pudding, while grounding his merely provisional statement of the view on *Symposium* 1.1, *Oeconomicus* 1.1, and *Apology* 1—to say nothing of *Hellenica* VI.1.9 and VI.5.9, and VII.3.4 and VII.4.1—taken together with *Memorabilia* I.1.19, IV.3.1, and *Anabasis* V.6.28. See *Socratic Discourse,* 86, 143.

4. See Gabriel Danzig, *Apologizing for Socrates: How Plato and Xenophon Created Our Socrates* (Lanham, MD: Lexington, 2010), 166; Sarah Brown Ferrario, "Xenophon and Greek Political Thought," in Flower, *Companion to Xenophon,* 61; Vivienne Gray, *The Framing of Socrates: The Literary Interpretation of Xenophon's "Memorabilia"* (Stuttgart: Franz Steiner Verlag, 1998), 91; David Johnson, "Xenophon's *Apology* and *Memorabilia,*" in Flower, *Companion to Xenophon,* 119; Donald Morrison, "On Professor Vlastos' Xenophon," *Ancient Philosophy* 7 (2012): 19; Nadon, *Xenophon's Prince,* 49; David Sedley, *Creationism and Its Critics in Antiquity* (Berkeley: University of California Press, 2007), 79.

5. See Eric Buzzetti, "The Rhetoric of Xenophon and the Treatment of Justice in the *Memorabilia,*" *Interpretation* 29, no. 1 (2001): 4–5; David Johnson, "Xenophon's *Apology,*" 124; Johnson, "Xenophon at His Most Socratic (*Memorabilia* 4.2)," *Oxford Studies in Ancient Philosophy* 29 (2005): 49; Kahn, *Plato,* 398; Lacey, "Our Knowledge of Socrates," 37n32; Paul Vander Waerdt, "Socrates in the Clouds," in *The Socratic Movement,* ed. Paul Vander Waerdt (Ithaca, NY: Cornell University Press, 1994), 85n96.

6. Strauss, *Xenophon's Socrates,* 9.

7. For the knots in which those who refuse to consider the simplest explanation for this have tied themselves up, see Alexandre Jakubiec, "Rites and Religious Beliefs of Socrates According to Xenophon," *Classical Quarterly* 67, no. 1 (2017): 291–93. As Jakubiec notes in passing, "nothing says that, by emphasizing Socrates' active practice of religious rituals, Xenophon proves Socrates' innocence" (293). See also Mark McPherran, "Does Piety Pay? Socrates and Plato on Prayer and Sacrifice," in Smith and Woodruff, *Reason and Religion,* 89.

8. See Christopher Moore, "Xenophon on 'Philosophy,'" in Danzig, Johnson, and Morrison, *Plato and Xenophon*, 144.

9. See Gray, *Framing*, 11–13.

10. See Gray, *Xenophon's Mirror*, 334.

11. See Gray, *Framing*, 27, 182; Thomas Pangle, *The Socratic Way of Life: Xenophon's "Memorabilia"* (Chicago: University of Chicago Press, 2018), 164.

12. See Gray, *Framing*, 84.

13. Neither IV.1.2 nor I.6.15 says, or means, that Socrates's students engaged in political affairs. In the case of I.6.15, which is a particularly good example of Xenophon's art of writing, what Socrates says merely calls upon us to repeat Antiphon's question on the level of Socrates's students. For the mistaken belief that I.6.15 says that Socrates's students engaged in political affairs, however, see Fiorenza Bevilacqua, "Socrates' Attitude Towards Politics in Xenophon and Plato," in Danzig, Johnson, and Morrison, *Plato and Xenophon*, 467; Louis-André Dorion, "Xenophon and Greek Philosophy," in Flower, *Companion to Xenophon*, 44; Dorion, "The Nature and Status of *Sophia* in the *Memorabilia*," in Hobden and Tuplin, *Xenophon*, 468n32; Lowell Edmunds, "Xenophon's Triad of Socratic Virtues," in Danzig, Johnson, and Morrison, *Plato and Xenophon*, 268. For the equally mistaken belief that IV.1.2 says as much too, see Vivienne Gray, *Xenophon on Government* (Cambridge: Cambridge University Press, 2007), 5.

14. See Donald Morrison, "Xenophon's Socrates as Teacher," in Vander Waerdt, *Socratic Movement*, 183; Carlo Natali, "Socrates' Dialectic in Xenophon's *Memorabilia*," in *Remembering Socrates*, ed. Lindsay Judson and Vassilis Karasmanis (New York: Oxford University Press, 2006), 6.

15. Euthydemos is a bad nature. About this, there is no room for doubt. For just the most obvious considerations, see Chapter 2, Section V. See also notes 16, 17, 22 in this chapter, notes 1, 3, 9, 18 and 22 in Chapter 2, and note 3 in Chapter 7.

16. Although Xenophon has only just told us that Socrates was not seriously interested in bodily beauty, Morrison seems to think that the beauty of Euthydemos speaks for—not against—the fact that Socrates was seriously interested in him. It is nothing short of remarkable that he says, "such a young man is just the sort to interest Socrates: *beautiful*, intelligent, ambitious" ("Socrates as Teacher," 185; emphasis added). Johnson admits that, while "Xenophon explicitly attributes good natures only to those with whom Socrates said, jokingly, that he was in love . . . [t]here is *nothing overtly erotic* about Socrates's conversation with Euthydemos" ("*Memorabilia* 4.2," 47n20; emphasis added). But that would make Euthydemos a bad nature, and Johnson resists this thought on the grounds that, because Euthydemos was beautiful, he "was apparently one of Socrates's so-called beloveds." He, too, fails to notice that the beauty of Euthydemos is an argument *against* the view that he was a good nature. Contrast Danzig, who keenly observes that Xenophon's claim, "that Socrates loved the young boys for their souls rather than their bodies, is not confirmed by the portrait that Xenophon actually provides" (*Apologizing*, 180).

17. In support of his view that Euthydemos "does not seem to have been especially gifted intellectually," Danzig performs a rare feat, he states the obvious: "Xenophon does not categorize him among those who possessed great natural abilities" (180–81). See David O'Connor, "The Erotic Self-Sufficiency of Socrates: A Reading of Xenophon's *Memorabilia*," in Vander Waerdt, *Socratic Movement*, 176n30: "none of the three conceited types fulfills the criteria for being a 'good nature' so that Xenophon never shows Socrates conversing with someone of the highest type. . . . [A]ll three types Xenophon discusses have some characteristic prejudice that limits their love of learning concerned with governing human beings well, and so to this extent they are

not 'good natures.'" See also Gray, *Framing*, 14, 150: Euthydemos "was unwilling to learn," whereas good natures are, by definition, "desirous of learning." But contrast Morrison, "Socrates as Teacher," 184: the problem with Euthydemos is "not that [he does] not [desire] knowledge, but that he mistakenly [thinks that he] already has the knowledge [he desires]." Contrast also Russell Jones and Ravi Sharma, who defer to Morrison, "Xenophon's Socrates on Justice and Well-being: Memorabilia iv 2," *Ancient Philosophy* 40, no. 1: 23n8: "The fact that Euthydemus initially considers his learning adequate . . . does not imply that he fails to qualify as a 'good nature.'" This is not a "fact," however, this is a figment of their imagination. The fact is that neither Xenophon nor Socrates ever says that Euthydemos desired, or was proud of, "learning" or "knowledge." See Chapter 2, Section V.

18. Strauss, *Xenophon's Socrates*, 93.

19. See Johnson, "*Memorabilia* 4.2," 54n32: "[IV.7.1] is considerably complicated by the passage that immediately precedes it, in which Xenophon outlines *two different Socratic methods*. In the first Socrates leads those who disagree with him back to first principles, a method perhaps comparable to that of Plato's Socrates (4.6.13–14); in the second, 'whenever he went through something himself in a speech . . . he produced listeners who agreed with him'" (emphasis added). See also Andreas Patzer, "Xenophon's Socrates as Dialectician," in Gray, *Oxford Readings*, 248–49. Patzer, however, translates *tēn asphaleian logou* as "the discussion's infallibility," and *asphalē rētora* as "unerring speaker," which is highly misleading. Among other things, when Homer called him an *asphalē rētora*, does anybody really believe that he was calling *Odysseus* a remarkable truth teller? Xenophon, as should go without saying, "compares [Socrates] to the inveterate *liar* Odysseus" (David Johnson, "Reply to Vivienne Gray," *Ancient Philosophy* 24, no. 2 [2012]: 447; "*Memorabilia* 4.2," 54–55n32; emphasis added). See also William Altman, "Dialectic in Xenophon's *Memorabilia*: Responding to 4.6," *Guairaca Revista de Folosofia* 34, no. 2 (2018): 118. After translating *tēn asphaleian logou* as "the discussion's infallibility" on one occasion, Patzer translates it as "the infallible *success of the discussion*" on another ("Socrates as Dialectician," 247). By "success," however, he seems to mean persuasive speech, and infallible or true speech is different from infallibly or rather—since Xenophon never said anything about infallibly or completely persuasive speech anyway—merely very persuasive speech. Gray translates *tēn asphaleian logou* as "sure method," before going on to translate *asphalē rētora*, more accurately than Patzer, as "safe speaker" (*Xenophon's Mirror*, 17–18). However, she obliterates the distinction between the dialectical method described in IV.6.13–15, which aims at "the truth," and the rhetorical one described in IV.6.15, which aims at "the most agreement"—even though she does speak of "rhetoric," apparently as distinguished from dialectic, elsewhere (*Framing*, 22, 27). If only in passing, she notes that Odysseus was seen as "the verbal trickster" (*Xenophon's Mirror*, 128), and that Antisthenes, for one, "concluded that [Odysseus's traditional epithet *polytropos*] showed how as orator he assumed different characters in addressing different audiences" (129n16). Recall *Memorabilia* I.2.58. For further discussion of Antisthenes's account of Odysseus's *polytropia*, which has come down to us via Porphyry's gloss on *Odyssey* I.1, see Silvia Montiglio, *From Villain to Hero: Odysseus in Ancient Thought* (Ann Arbor: University of Michigan Press, 2011), 21–22:

> It could be thought, Antisthenes says, that Homer does not praise Odysseus more than he blames him, when he calls him *polytropos*. Indeed, Homer did not make Agamemnon and Ajax *polytropoi* but simple [*haplos*] and noble. Nor, by Zeus, did he give the wise Nestor a deceptive and changeable character: quite the contrary, Nestor was sincere when he consorted with Agamemnon and everyone else, and if he knew

> something good for the army, he advised them without hiding it away. Achilles was so far from approving that kind of character (*tropon*) that he held that man as hateful as death 'who hides one thing in his heart and speaks another' (*Iliad* IX.313). Antisthenes solves the difficulty by saying: What then? Is Odysseus bad because he is called *polytropos*? Is it not because he is wise (*sophos*) that Homer has given him that name? . . . If wise men are skilled at discussing, they also know how to express the same thought in many ways (*tropos*), and since they know many turns of speech (*tropous logōn*) to say the same thing, they could be called *polytropoi*. . . . For this reason Homer says that Odysseus, being wise (*sophon*), is *polytropos*, because he knew how to consort with people using many turns of speech.

Antisthenes, however, does not "solve the difficulty," except insofar as Homer, by this account, blames Achilles for being "simple" or "straightforward" (*haplos*) and "noble," and praises Odysseus for being *polytropos* and "wise."

20. Morrison, "Socrates as Teacher," 191.

21. Patzer notes, correctly, "how reminiscent the phrasing [found in Plato, *Phaedo* 101d2] *to asphalēs tēs hupotheseōs* is of the *asphaleia logou* [found here, in *Memorabilia* IV.6.15]" ("Socrates as Dialectician," 250). But Plato and Xenophon both have rhetoric, not dialectic, in mind. As for dialectic, Patzer's remarks to the effect that "the difference [between what Plato and Xenophon have to say about . . . Socratic dialectic] could not be greater" (249) could not be further from the truth. Compare Chapter 3, Section II and Chapter 8, Section III with Sebell, *Socratic Turn* 106–143. See also, for Aristotle on Socratic dialectic, 189–90n77.

22. See Gray, *Xenophon's Mirror*, 363: "We know that Socrates differentiated," in IV.2.13–18, "theft as being always good when practiced on enemies, sometimes good when practiced on friends to their benefit, never good when done to get the advantage over them." It follows that "we know," too, that lying to or deceiving friends is sometimes just or good according to Socrates. For Socrates argued, in almost the same breath, that if a general were to lie to and deceive his army when they are "depressed," say, that would be just or good (IV.2.17). As Danzig points out, "the mere mention of slavery and depression as examples in the argument is significant since, as we will see, Socrates uses the conversation to induce depression by persuading Euthydemos that he is slavish" (*Apologizing*, 187). If Socrates thought that it would be just or good if a general were to lie to and deceive his army when they are "depressed," did he think that it would be just or good for him to lie to or at least deceive Euthydemos, too, when he is "depressed" (IV.2.23, IV.2.39, IV.3.15)? Again, by Gray's account, that follows. Danzig goes so far as to say that "while Socrates does not speak here," at IV.2.17, "of enslaving one's friends, a little thought shows that beneficial enslavement would be just also in regard to a friendly city or individual" (*Apologizing*, 187).

23. See Morrison, "Socrates as Teacher," 208.

24. See Christopher Moore, *Socrates and Self-Knowledge* (Cambridge: Cambridge University Press, 2015), 223: Socrates "practices indirection" with Euthydemos. See also Morrison, "Socrates as Teacher," 186.

25. How, then, could the gentlemanly associates mentioned at I.2.48 be good friends? Compare I.2.8 and I.2.48 with II.3. Contrast Dorion, "Fundamental Parallels," 532.

26. See Danzig, *Apologizing*, 181, 184: "In seducing Euthydemus, Socrates makes use of many of the same techniques that he recommended to Theodote."

27. Contrast Pangle, *Socratic Life*, 167. Pangle's statement that "Socrates's more thorough or penetrating tutoring of truly promising youths" is "missing" from *Memorabilia* IV (166–67) contradicts his true statement that, in *Memorabilia* IV, "Xenophon undertakes the task of portray-

ing [the] peak, beneficial, Socratic activity" (164). Despite himself (257n12), Pangle repeatedly falls back on the "catch-all" explanation that Socrates educated Euthydemos for the benefit of onlookers (202, 205, 207).

CHAPTER 2

1. Xenophon only ever says that Euthydemos collected or gathered books; yet the vast majority of classicists, "reading between the lines," would have us believe that he read them. See Altman, "Dialectic," 130; Gray, *Framing*, 37; Johnson, "*Memorabilia* 4.2," 47; Moore, *Socrates*, 231; Moore, "Xenophon on 'Philosophy,'" 135; David O'Connor, "Xenophon and the Enviable Life of Socrates," in *The Cambridge Companion to Socrates*, ed. Donald Morrison (Cambridge: Cambridge University Press, 2011), 68.

2. "[Socrates] argues that even thoroughbred horses, from excellent stock, need improvement. Men too need to gain knowledge of what they have to do" (Moore, *Socrates*, 222). But to say that men "too" need to gain knowledge makes no sense. See George Grote, *Plato and the Other Companions of Sokrates*, 4 vols. (London: John Murray, 1865), 2:269n: "Both the Platonic Sokrates and the Xenophontic Sokrates, frequently illustrate the education of men by comparison with the bringing up of young animals as well as with the training of horses." Moreover, "this comparison occurs so frequently, that it excites much displeasure among various modern critics, who seem to consider it as unseemly and inconsistent with 'the dignity of human nature.'" Critics today are too sophisticated or too naïve to feel the force of the comparison. See, for example, Johnson, "*Memorabilia* 4.2," 47: "The analogy with animals is a typically Xenophontic touch."

3. See Danzig, *Apologizing*, 182n52: "Strauss comments that 'all took place appropriately in a bridle-maker's shop,' but he does not explain what is appropriate about that. . . . [P]erhaps it signifies the fact that Socrates will tame and control the young man as one does with a young horse." While that is indeed what Strauss and Xenophon were getting at, the fact that Danzig understands IV.2.2 to suggest "a positive answer to the much-debated question" with which that passage has to do is one indication that he does not appreciate the significance of this. See note 2 in this chapter.

4. Socrates did "lead" (*agein*) to gentlemanliness (I.6.14). At I.4.1, however, Xenophon spoke of what I translate as "leading all the way toward" (*proagein*) virtue. For the latter term, see I.2.22—the deceptively simple passage in the light of which the appearance of the term in I.4.1 must be understood. If I am not mistaken, these are the only appearances of *proagein* in the *Memorabilia*. See Buzzetti, "Rhetoric of Xenophon," 6–7: "Socrates' final exhortation to self-control in the *Memorabilia* is prefaced by what is in effect a telling admission: 'when [Socrates] conversed, he *turned* (*protrepein*, rather than *proagein*) his companions most of all toward self-control." See also Bandini and Dorion, *Mémorables III*, 228–29n7.

5. See Gray, *Framing*, 44: "[This] looks like the usual disclaimer of knowledge." For the view that Socrates emphatically denied being a teacher of virtue, see also John M. Cooper, *Reason and Emotion: Essays on Ancient Moral Psychology and Ethical Theory* (Princeton, NJ: Princeton University Press, 1999), 22; Morrison "Socrates as Teacher," 203.

6. Contrast Louis-André Dorion, "On the Different Reasons That Socrates Always Obeys the Law," in Danzig, Johnson, and Morrison, *Plato and Xenophon*, 492–93: "Socrates seems to concede that no one is an expert in the field of justice. . . . But Socrates does not say that there are no experts in the field of justice; he says that he is surprised that nobody knows who to go to in order to learn what justice is. But this expert in matters of justice does exist—it is Socrates

himself." Note, what he himself fails to mention, that Dorion's reading requires us to reject the authority of the manuscripts and accept a reading of Stobaeus. Even then, rejecting the authority of the manuscripts is not enough to justify Dorion's claim that "this expert in matters of justice . . . is Socrates himself." For even if it were true that Socrates had only said—what he did not say, according to the manuscripts—that "nobody knows who to go to in order to learn what justice is," Socrates would seem to include himself among those who do not know who to go to; after all, "nobody knows." Either way, Socrates never once said that he was "this expert." Well, why not? Dorion would seem to imply that Socrates withholds the truth from everyone, since, to repeat, "nobody knows" that he is "this expert." Why, then, would Socrates do that? Dorion does not say. In defense of "reading between the lines," or for rejecting them outright and then "reading between the lines" of Stobaeus, he mentions just two considerations. First, he refers to IV.2.2–7 in the belief that, there, "Socrates explains that political competence is just like any other type of expertise: it must be learned from an expert . . . Socrates lets his interlocutors know he is an expert in the field of politics and is able to teach it (cf. *Mem.* I.6.15, 4.3.1)." As we are about to see, however, this is just the opposite of what IV.2.2–7 says or means. Besides, if "Socrates lets his interlocutors know he is an expert in the field of politics," what are we to make of the fact that (according to Stobaeus) he was *always* saying (IV.4.6) that "nobody knows who to go to in order to learn what justice is"? For further discussion of I.6.15, which, like IV.2.2–7, does not mean what Dorion thinks it means, see note 13 in Chapter 1. As for IV.3.1, if Dorion believes that anything is said there to the effect that Socrates was a teacher of justice or moderation, he is, again, simply mistaken. See also note 2 in Chapter 7. Second, Dorion says, "If Socrates had wanted to say that no one has the expertise to teach justice, then it becomes difficult to understand how he can give Hippias a long lecture on . . . justice" (493). But maybe Socrates is difficult to understand. See Chapter 2, Section VII.

7. See Marina Tamiolaki, "Athenian Leaders in Xenophon's *Memorabilia*," in "Aspects of Leadership in Xenophon," ed. Richard Fernando Buxton, *Histos*, suppl. 5 (2016): 26–27: "Socrates's view of Themistocles runs counter to a whole tradition about the Athenian leader, according to which his success was due to his exceptional innate abilities. . . . There was no tradition in antiquity about him having received an excellent education or having associated with famous teachers, such as was the case, for instance, with Pericles."

8. Morrison, "Socrates as Teacher," 186. See also Danzig, *Apologizing*, 182; Moore, *Socrates*, 231.

9. Later, Euthydemos "reverts to his earlier silence, this time thoroughly convinced that he has nothing to say of interest on any subject whatsoever" (Gray, *Framing*, 152). Compare IV.2.6 with IV.2.39. Euthydemos will not speak when he fears he does not know, just as he will not speak when he believes he does know.

10. See Gray, *Framing*, 151; Morrison, "Socrates as Teacher," 186. Contrast Pangle, *Socratic Life*, 170: "This time . . . Socrates said nothing about teachers of the arts. He spoke instead in terms of something like apprenticeship with the most reputable practitioners."

11. Morrison, "Socrates as Teacher," 186. See also Moore, *Socrates*, 231.

12. See Bevilacqua, "Socrates' Attitude," 465; Gabriel Danzig, "Xenophon and the Socratic *Elenchos*: The Verbal Thrashing as a Tool for Instilling *Sophrosune*," *Ancient Philosophy* 37, no. 2 (2017): 316; Danzig, *Apologizing*, 185n58, 186, 196–99; Gray, *Framing*, 14, 37, 81, 152; Gray, *Xenophon's Mirror*, 333; Genevieve Lachance, "Xenophon and the *Elenchos*: A Formal and Comparative Analysis," in Danzig, Johnson, and Morrison, *Plato and Xenophon*, 181; Morrison, "Socrates as Teacher," 188.

13. See Danzig, *Apologizing*, 184n56; Johnson, "*Memorabilia* 4.2," 50n26; Morrison, "Socrates as Teacher," 188.

14. See Dorion, "Nature of *Sophia*," 464: "moral *sophia*," rather than knowledge.

15. Morrison, "Socrates as Teacher," 186.

16. See Pangle, *Socratic Life*, 234n32.

17. O'Connor, "Self-Sufficiency," 177, 175.

18. See Johnson, "*Memorabilia* 4.2," 51: "Socrates speaks of reading texts . . . in common with his friends, i.e., of reading together in conversation," whereas, since Euthydemos refused to converse, "[he] did not read his texts in this interactive way." See also Moore, "Xenophon on 'Philosophy,'" 135.

19. See David Johnson, "The Rational Religion of Xenophon's Socrates," in *Resemblance and Reality in Greek Thought*, ed. Arum Park (New York: Routledge, 2017), 191: "[Euthydemos] was apparently rather wealthy, wealthy enough to have accumulated a large library."

20. See Danzig, *Apologizing*, 184; Gray, *Xenophon's Mirror*, 17; Johnson, "*Memorabilia* 4.2," 50; Morrison, "Socrates as Teacher," 186.

21. See Gray, *Xenophon's Mirror*, 19; Gray, *Xenophon on Government*, 6: "Euthydemos learned the 'kingly art' . . . from Socrates." Gray is not alone in collapsing virtue into art. See also Danzig, *Apologizing*, 185; Moore, *Socrates*, 219; Morrison, "Socrates as Teacher," 187; O'Connor, "Self-Sufficiency," 178. Johnson and Phillips, by collapsing art into virtue, make just the opposite mistake. See Johnson, "*Memorabilia* 4.2," 47n20, 55; John Phillips, "Xenophon's 'Memorabilia' 4.2," *Hermes* 117, no. 3 (1989): 367.

22. The fact that art and virtue switch places in IV.1.2 and IV.2.11 is rarely, if ever, appreciated. See, for example, Johnson, "*Memorabilia* 4.2," 47n20; O'Connor, "Self-Sufficiency," 177.

CHAPTER 3

1. See Moore, *Socrates*, 225: "There is something significant about the joke" that self-knowledge is knowing one's name. The significance, to which the distinction between names and numbers in IV.4.7 also draws our attention, follows from the fact that names are by convention. Is the self, having been born and raised in a city, by convention?

2. For further discussion of the contest over wisdom between Socrates and Apollo, see Eric Buzzetti, *Xenophon's Socratic Prince: The Argument of the Anabasis of Cyrus* (New York: Palgrave Macmillan, 2014), 54–58.

3. See Dustin Sebell, "The Problem of Political Science: Political Relevance and Scientific Rigor in Aristotle's 'Philosophy of Human Affairs,'" *American Journal of Political Science* 60, no. 1 (2016): 85–96.

4. Vlastos gives expression to the generally accepted opinion (that justice is not so much a matter of speaking, explaining, or knowing as of doing) when he says

> what Socrates called "knowledge" he thought both necessary and sufficient for moral goodness. I think it neither. Not necessary, for the bravest men I ever met would surely have flunked the Socratic examination on courage. Why this should be so would take long to unravel, and I have no confidence I could do it successfully. But I don't need to for the point at issue. For this I need only to stick to the fact: that a man can have great courage, yet make a fool of himself when he opens his mouth to explain what it is that he has. I am not saying that it would not be a fine thing if he could talk better, and know more . . . I am only saying it is not necessary for what Socrates did think it necessary. ("Paradox of Socrates," 15)

5. See Strauss, *Xenophon's Socrates*, 106, 108, 96.

6. Johnson sees that the writing stops at some point, but he thinks that it stops much earlier than it does merely, it seems, because some erasing must be done ("*Memorabilia* 4.2," 53). But surely Socrates was writing in the sand (consider Plato, *Meno* 82b9-10ff.). There is a general lack of awareness of the seismic shift that occurs at this point in the conversation: the refutation, strictly speaking, is over. See Danzig, *Apologizing*, 188; Lachance, "Xenophon and the *Elenchos*," 172.

7. See Roslyn Weiss, "Pity or Pardon," in Danzig, Johnson, and Morrison, *Plato and Xenophon*, 300n45: "Xenophon's Socrates blurs the distinction between the question of *which* is more unjust—intentional or unintentional deception—and the question . . . *who* is the more just man."

8. See Lachance, "Xenophon and the *Elenchos*," 173: "these two examples [grammar and justice] cannot be considered equally."

9. Leo Strauss, "The Origins of Political Science and the Problem of Socrates," *Interpretation* 23, no. 2 (1996), 170.

10. See Lachance, "Xenophon and the *Elenchos*," 173n24, 181: "It is possible that Xenophon has not presented explicitly the absurd conclusion of this reasoning because of its scandalous nature."

11. Contrast Pangle, *Socratic Life*, 176–77: Euthydemos made "the devastating discovery that his convictions about justice were incoherent," but "he lacked the heart" to live with this. The view that one can know one's ignorance and yet, owing to lack of "heart," not live with this knowledge is the tragic view of life, according to which one can know what is best and yet not do it. Knowledge, on this view, is not enough. For there can be knowledge, knowledge of ignorance, without continence. According to Socrates, however, continence is the foundation of such knowledge. See Chapter 7, Section II. See also David Bolotin, "Delphic Examinations," *St. John's Review* 53, no. 1 (2011): 87–88. Relatedly, what Pangle says about "the true, serious meaning of the famous Socratic thesis, 'virtue is knowledge'" is far from clear to me; but it is clear enough—from what he says about "opinion about the good only [being] 'knowledge' (in the Socratic sense) when that opinion is held by a consciousness in which practical reason has achieved domination over the passions"—that virtue, on his view, is not so much knowledge (in the usual sense) as continence (Thomas Pangle, *Socrates Founding Political Philosophy in Xenophon's "Economist," "Symposium" and "Apology"* [Chicago: University of Chicago Press, 2020], 18; contrast 113). Pangle arrives at his view because of the way in which Socrates "playfully personified," in *Oeconomicus* 1, "as evilly despotic demons or divinities, the psychological forces that make humans who . . . *wish* to do what they think they know will make them happy, do in fact the opposite." But the despots in question are not who, or what, he thinks ("passions"). For a good indication of their true identity, compare the last sentence or so on page 99 in Strauss, *Socratic Discourse* with the top of page 96 ("This is confirmed . . ."), the top of page 98 ("We see again . . ."), and the bottom of page 98 ("This rejoinder is strange . . .").

12. The final round of questioning is just a sophistical refutation of the fundamental assumption's necessary consequence. Pangle, by contrast, regards it as a "Socratic refutation" (*Socratic Life*, 175). But it is not the "positive," Socratic teaching—see note 27 in Chapter 1—it is the peak of the "negative," Socratic teaching that is all but missing from *Memorabilia* IV.

13. To Moore, too, "deliberate versus accidental misreading" stands out ("Xenophon on 'Philosophy,'" 135).

14. See Johnson, "*Memorabilia* 4.2," 50–51: "The limitations of writing" is "an implicit theme" of the conversation; "Plato's discussion of Socrates' views on the written word are well known. Socrates himself wrote nothing, and in the *Phaedrus* Plato has Socrates explain the limitations of writing (274B-277A; cf. *Epist.* VII 341B-344C) . . . Xenophon understood the limita-

tions of writing in much the same way that Plato did." To see that Xenophon understood the weakness of writing in the same way that Plato did, ultimately because he understood justice, self-knowledge, and the good in the same way that Plato did, compare David Levy, "Socrates' Self-Knowledge," in *Socrates in the Cave: On the Philosopher's Motive in Plato*, ed. Paul Diduch and Michael Harding (New York: Palgrave Macmillan, 2019), 77–106.

CHAPTER 4

1. According to Johnson ("*Memorabilia* 4.2," 67), "the treatment of health here is rather surprising, given the high praise Xenophon's Socrates bestows on health elsewhere. In *Memorabilia* 3.12 Socrates persuades his interlocutor to take better care of his body (cf. *Mem.* 4.7.9)." But the treatment of health is only surprising at first glance. In fact, there is perfect agreement between "the treatment of health here" and "the high praise Xenophon's Socrates bestows on health elsewhere."

2. See Bandini and Dorion, *Mémorables III*, 100n5: Before destroying Palamedes, "Odysseus simulates craziness to escape his obligations. . . . To thwart Odysseus's ploy, Palamedes . . . places the young Telemachus in front of the plow. In order to avoid crushing his son, Odysseus had to put an end to his plot. From this moment on, Odysseus dedicates himself to a tenacious hate for Palamedes."

3. The failure to see this distinction, together with the closely related assumption that Plato saw wisdom as "always good" (Johnson, "*Memorabilia* 4.2," 67), leads many classicists to believe that the argument is a "fallacy" or "a garbled version of . . . Platonic arguments" (Johnson, 68; Kahn, *Plato*, 397). Pangle, similarly, claims that "Socrates did not affirm in his own name that the goodness of wisdom is qualified or disputable"—he fails to see the distinction between "qualified" and "disputable" (consider *Socratic Life*, 179–80)—and he claims that classicists who read Socrates as speaking affirmatively ignore the "playfully ironic, tutorial dialectic" context (258n22), apparently because he believes that there is something contradictory in asserting that the greatest good for man is ambivalent or ambiguous. See, however, Dorion, "Nature of *Sophia*," 461: "There is nothing contradictory in asserting that *sophia* is the greatest good for man (4.5.6) and yet is ambivalent." Note, too, Socrates never asserted that it was good, much less unambiguously good, for him to die when he did; death was, he asserted, "better" (IV.8.6). But Pangle finds Socrates's death lacking in goodness and thus inexplicable—had it not become "gloriously shining and beneficial to humanity," at least—because he confuses its "asserted goodness" with "unambiguous goodness" (*Socratic Life*, 214; contrast 215 with 78).

4. For another reading of I.1.9, see Dorion, "Nature of *Sophia*," 471: "Men cannot trust exclusively to human knowledge for the conduct of their affairs and . . . they must call upon divination." To quote Dorion's own translation of the passage, however, "It is no less irrational to seek the guidance of heaven in matters which men are permitted by the gods to decide for themselves by study: to ask, for instance, Is it better to get an experienced coachman to drive my carriage or a man without experience? Is it better to get an experienced seaman to steer my ship or a man without experience?" So it is better to get an experienced coachman or seaman to guide you than a man, say, a diviner, without experience; and to "call upon divination," or not to "trust exclusively to human knowledge," is irrational. As for I.1.7–8, which Dorion also reads in the cursory manner, see Chapter 5, Section VII.

5. See O'Connor, "Self-Sufficiency," 178–79: "The mention of prayer reinforces the connection between 'the disputable things,' which reveal Euthydemus' ignorance, and 'the hidden things,' which are the objects of divination." See also Jones and Sharma, "Socrates on Justice," 32n22.

6. According to Pangle, by giving the best answer to the question of what a god is (*Socratic Life*, 19), "the art of *refutational* exposure and clarification of moral opinions . . . or its psychological results, provides the . . . foundation . . . for all rational science" (200, 204). "The refutations," by Pangle's account, "had as their consequence a profound change in Euthydemus's piety and praying, that is, in his religious experience of divinity" (181); "the manifest empirical consequence of Socrates's refutations was that Euthydemus," previously guided by piety, "no longer had any confidence that he should, or could, pray" (180). And "Euthydemos did not or could not find satisfactory guidance for his life by returning . . . to his pre-Socratic prayerful piety" (182) allegedly because, "as a consequence of the Socratic refutations," there was a "disintegration" of "[his] religious belief" (183). Now, according to Pangle, "Socrates tested to see if Euthydemus would react to the devastating discovery that his convictions about justice were incoherent by throwing himself into service to and guidance by . . . divinity" (177). It was supposedly this, then—that, "as a matter of empirical fact, nothing like this happened"—that Socrates "needed to learn, or to confirm, that he could not learn or confirm by confining himself to the education of the good natures," or it was supposedly the "philosophic need" to confirm this, then, that "made him spend so much time and energy on the philosophically unpromising" (168). But Pangle rests his case for a "disintegration" of Euthydemos's religious beliefs solely on the fact that Euthydemos said on this one occasion that he did not know what to pray to the gods for. And that just means, to quote Pangle's only defensible statement about the matter, "[his] *praying* had *in some measure* become paralyzed" (180; emphasis added). Besides, Euthydemos said that he did not know what to pray to the gods for precisely because he still continued to believe he knew that there was somewhere, he knew not where, something always good. In other words, by saying that he did not know what to pray to the gods for, Euthydemos gives overwhelming evidence that his religious beliefs easily withstood Socrates. Now, there is no evidence that Socrates disintegrated Euthydemos's religious beliefs—there is overwhelming evidence that he did no such thing—for the simple reason that Socrates did not disintegrate them. And he did not do so, first of all, because he had no wish to confirm that, "as a consequence of the Socratic refutations," there was a "disintegration" of Euthydemos's religious beliefs and, second, because Socrates had no expectation that the refutations of the unpromising would, "as a matter of empirical fact," have this consequence.

7. When Johnson says, "so long as we do not add disputable goods to happiness, then, happiness can remain an indisputable good" ("*Memorabilia* 4.2," 70), he is, unwittingly, giving expression to the problem of happiness, as Xenophon, Plato, and Aristotle saw it. See Plato, *Republic* 505e1–4; Sebell, "Political Science," 90ff.

8. See Pangle, *Socratic Life*, 182: "Xenophon does not show Euthydemus being thus led to disenchantment with democracy. Xenophon shows him being led to contempt for himself."

9. Johann Wolfgang von Goethe, *Conversations with Eckermann* (New York: M. Walter Dunne, 1901), 25.

10. "The 'know your powers' view [of self-knowledge] frequently attributed to Xenophon's Socrates wrongly takes the initial interpretation by Socrates' interlocutor, Euthydemus, as the view articulated throughout the entire conversation" (Moore, *Socrates*, 216). See, for various proponents of "the 'know your powers' view," Brickhouse and Smith, *Philosophy of Socrates*, 44; Dorion, "Xenophon and Greek Philosophy," 53; Johnson, "*Memorabilia* 4.2," 53, 63; Mario Montuori, *Socrates: Physiology of A Myth* (Amsterdam: J. C. Gieben, 1981), 129; Pangle, *Socratic Life*, 177–78.

11. Strauss, *Socratic Discourse*, 98.

12. Both Danzig, when he says that "without [self-knowledge] success in *private* and *political life* is impossible," (*Apologizing*, 191; emphasis added), and Johnson, when he says that "those with self-knowledge therefore *flourish* and are *honoured* ("*Memorabilia* 4.2," 63; emphasis added),

show some awareness of the monologue's central division. Annas, wholly unaware of it, collapses the first part of the monologue into the second ("the social penalties of ridicule and contempt"). See Julia Annas, "Self-Knowledge in Early Plato," in *Platonic Investigations*, ed. Dominic O'Meara (Washington, DC: Catholic University of America Press, 1985), 121. Jones and Sharma, also wholly unaware of it, collapse the second part of the monologue into the first ("human flourishing"). See Jones and Sharma, "Socrates on Justice," 33, 27–28. Pangle apparently cites Strauss's observation that "[Socrates] makes here a clear, if tacit, distinction between the good things and the noble ones" in support of his own claim that "in his speech Socrates had not mentioned the just and the noble things . . . the just and noble now suffered a partial eclipse" (*Socratic Life*, 178). But Strauss's observation, to say nothing of his account of the monologue concerning self-knowledge, undermines Pangle's claim. According to Strauss, "Socrates makes here . . . *a clear distinction*," specifically, "Socrates makes clear . . . that through self-knowledge . . . [men] acquire *the good things* and guard against the bad ones; through their knowledge . . . they become *famed and honored* and are desired as protectors, nay, rulers (*Xenophon's Socrates*, 98; emphasis added). Although Pangle claims that self-knowledge is conceived of, in this case, "as knowledge of one's own power to obtain for oneself most *good things*," nevertheless, like Danzig and Johnson, he admits in passing that self-knowers not only "provide *the good things*," according to the monologue, but also "become of *good repute and honored*" (*Socratic Life*, 177–78; emphasis added). Since he counts the latter, "being honored," among "the noble things" (40–41, 112, 117, 168), noble things had been mentioned, even by his own admission, after all. Finally, as for his claim that Socrates had not mentioned the just things, Strauss indicated the truth of the matter, as we will soon see, by observing that self-knowers "are desired as protectors, nay, *rulers* (*Xenophon's Socrates*, 98; emphasis added).

13. See Johnson, "*Memorabilia* 4.2," 64: "[Xenophon] seems to grant those who are ignorant of themselves too much knowledge. . . . [W]e have the mystery of how those who lack self-knowledge can nevertheless be sensible enough to want the self-knowers to rule them."

14. Either because he does not find it strange enough or, more probably, because he finds it too strange, Moore pays no attention to the one and only example of self-ignorance, or self-knowledge, ever given in *Memorabilia* IV.2. See Christopher Moore, "Self-Knowledge in Xenophon's *Memorabilia* 4.2," *Classical Journal* 110, no. 4 (2015): 397–417; Moore, *Socrates*, 219n6. See also, for this error of omission, Johnson, "*Memorabilia* Book 3," 483, 485–86.

15. See Gabriel Danzig, "Big Boys and Little Boys: Justice and Law in Xenophon's *Cyropaedia* and *Memorabilia*," *Polis* 26, no. 2 (2009): 295n70: "Justice is only one of the causes of military victory. There is nothing to preclude the possibility that a small just nation . . . could nevertheless be destroyed by vastly inferior but numerous unjust nations."

CHAPTER 5

1. The other animals can see, taste, touch, smell, hear (I.4.5–6). Only man, only man's *soul*, has any perception of the gods (I.4.13). Learning depends on sense perception (IV.3.11).

2. References to the fragments of the "pre-Socratic" philosophers follow the standard "Diels–Kranz" numbering system found in Hermann Diels, *Die Fragmente der Vorsokratiker*, 3 vols., ed. Walther Kranz, 9th ed. (Berlin: Weidmannsche Verlagsbuchhandlung, [1952] 1882).

3. For the sake of brevity, I am glossing over an important point: Socrates does not say anything about "the god," much less "the gods," until Aristodemos forces the issue about halfway through the conversation (I.4.9–11ff.).

4. With few, if any, exceptions (I.4.17–18, for example, is not an argument by any stretch of the imagination), Socrates is not advancing arguments in his own name; he is merely asking questions. And yet it is generally believed that Socrates is advancing arguments in his own name. See Joseph DeFilippo and Phillip Mitsis, "Socrates and Stoic Natural Law," in Vander Waerdt, *Socratic Movement*, 256; Sedley, *Creationism*, 83–85; Vander Waerdt, "Socrates in the Clouds," 85.

5. Sedley, by contrast, comes to the conclusion that "Xenophon's Socrates is a fundamentally anti-scientific creationist," whose argument "purports to demonstrate, by citing evidence of rational design in the natural world, the existence of *a creator god*" (*Creationism*, 78–86). But Sedley, who seems to think that trying "to demonstrate" something "by citing evidence" is "anti-scientific," has no grasp of the terms of the debate between creationism and its critics. If, say, "the channel through which excrement is voided was located as far away from our noses and eyes *as could be managed*" (81; emphasis added), the so-called god cannot possibly be a creator. Sedley is not alone. Just as it is generally believed that Socrates is advancing arguments in his own name, when, in fact, he is merely asking questions, it is generally believed that Socrates is arguing for a creator god, when, in fact, nothing could be further from the truth. See Gray, *Framing*, 37; Guthrie, *Socrates*, 155–56. For a vastly superior treatment of the issue, as it arises in Plato's *Timaeus* at least, see R. J. Hankinson, *Cause and Explanation in Ancient Greek Thought* (Oxford: Oxford University Press, 1998), 109: "Plato's Artisan is not, like the God of Genesis, a creator ex nihilo. He is an organizer, working with preexisting materials which impose material constraints on what he can produce."

6. See Leo Strauss, *On Tyranny*, ed. Victor Gourevitch and Michael Roth (Chicago: University of Chicago Press, 2000), 115–16n40: "It is an open question whether Simonides, or Xenophon, considered the deity an incorporeal being. As for Xenophon's view of this subject, compare *Memorabilia* I.4.17 and context (for the interpretation consider Cicero, *De Natura Deorum* I.12.30–31 and III.10.26–27)." See also Werner Jaeger, *The Theology of the Early Greek Philosophers* (Oxford: Clarendon Press, 1947), 169: "The relation between soul and body corresponds exactly to that between God and the world."

7. See W. E. Higgins, *Xenophon the Athenian: The Problem of the Individual and the Society of the Polis* (Albany: State University of New York Press, 1977), 32, 34: "One of Aristodemos' most penetrating complaints [is] do the gods care for the *individual* man?" Nevertheless, "[Socrates] does not answer with forthright assurance Aristodemos' question about the gods' philanthropy to the *individual* man" (emphasis added). See also Pangle, *Socratic Life*, 53.

8. Accordingly, Socrates was accused of bringing in new *daimonia* "especially" (*malista*)—not solely—because he said the *daimonion* gave him signs (I.1.2). See Mark McPherran, *Religion of Socrates* (University Park, PA: Penn State University Press, 1996), 278–79n101. See also Johnson, "Rational Religion," 178.

9. Contrast Dorothea Frede, "Theodicy and Providential Care in Stoicism," in *Traditions of Theology: Studies in Hellenistic Theology, Its Background and Aftermath*, ed. Dorothea Frede and Andre Laks (Leiden: Brill, 2002), 86: "[Socrates] made a convert of his associate Aristodemus by a highly refined argument from design." In fact, "[Xenophon] does not say that Aristodemus learnt his lesson on this occasion" (Johnson, "*Memorabilia* 4.2," 42).

10. For this reason, while Socrates may have said on other occasions that the gods offer *him* advice they withhold from all other human beings, he did not do so here, just where one would most expect him to. See Pangle, *Socratic Life*, 53–54: "Socrates dodges the challenge [to articulate a convincing account of the *daimonion*] . . . doubtless confirming Aristodemus's disbelief in his master's claims about [it]."

11. See Gabriel Danzig, "Xenophon's Wicked Persian, or What's Wrong with Tissaphernes? Xenophon's Views on Lying and Breaking Oaths," in *Persian Responses: Political and Cultural*

Interaction with(in) the Archaemenid Empire, ed. Christopher Tuplin (Swansea: Classical Press of Wales, 2007), 48n28: "According to the logic of Socrates' question, it is only those who believe that the gods have implanted such a belief in us who must confess their power."

12. Do the gods *do* anything (I.1.19)? Or are they gentlemen in the strict sense (I.1.16)? Contrast I.4.16 and *Oeconomicus* 7.31.

13. *Guide of the Perplexed*, trans. Shlomo Pines (Chicago: University of Chicago Press, 1963), III.17.

14. See McPherran, *Religion of Socrates*, 278n99; J. D. Mikalson, *Athenian Popular Religion* (Chapel Hill: University of North Carolina Press, 1983), 39; Nathan Powers, "The Natural Theology of Xenophon's Socrates," *Ancient Philosophy* 29, no. 2 (2009): 250.

15. *Summa Contra Gentiles*, trans. Anton Pegis (Garden City, NY: Doubleday, 1955), I, ch. 9, ¶2.

16. Notwithstanding his own translation of I.1.11 ("he did not discourse about the nature of the physical universe, as most of the other philosophers did")—not to mention, among other things, I.1.16 ("and about the other [nonhuman] things"), IV.6.1, IV.6.7, IV.7.3, IV.7.5, I.4, IV.3, *Oeconomicus* 11.3, and *Symposium* 6.6–7.2ff.—Dorion believes that Xenophon had claimed there, in I.1.11, that Socrates's "interest in questions dealing with human matters" was "exclusive" ("Xenophon and Greek Philosophy," 40). See also Vander Waerdt, "Socrates in the Clouds," 80; Vlastos, "Socratic Piety," 57. But contrast Johnson, "Rational Religion," 196n23: "Xenophon says not that Socrates did not study the cosmos, but that he did not study it *like the sophists do* (i.e., like the Presocratics)." Contrast also DeFilippo and Mitsis, "Natural Law," 259: "The inconsistency [between *Memorabilia* I.4 and I.1] begins to dissolve when one recognizes that in *Memorabilia* I.1 Xenophon qualifies the claim that Socrates eschews the study of nature as a whole."

17. For the use of the term "revelation" in the Greek context, see Asli Gocer, "A New Assessment of Socratic Philosophy of Religion," in Smith and Woodruff, *Reason and Religion*, 123–25; Mark McPherran, "Socratic Reason and Socratic Revelation," *Journal of the History of Philosophy* 29, no. 3 (1991): 345–73; Vlastos, "Socratic Piety." See also note 20 in this chapter.

18. See also Pangle, *Socratic Life*, 233n19.

19. Since he treats both shortcomings together in the person of Aristodemos, Xenophon's suggestion would seem to be that only those whose thoughts are not what they should be openly reveal them in speech, much less in deed. See Chapter 6, Section V.

20. See McPherran, *Religion of Socrates*, 275n91:

> Although we never see Socrates make the sort of distinction between "natural" theology and "revealed" theology the natural theologians of the seventeenth and eighteenth centuries employed, the basic distinction between the two appears to be recognized by Socrates *in practice*. For although on the one hand we see here (and elsewhere) an attempt to develop and justify a conception of divinity through the unaided use of "secular reason," we have seen that Socrates also retains an important role in his philosophizing for the extrarational incursions by the divine recognized by ancient religious tradition. These sources are properly termed "extrarational"—and in a sense comparable to modern talk of "revelation."

21. See McPherran, 276: "Even the motion of the sun and earth seem providentially coordinated to serve the needs imposed by our (*necessary?*) human frailty (and presumably those needs imposed on animals)" (emphasis added).

22. Contrast Pangle, *Socratic Life*, 185.

23. As the reference to "unenviously" given air goes to show, whoever was responsible for the interpolation found here in the Vatican manuscript understood Xenophon very well—so well, in fact, that one wonders whether this really is an interpolation. See Bandini and Dorion, *Mémorables III*, 124n1: "the passage was considered to be authentic by many classicists at the end of the eighteenth and beginning of the nineteenth centuries."

24. Anthony Ellis, "A Socratic History: Theology in Xenophon's Rewriting of Herodotus' Croesus *Logos*," *Journal of Hellenic Studies* 136 (2016): 81. See also Pangle, *Socratic Life*, 185: "Socrates broke with a cardinal belief of traditional Greek faith and piety, which expresses the envy and hostility of Zeus toward humanity."

25. See, ad loc., Bandini and Dorion, *Mémorables III*; Marchant, *Xenophon*. Contrast Karl Hude, *Xenophontis Commentarii* (Stuttgart: Teubner, 1934), ad loc.

26. See McPherran, *Religion of Socrates*, 285: "The teleological argument preserved by Xenophon is in a sense a *political* argument: the existence of well-ordered human communities argues for the existence of what is a necessary condition of such order, namely, a divine lawgiver, a being who provides the foundations for conventional legislation." But what sort of "teleological argument" is that, then? "The necessary condition of such order" is really only widespread belief in a divine lawgiver, which is to say, revealed theology. See Gabriel Danzig, "Plato, Aristotle, and Xenophon on the Ends of Virtue," in Danzig, Johnson, and Morrison, *Plato and Xenophon*, 344: "The assistance of the gods is necessary precisely because virtue aims at political success but cannot guarantee it." See Chapter 6, Section IV.

27. Despite saying that "Socrates uses *theoi* or *to daimonion* indifferently to designate the gods" (Bandini and Dorion, *Mémorables III*, 130–31n10), Dorion also says that "Socrates distinguishes, in §13, *the gods* dispensers of goods . . . from *the god* who orders and maintains all of the universe" (128n6). See, for additional examples of equivocation on this point, Guthrie, *Socrates*, 155; McPherran, *Religion of Socrates*, 278; Sedley, *Creationism*, 79, 149n33. See also note 5 in this chapter.

28. In *Memorabilia* IV.3, as the constant repetition of *deometha* goes to show, the emphasis is on the fact that, given human nature, the world is designed to satisfy our natural needs, whereas in I.4 the emphasis is on the fact that human beings are designed to get by in the given, natural world. For example, IV.3 begins with Socrates saying that we need light (for our eyes) to see what can be seen, whereas I.4 begins with Socrates saying that we need eyes to see what can be seen. See also Section IV in this chapter. The difference of emphasis—on account of which the two conversations form a vicious circle, where the world depends on human nature and human nature depends also, or instead, on the world—serves to bring out the element of chance, or the role played by "the god," in any and all "natural theology."

29. Contrast David Leibowitz, *The Ironic Defense of Socrates: Plato's Apology* (Cambridge: Cambridge University Press, 2010) 92–99; Leibowitz, "Reply to Levy: Socrates's Post-Delphic Refutations," *Interpretation* 39, no. 1 (2012): 95–102. According to Leibowitz, Plato's Socrates suspects that all religious beliefs derive from moral beliefs, "but not being certain, he is eager for confirmation" (*Ironic Defense*, 93). However, since Leibowitz does not distinguish this suspicion from the very different suspicion that "believers, whether they know it or not, expect the gods to be bound by some kind of humanly intelligible law or justice," he thinks that Socrates is eager for confirmation of this—that "believers . . . expect the gods to be bound by some kind of humanly intelligible law or justice" (*Ironic Defense*, 71–72, 93–95; David Levy, "Reply to Leibowitz," *Interpretation* 39, no. 2 [2012]: 225). Now, on this score, we have already been given reason to doubt that Leibowitz's Socrates is Plato's. See David Levy, review of *The Ironic Defense of Socrates*, by David Leibowitz, *Interpretation* 38, no. 3 (2011): 261–76; "Reply to Leibowitz," 223–

30. On one hand, I have nothing to add to what Levy said there. On the other hand, since Leibowitz is aware that there are no fundamental differences between Plato's Socrates and Xenophon's (*Ironic Defense*, 76ff., 97n70, 100n74, 105n82, 183), let me add to Levy's reasons for doubting that Leibowitz's Socrates is Plato's just one or two of the same reasons for doubting that Leibowitz's Socrates is Xenophon's. First, whereas Leibowitz's Socrates tries to confirm that religious beliefs derive from moral beliefs by trying to confirm that believers are "unable to believe that the [divine] command either possesses a moral perfection that eludes the grasp of human reason or is divine despite being morally imperfect," Xenophon's Socrates, like Plato's, does no such thing (*Ironic Defense*, 93; Leibowitz, "Reply to Levy," 99; see Levy, "Reply to Liebowitz," 225–26). According to Leibowitz, "in his post-Delphic refutations Socrates must sometimes have brought up the gods" ("Reply to Levy," 96–97). As Pangle observes, however, "[the refutations] were not about religious subjects," by Xenophon's account (*Socratic Life*, 183, 181). And Xenophon's Socrates does not try to confirm that religious beliefs derive from moral beliefs in this way, by bringing up the gods, not only because he feels no need to do so but also because he does not suspect that "believers . . . expect the gods to be bound by some kind of humanly intelligible law or justice." Second, that is, Xenophon's Socrates is certain that if indeed religious beliefs derive from moral beliefs in the manner indicated here, in IV.3, to say nothing of Plato's *Euthyphro*, Leibowitz's "fundamental point" misses the mark: as even he concedes (*Ironic Defense*, 95, 99n72), the believer *need not* raise, and—one might add—maybe even cannot exactly raise, "the claim that the god's commandments and actions are just" (*Ironic Defense* 94–95; "Reply to Levy," 98–99; see Levy, "Reply to Leibowitz," 228). First, then, by making them do more work than Socrates needed them to do, Leibowitz underestimates the Socratic refutations (and overestimates revealed religion); second, by refusing to acknowledge the very real possibility of superhuman wisdom, which, by definition, "eludes the grasp of human reason," Leibowitz underestimates revealed religion (and overestimates the Socratic refutations) (Levy, "Reply to Leibowitz," 226–27n8). And he both underestimates and overestimates the Socratic refutations, as it seems to me, because he does not understand moral beliefs, or the manner in which religious beliefs derive from moral beliefs, as Socrates did. Another indication of this is that Leibowitz neither saw the need to answer nor understood the question of how religious beliefs derive from moral beliefs. See Leibowitz, "Reply to Levy," 100–102; Levy, "Reply to Leibowitz," 230.

30. Dorion, who makes every effort to cast this in the best possible light, cannot help but notice that to offer sacrifices to the gods "according to one's power" is to offer them less—infinitely less—than they deserve (*Mémorables III*, 131–32n2).

CHAPTER 6

1. See Vivienne Gray, "Xenophon's Socrates and Democracy," *Polis* 28, no. 1 (2011): 13.

2. See Dorion, "Straussian Exegesis," 311–12: "We might believe that Socrates' disobedience concerns only the episode of Leon of Salamis. Since the text is clear that Socrates 'alone did not obey,' several people must have had the opportunity to disobey; so it was the order to arrest Leon of Salamis, which was given to Socrates 'and some others of the citizens.' The expression 'alone did not obey' therefore does not seem to refer to the ban against conversing with the city's youth. Moreover, the ban on teaching the art of argument exclusively and directly targets Socrates (I 2, 31); in this case, it would be strange to specify that he was the only one who refused to obey." See also David Johnson, "Xenophon's Socrates on Law and Justice," *Ancient Philosophy*

23, no. 2 (2012): 276: "Xenophon does not tell us here whether Socrates obeyed this law once it had been explained to him. At iv 4.3 Xenophon implies that Socrates disobeyed, but his language there is just vague enough to leave open the possibility that he did obey. Certainly Xenophon does not stress Socrates' disobedience, if disobey he did. Perhaps Socrates disobeyed only in private, or otherwise managed to restrain himself for the short time the Thirty had left in power." Since Socrates was not put to death by the Thirty (I.2.37), it is safe to assume that he obeyed the law. See, finally, Darrel Colson, "On Appealing to Athenian Law to Justify Socrates' Disobedience," *Apeiron* 19, no. 2 [1985]: 139: "No commentator, either ancient or modern, has followed Xenophon's lead in declaring the law about teaching to be illegal. I am not even sure on what grounds such a declaration could be made." But again, Xenophon made no such declaration.

3. See Dorion, "Different Reasons," 507: "The appeals to pity are not in themselves illegal; what is illegal is their use to incite the judges . . . to break their oath to judge the case in accordance with the law."

4. The suggestion that jurors will no longer be divided in their votes stands out (compare IV.4.8 with IV.4.11), especially because the trial of Socrates was only just mentioned. According to Socrates, if knowledge of justice were universal, would jurors not be divided on the injustice of not believing in the gods?

5. See Bandini and Dorion, *Mémorables III*, 139n11.

6. Richard Rorty, *Contingency, Irony, Solidarity* (Cambridge: Cambridge University Press, 1989), 46.

7. See Weiss, "Pity or Pardon," 299: "Socrates' account of justice is not one of those moral lessons he purportedly offers freely and generously to all comers," "[Socrates] offers a definition of justice only under duress." See also, for this view, Gray, *Xenophon's Mirror*, 364; Johnson, "Intertextual Socrates," 84; Moore, "Socratic Education," 510.

8. See Colson, "Socrates' Disobedience," 142–43:

> There was no anguish over poor Leon's plight. Did Socrates try to warn him? There is no indication that he did. . . . Did he try to talk them out of making the arrest? There is no evidence that he did. *Did he object in the presence of those among the Thirty who issued the command?* Here again, no evidence. If indeed he tried at all to avert Leon's tragedy, his efforts were not considered significant enough to mention by either Plato or Xenophon. All we know is that Socrates absented himself from the situation. . . . The disobedience or defiance is self-centered, and it seems to ignore the suffering to be endured by Leon (emphasis added).

As for the Arginusae generals, Colson concludes that we are encouraged, by Plato and Xenophon,

> to envision Socrates fighting fiercely against the mob, first opposing their base intentions, then voting against their resolutions. But if the Hellenica is to be believed, and it is virtually our only historic account of this trial, Socrates' "opposition" simply was his "voting against" the proposal of Callixeinus . . . and this is the intriguing point, Socrates does nothing more. But the curiosity is that he really did not make any effort to avert the disaster. Why did he not join with Euryptolemus in bringing the *graphē paranomon*? . . . For that matter, why was Euryptolemus alone when he "mounted the platform and spoke . . . in defence of the generals"? *Why did Socrates not mount the platform and attempt to convince the Assembly to reconsider its plan?* . . . Once again, we are confronted with Socrates' "lack of love" (146–47; emphasis added).

See also Anderson, *Xenophon*, 47n1; Johnson, "Law and Justice," 276.

9. Dorion takes the view that, for Socrates and Xenophon, "a man's virtue is measured and shown more by his actions than his discourse" ("Straussian Exegesis," 301). But he is not aware of the conversation's many subtle, and not so subtle, references to intentionality, including even Socrates's own redefinition of justice in terms of . . . intentionality.

10. For the fact *that* Hippias is bewildered, see Moore, "Socratic Education," 511; Donald Morrison, "Xenophon's Socrates on the Just and the Lawful," *Ancient Philosophy* 15, no. 2 (2012): 329. But *why* is Hippias bewildered? The plot thickens when, as we will see, Hippias so readily agrees with the conclusion that the lawful and the just are one and the same thing (IV.4.18). Such a sudden reversal (if it is one) is astonishing, "given Hippias' status as a sophist, and his negative attitude toward the positive law of the city" (Johnson, "Law and Justice," 272; see also Bandini and Dorion, *Mémorables III*, 139n11), on one hand, and given that Socrates's argument makes virtually no mention of justice, on the other (IV.4.15–17). Why does Hippias so readily agree? Both questions, the question of why Hippias is so bewildered and the question of why he so readily agrees with Socrates, point to what is really at issue in the conversation. Pangle mistakes Hippias's bewilderment at what Socrates said for doubt that Socrates "meant it" (*Socratic Life*, 193) because he wrongly assumes that "the *identification* of the legal with the just must be an *exoteric* teaching of Socrates" (190–91).

11. See Danzig, "Big Boys," 182: "Taken literally this identification of the lawful and the just implies that there is no standard of justice other than the law." But that is only one possibility. Better, at least in this respect, was Danzig's earlier statement concerning *Cyropaedia* I.3.16–17: "By saying the *nomimon* is just, Cyrus' teacher means simply to identify the two. This could mean *either* assimilating the just to the lawful and adopting a positivist legal position which claims that whatever is established by law must be considered just; *or* it could mean assimilating the lawful to the just, adopting what Morrison calls an idealist position and claiming that whatever is just must be considered lawful" (280; emphasis added). In another respect, however, this statement is worse than his later one. For the "positivist" position would then seem to mean that "positive laws are to be obeyed precisely because they have been adopted by the community" (Johnson, "Rational Religion," 187). And this is not what the anti-idealist position means—see note 12 in this chapter—this is what the modern and, to put one of Johnson's remarks to good use, "strikingly naïve version of legal positivism" means (188). See, for a better discussion of the "positivist" and "idealist" positions, Leo Strauss, *Liberalism, Ancient and Modern* (New York: Basic Books, 1968), 67: "In a way law and justice seem to be interchangeable; hence law will be something high. But a city's opinions may be low. We are confronted then with a contradiction between the two most audible opinions which are so audible because they are opinions of the city: the opinion that the law is the opinion of the city and the opinion that the law is something high." The issue here, as we will soon see, is whether or not the law is "something high" or, to use Hippias's word, "serious." See also Johnson, "Law and Justice," 272.

12. See Leo Strauss, *The City and Man* (Chicago: University of Chicago Press), 75–76: "If the just is identical with the legal, the source of justice is the will of the legislator. The legislator in each city is the regime: the tyrant, the common people, the men of excellence, and so on. Each regime lays down the laws with a view to its own preservation and well-being, to its own advantage. From this it follows that obedience to the laws or justice is not necessarily to the advantage of those who do not belong to the regime or to the ruled or may be bad for them."

13. Strauss, *Xenophon's Socrates*, 111.

14. See Strauss, 113: "Disparaging the laws on the grounds which [Hippias] adduced is tantamount to disparaging patriotic war efforts."

15. See Higgins, *Xenophon the Athenian*, 132: "[Socrates] succeeds in doing what Socrates elsewhere called next to impossible: he praises [the Spartans]," and blames the Athenians, "to Athenians."

16. Dorion claims that Socrates said, at IV.4.15, that "the best leaders are law-abiding" ("Different Reasons," 495). But of course, since the rulers make the laws, Socrates never said that. Relatedly, Socrates spoke finally of concord in cities and concord in households as if they were no different from one another (IV.4.16). Households, however, are not ruled by law.

17. A lot would be required to show how carefully worded and arranged the twelve questions are. So let me leave it at mentioning only the list's two most important puzzles. First, Socrates moves from the benefits a lawful man receives from others to the benefits a lawful man gives to others. Second, about halfway through, Socrates suddenly, and quite shockingly, treats the lawful man as if he were a lawful *army* or a lawful *city* unto himself, making peace with other *armies* or *cities*, forming alliances with them and leading the allies (IV.2.15–17, IV.2.29, and consider, also, IV.5.2). The list turns out to have some bearing on the question, to which Socrates's first argument impels one (IV.4.15–16), "What is a city?" See Pangle, *Socratic Life*, 194: "[Socrates is] preoccupied with the threat of and from one's enemies, and hence the need for friends and allies, in a state of war. . . . Socrates almost sounds like Hobbes."

18. Socrates is merely asking questions. As before (see note 4 in Chapter 5), however, it is generally believed that he is advancing arguments in his own name. See, for example, Dorion "Different Reasons," 495; Gray "Socrates and Democracy," 10; Morrison "Socrates on the Just," 336. According to Dorion, "Socrates presents his demonstration in §17 in the form of a long sequence of questions that are in fact so many affirmations" (*Mémorables III*, 157n2). Since when, however, is a long sequence of questions a "demonstration," and not . . . a long sequence of questions? See also Johnson, "Law and Justice," 273.

19. See Colson, "Socrates' Disobedience," 143: "Two [of the Arginusae generals] saw the writing on the wall and did not return to Athens."

20. Gray is simply unaware that to prove that "obedience to the laws is the foundation of the success of entire communities" is not to prove that lawfulness is essential to an individual's "success" (*Xenophon's Mirror*, 364; *Xenophon on Government*, 10; "Socrates and Democracy," 3). See also Ferrario, "Xenophon and Greek Political Thought," 61. "On this view," however, "an argument could be made to justify occasional deviation from the law when such deviation would bring significant or preponderant benefit" (Danzig, "Big Boys," 282).

21. It is not at all true to say that "Socrates actually argues," in IV.4.13–17, "that it is always just to obey the law" (Danzig, "Big Boys," 282). See also Vander Waerdt, "Socratic Justice," 45. Justice is never mentioned—except once, remarkably, in a question that would seem to suggest that the lawful are not the most likely to receive the just (good) things from others (IV.4.17). Johnson says, more accurately, "Socrates does not present any argument to show that the just and the lawful in fact coincide, as we might have expected; instead, he argues that the laws of the city are *a serious matter* by showing how beneficial it is to obey them" ("Law and Justice," 272; emphasis added). On this, however, even he wavers (279). The widespread failure to grasp what it might mean to say that the lawful and the just are the same thing—for which "the strikingly naïve version of legal positivism" peculiar to modern political thought is largely to blame (consider Strauss, *City and Man*, 43–44)—has led to the equally widespread failure to grasp that what is at issue in the conversation is whether or not the lawful is something high or serious, *not* whether the lawful and the just are the same thing. See Danzig, "Big Boys," 282; Gera, *Xenophon's "Cyropaedia,"* 75; Morrison, "Socrates on the Just," 337.

22. See Gisela Striker, "Origins of the Concept of Natural Law," in *Proceedings of the Boston Area Colloquium of Ancient Philosophy* 2 (1986): 88–89: "What Xenophon has to offer in support of Socrates' alleged definition of justice are in fact arguments to support the quite different thesis that it is just and beneficial to obey the law of one's city. . . . Next, without explaining the connection, Socrates is made to introduce the so-called 'unwritten laws.'" Striker is not entirely wrong; however, she fails to appreciate that Xenophon knew better than anyone that Socrates's arguments support a "quite different thesis," on one hand, and that the connection between the written laws and the unwritten laws is fully explained, on the other, by the fact that Socrates's arguments do not adequately support the thesis in question. Note that Dorion initially says, "[Socrates] tries to show that obedience to the laws is *always advantageous* to the state and the individual. The rewards of obedience to the [human] laws are reasons to obey them," before going on to say, shortly thereafter, "the great advantage of the divine laws over human ones, for Xenophon's Socrates, lies in the fact that the transgressor cannot avoid divine punishment (cf. 4.4.21), which by implication means that it is not only possible to break human laws *with impunity*, it is also possible to break human laws *without incurring any harm whatsoever*" ("Different Reasons," 495, 497; emphasis added). Unless he really meant that Socrates tries, *and admittedly fails*, "to show that obedience to the laws is always advantageous," Dorion contradicts himself. Either way, even by his own admission, there are not always reasons to obey the human law after all. And Socrates "is made to introduce the so-called 'unwritten laws'" in order to solve the problem of the rationality of the written laws. As it turns out, while Dorion may not be entirely wrong to say that "we do not have a single good reason to doubt that Xenophon's Socrates was a legal positivist" (Bandini and Dorion, *Mémorables III*, 146n3), he has no idea what he is saying. Despite his vague misgivings about legal positivism (168n1; "Different Reasons," 498, 489; "Straussian Exegesis," 316), a legal positivist, by his "strikingly naïve" account, always obeys the law. Elsewhere, in "a list of sixty-two points of convergence," real or imagined, "between [Socrates and Ischomachus]," which Dorion compiled, "to show that the Straussian reading of the *Oeconomicus* has little to recommend it, given the more or less complete agreement between Socrates and Ischomachus," he makes one mistake after another ("Fundamental Parallels," 522). And one particularly big mistake is relevant here. For Dorion refers to *Oeconomicus* 7.31, on one hand, and *Memorabilia* IV.4.21–24, on the other, in the belief that they show convergence between Ischomachus and Socrates on the view that "acting contrary to a natural disposition is *automatically punished*" (524; emphasis added). However, while Socrates speaks here, in IV.4, of laws that are automatically punished, what Ischomachus said, in *Oeconomicus* 7.31, was that lawbreakers are "perhaps" (*isōs*) noticed by the gods and punished. Accordingly, Socrates does not say, what Ischomachus stresses, that the law "praises" (7.16, consider 14.3–10). In any event, lest one make the further mistake of thinking that one little "perhaps" makes no difference, let me add that *the* difference between the written and the divine laws in IV.4 is . . . one little "perhaps." Those who act contrary to the written laws are *perhaps* (noticed by human beings and) punished, whereas those who act contrary to the divine laws are *definitely* punished. See note 29 in this chapter.

23. See John Locke, "A Letter Concerning Toleration," in *Two Treatises of Government and A Letter Concerning Toleration*, ed. Ian Shapiro (London: Yale University Press, 2003), 231: "How easily and smoothly the clergy changed their decrees, their articles of faith, their forms of worship, everything, according to the inclination of those kings and queens. Yet were those kings and queens of such different minds, in points of religion, and enjoined thereupon such different things, that no man in his wits, *I had almost said none but an atheist*, will presume to say that any sincere and upright worshipper of God could, with a safe conscience, obey their several decrees" (emphasis added).

24. See Danzig, "Big Boys," 283n41: "The unwritten law seems to be a general principle expressed differently in different societies. While the unwritten law obliges worship of the gods, the particular form of worship is determined by the local written law."

25. See Danzig, 285; Morrison, "Socrates on the Just," 340.

26. Johnson, "Law and Justice," 264–65. See also Bandini and Dorion, *Mémorables III*, 164n1; Danzig, "Big Boys," 283–84; Gray, "Socrates and Democracy," 11.

27. See Danzig, "Big Boys," 283n42; Dorion, "Straussian Exegesis," 309; Gray, "Socrates and Democracy," 11.

28. For example, Socrates was punished by a city for teaching, and for thinking, that there was nothing wrong with a (wise) son enslaving his (unwise) father (I.2.49–50) and for saying that (unwise) parents are undeserving of honor (I.2.51–55). See Danzig, "Big Boys," 284, 284–85n45: "Xenophon saw moral and religious failings as causes of damage . . . to the individual. . . . Neglecting one's parents *may* bring the loss of allies who despite physical infirmity *may* be a source of valuable wisdom" (emphasis added). Danzig thus unwittingly makes the case that honoring parents is not a law enacted by the gods. See also Johnson, "Law and Justice," 272.

29. See Bandini and Dorion, *Mémorables III*, 159–60n1: "It would be difficult, nay, impossible to assimilate the three other unwritten laws (honor the gods, honor parents, be grateful) to the laws of *physis*, so that it is clearly inappropriate to affirm that these laws 'come principally from *physis*.'" But then, by Dorion's own admission, these unwritten laws—and thus the written laws with which they are "in perfect accord" (see, for example, "Straussian Exegesis," 308)—are not by nature. This offhand remark, with which he, unawares, seconds Hippias's antinomianism, is the closest that Dorion ever comes to grasping what is at issue in the conversation.

30. Strauss, *Xenophon's Socrates*, 109.

31. For further discussion of "ancient" and "modern" sophistry, see Christopher Bruell, *On the Socratic Education: An Introduction to the Shorter Platonic Dialogues* (Lanham, MD: Rowman and Littlefield, 1999), 76–78.

CHAPTER 7

1. See Edmunds, "Xenophon's Triad," 257: "The first . . . virtues are moral, the rest are intellectual."

2. Contrast Bandini and Dorion, *Mémorables III*, 133n8: "The program set in §2 is thus fulfilled. Socrates's first objective is indeed to render his companions moderate; in order to reach this end, he shows them to what extent the gods are at once powerful . . . and benevolent. . . . This demonstration has for its effect to render them moderate . . . and pious." There is no denying that Xenophon wrote in a way calculated to give cursory readers the impression that Dorion, among others, comes away with. But nor is there any denying that Dorion is reading, involuntarily, "according to the principle that what Xenophon says is . . . the opposite of what he means" (Flower, "Introduction," 7). For what Xenophon says in IV.3.18 is that the program, as set in IV.3.2, remains unfulfilled.

3. See Gray, *Framing*, 81: Euthydemos was only "*imitating* [Socrates's] *practices*" (emphasis added). See also Morrison, "Socrates as Teacher," 188: "[Euthydemos] hangs out with Socrates as much as he can, and even begins to *imitate* some of Socrates' *practices*" (emphasis added). Of course, Xenophon does not say that Socrates taught Euthydemos to converse (contrast IV.2.40 with IV.3.1, IV.5.12, and IV.6.1). Moreover, Euthydemos never left Socrates's side, unless there was "some necessity" (IV.2.40). But Socrates's "*daimonion*" was just such a necessity (*Symposium* 8.4). Because Socrates refused payment, Euthydemos could not "collect" him, just as he collected books

of men reputed to be wise (I.2.6, I.6.5). On the other hand, by remembering Socrates, Xenophon was benefitted even when Socrates was not present (IV.1.1, consider I.2.21). Xenophon did not always remain by Socrates's side. For *the* treatment of Xenophon's absence from Socrates in the *Anabasis*, see Buzzetti, *Xenophon's Socratic Prince*.

4. See O'Connor, "Self-Sufficiency," 179: "The self-knowledge Socrates provided to his gentlemanly friends is primarily a pious acknowledgment of human limitation in the face of the divine, rather than the empowering kingly art they so coveted at the beginning of their intercourse with him. . . . [P]olitical ambition [transmutes] into pious humility." See also O'Connor, "Enviable Life," 70: "We hear no more of Euthydemus's pursuing his grand ambitions . . . Socrates teaches him that this knowledge [of what kingship requires] is not humanly available—it depends on divination . . . Euthydemus will have to rethink his ambitions in light of this chastening understanding of the divine."

5. See Danzig, *Apologizing*, 192; Danzig, "Socratic *Elenchos*," 313.

6. Contrast Moore, "Socratic Education," 501: "For Socrates as educator, *sōphrosunē* always came first."

7. See Natali, "Socrates' Dialectic," 11.

8. For the interpretation of I.5.3, see Strauss, *Xenophon's Socrates*, 27: "While greed is thought to be harmful only to others but helpful to oneself, incontinence is harmful to others but still more so to oneself; greed is compatible with continence and perhaps even calls for it (cf. also *Oeconomicus* XII.11–16)." Recall that making immoderate youths skilled in action would only make them even more unjust and more capable of evildoing (IV.3.1–2). See also, for further discussion of continence in the *Memorabilia*, Eric Buzzetti, "The 'Middle Road' of Socratic Political Philosophy: Xenophon's Presentation of Socrates' View of Virtue in the *Memorabilia*" (PhD diss., Boston College, 1998), 42–66.

9. On the other hand, to define continence by reference to "the most excellent things," for example, is not to say that continence is among "the most excellent things." Contrast Dorion, "Nature of *Sophia*," 474–75: "self-mastery is the fundamental basis of virtue. . . . In this one sees again that *enkrateia* takes precedence over *sophia*." To say that "self-mastery is the fundamental basis of virtue," or "the necessary condition for . . . [*sophia*]" (458), is to say that self-mastery is not virtue or *sophia*. Virtue or *sophia*, as the end to which *enkrateia* is a means, takes precedence over *enkrateia*. But of course, having said that, the means comes before the end. See Chapter 2, Section VI.

10. See Strauss, *Xenophon's Socrates*, 115: "Moderation differs from wisdom as caring, practice, assiduity differ from knowledge. The silence here on piety and justice does not require further explanation." Consider, on the bottom of page 114 in *Xenophon's Socrates*, Strauss's use of *or*.

11. See note 11 in Chapter 3. As for "the preventers" (*tous kōlusontas*) mentioned at IV.5.3, their identity is almost as shocking as the true identity of the beast-like or cattle-like men mentioned at IV.5.11. For the identity of the latter, see, for example, Bruell, "Strauss on Xenophon's Socrates," 301. Consider IV.5.4–5 and *Oeconomicus* 5.13 for the identity of the former.

CHAPTER 8

1. Contrast Strauss, *Xenophon's Socrates*, 116–17. Considering IV.7.8 (*suneskopei, sundiexēei*), the *en* of manuscript B should, I think, be rejected. As was partly indicated once already, and as we will see much more clearly soon enough, IV.7.8 refers back to IV.6.1 and IV.6.13–15.

2. Patzer also sees that IV.6.1 and I.1.16 are closely connected ("Socrates as Dialectician," 242–43).

3. Strauss, *Xenophon's Socrates*, 177.

4. See Grote, *Plato*, 4 vols., 1:248, 260n.

5. Despite the striking resemblance to IV.2.31–36, it is generally believed that the previous occasion on which Socrates refuted Aristippus was II.1. See Danzig, "Socratic *Elenchos*," 303; Gray, *Framing*, 143; David Johnson, "Aristippus at the Crossroads: The Politics of Pleasure in Xenophon's *Memorabilia*," *Polis* 26, no. 2 (2009): 204–22. However, Aristippus tries to refute Socrates in III.8 just as he himself had been refuted by Socrates earlier (*hōsper autos hup' ekeinou to proteron ēlenkheto*), and Socrates had not refuted Aristippus in II.1 at all, much less in the same way that Aristippus tries to refute Socrates in III.8.

6. See Bandini and Dorion, *Mémorables III*, 229n8.

7. See Danzig, "Socratic *Elenchos*," 296n6, 312.

8. See Johnson, "Intertextual Socrates," 82–83; Pangle, *Socratic Life*, 192; Vander Waerdt, "Socratic Justice," 37n101. Contrast Bandini and Dorion, *Mémorables III*, 142n3: "the only interlocutor that Socrates refutes in the *Memorabilia* is Euthydemos . . . so that it would seem clearly inappropriate to maintain that Socrates 'refutes everyone.'" As Moore observes, however, "Xenophon never in his own voice calls Socrates a philosopher" ("Xenophon on 'Philosophy,'" 128). And would it seem "clearly inappropriate," to Dorion, to maintain that Socrates is a philosopher? As Moore also observes, "Xenophon recognizes that much of the populace despises philosophy" (148), hence, "Xenophon could have had a strong strategic reason for dissociating Socrates from it" (139, 145). But Xenophon had no less reason for "dissociating" Socrates from the refutations on which his new and different way of philosophizing came to depend. According to Santas, "What upset the Athenians was the central thing that Socrates did day in and day out: the *elenchus* . . . he attacked the most fundamental principles of Athenian life, the Greek ideals of moderation, courage, justice, piety . . . he cut to pieces the intellectual foundation of the body politic" (*Socrates*, 5). The "theory of ideas" was the price that Plato had to pay for not allowing the refutations to recede into the background of his writings. See Sebell, *Socratic Turn*, 191n83.

9. See Weiss, "Pity or Pardon," 299: "Section 4.6.6 is a clear instance of Socrates' tailoring an argument to suit the interlocutor."

10. See Altman, "Dialectic," 125: "[Socrates's] arguments are deliberately flawed." And they are "flawed *deliberately*," according to Altman, to provoke the reader, "the more dialectical companion of Socrates who will and can never appear in the text" (121), "to explain clearly . . . how one might effectively contradict . . . those arguments" (131, 129).

11. Socrates drops the article from *tous theous* only here. And nothing is said, just now, of law. To understand this, recall that Socrates had predicted that good natures would go on to honor the *daimonion*, if not the gods, by learning and learning alone (IV.3.14). See Strauss, *On Tyranny*, 104: "Just as [Socrates] admits a translegal justice, although his Socrates identifies justice with legality, so he admits a piety which emerges out of the contemplation of nature which has no necessary relation to law; a piety, that is, whose possibility is virtually denied by the definition by his Socrates," in IV.6. Gray papers over the tension between the definition given in IV.6 and the impression left by I.4 and IV.3 by defining piety as "a matter of knowing the 'works' for which the gods should be honored *and* understanding what is 'lawful' regarding the worship of the gods" (*Framing*, 185; emphasis added). But which is it? Elsewhere, she admits that "Socrates teaches men to honour the gods without political reference (I 4 and IV 3)" ("Socrates and Democracy," 21n7). In any event, making the same mistake as Euthydemos, Gray's definition of piety means that someone who does

not honor or worship the gods can be pious (see Altman, "Dialectic," 123n45). Perhaps dimly aware of the absurdities that follow if piety is made to depend on the (many, mutually exclusive) laws—Zeus, say, is not worshipped in Egypt: see note 23 in Chapter 6—Gray envisions, somehow, "ever higher levels at which Socrates might be capable of operating. Knowledge of the laws about the gods could be theorized *above the level of the law of the state* to some higher and abstract realm" (*Framing*, 40; emphasis added). Oddly enough, she is not entirely wrong.

12. See Weiss, "Pity or Pardon," 300: "There is in this argument the bizarre implication that everyone who simply knows the rules will obey them and will, as a result, be pious and just.... [O]n this definition of piety and justice, almost everyone would be pious and just.... Moreover, there is equivocation on 'ought': is the 'ought' in knowing what ought to be done the same 'ought' in people's doing what they think ought to be done? In the first case it is what is prescribed by the laws; in the second it is one's own estimation of the best way to proceed." On this last point, which is crucial, see also Altman, "Dialectic," 123.

13. Only here, throughout IV.6.7, and at the very end of IV.6.11, does "to know" translate *epistamai*: to truly, genuinely know. Elsewhere, "to know" translates *eidenai*. Wisdom and courage, it turns out, involve knowledge of one thing; piety and justice involve knowledge—of another sort—of something else.

14. Contrast Dorion, "Nature of *Sophia*," 466; Kahn, *Plato*, 79; Cooper, *Reason and Emotion*, 25.

15. Strauss, *Xenophon's Socrates*, 199.

16. For further discussion, see Buzzetti, "'Middle Road,'" 149–78.

17. See Patzer, "Socrates as Dialectician," 246–47: "Here the conversation breaks off; for Xenophon can trust the readers to complete the conversation for themselves."

18. For which, see, for example, Jones and Sharma, "Socrates on Justice," 35: "By virtue of her knowledge of justice, the just person is aware that there is in fact no benefit to be had by [unjust] action." Note, while they cannot find this thesis "signaled explicitly," they find it operating "behind the scenes" (24), "presented only indirectly" (27), or "beneath the surface" (34), in *Memorabilia* IV.2.

19. See Strauss, *Socratic Discourse*, 89: "In Xenophon's enumeration of Socrates' virtues manliness, the virtue of war, is not mentioned.... Socrates was a man of peace rather than of war." See also Strauss, 136: "We might even think that Ischomachus is addressing Socrates 'O woman.'" As we saw twice before, Socrates used to swear, like a woman, "by Hera," when praising the philosophic life. And his friends are, somehow, female (III.11.16). Compare *Cyropaedia* III.1.42–43, IV.2.25, and VIII.4.24 with VII.2.26ff.

20. See Altman, "Dialectic," 125: "the law-based conceptions of both the pious man and the just men began ... by ruling out the possibility that one can honor the gods or treat human beings 'in whatever manner one might wish.'"

CHAPTER 9

1. See Pierre Pontier, "How to Defend the Defense of Socrates? From the *Apology* to *Memorabilia* Book 1," in Stavru and Moore, *Socrates and the Socratic Dialogue*, 447: Pontier realizes that "Xenophon's defense aims at showing," contra Hippias, "that Socrates did not at all conceal his opinion," but he does not seem to realize that IV.7.1 refers to IV.4.9 and IV.4.11.

2. See O'Connor, "Self-Sufficiency," 167–68: "Socrates' self-sufficiency was different from the self-sufficiency of his associates," specifically, "Socrates' own self-sufficiency was of a different

character from the self-sufficiency of his *gentlemanly* associates" (emphasis added). See also Edmunds, "Xenophon's Triad," 257: "Self-sufficiency is clearly not a moral virtue."

3. See Morrison, "Socrates as Teacher," 204: "Xenophon's claim is compatible with Socrates teaching nothing, if there is nothing that he knows."

4. For the view that Socrates sought knowledge for its own sake, see O'Connor, "Self-Sufficiency," 169. See also Gray, *Framing*, 183; Alexander Nehemas, *Virtues of Authenticity* (Princeton, NJ: Princeton University Press, 1999), 86–87; Pangle, *Socratic Life*, 208; Vander Waerdt, "Socrates in the Clouds," 50n8. For the opposite view, see Danzig, "Plato, Aristotle, and Xenophon," 346, 349, 363; Dorion, "Xenophon and Greek Philosophy," 40; Johnson, "Xenophon's *Apology*," 128.

5. See McPherran, *Religion of Socrates*, 285: "Socrates does not reject all reasoning about the cosmos, but . . . only the epistemologically presumptive and *mechanistic* sort, the sort propounded by the *phusiologoi*." But how did Socrates come to see that mechanistic reasoning about the cosmos is "epistemologically presumptive," if not by trying his hand at it?

6. See O'Connor, "Self-Sufficiency," 169: "Xenophon tells the reader that despite [his] advice Socrates himself *was* familiar with the more theoretical parts of [geometry and astronomy]. Similarly, Socrates turned his associates away from imitating Anaxagoras and becoming concerned with heavenly phenomena, yet the immediately following critique of Anaxagorean theories shows that Socrates himself *was* quite familiar with speculation on such subjects." See also Burnet, *Plato's Phaedo*, xxxviii: "Socrates cannot have stood aloof from the scientific movement of [his] time. Xenophon does *not really* say that he did. He tells us, indeed, that Socrates dissuaded *his friends* from spending their lives in the study of higher mathematics and astronomy, but he adds in both cases that *Socrates* was not unversed in these subjects himself" (emphasis added). See note 62 in the Introduction.

7. The open-endedness of the remark is rarely, if ever, appreciated. See Dorion, "Xenophon and Greek Philosophy," 38–39.

8. See, for further discussion, Sebell, *Socratic Turn*, 45–60.

9. Like what he says about oil and water, what Socrates says at *Symposium* 7.4—about the lamp, which gives light, and brass, which merely reflects (the lamp's) light—shows how he thinks about the sun. For, according to Anaxagoras, the moon merely reflects the light of the sun, like brass (Diels–Kranz 59B.18, 59A.42, 59A.76). Consider, along with this, *Symposium* 6.6–8. Some people, Socrates said, are pious toward rocks (I.1.14).

10. So far, the useful has not limited Socrates's learning, only his teaching. To teach too much, in this case, would be foolish (consider I.3.1). Anaxagoras, who went so far as to teach that the sun is a fiery rock, was called "the atheist" (Diels–Kranz 59A.113, 59A.17; consider Diels–Kranz 59A.18). But Socrates, Xenophon indicates, learned astronomy from an astronomer (IV.7.5, contrast IV.7.2).

11. See Dorion, "Xenophon and Greek Philosophy," 39: "This criticism of Anaxagoras probably has an apologetic dimension to the extent that, according to certain accounts, Socrates was a pupil of Anaxagoras and/or Archelaus, the latter having been himself a disciple of Anaxagoras." See also Burnet, *Plato's Phaedo*, xl–xli; Reginald Hackforth, *Plato's Phaedo* (Cambridge: Cambridge University Press, 1972), 128; A. E. Taylor, "On the Date of the Trial of Anaxagoras," *Classical Quarterly* 11, no. 2 (1917): 85.

12. Dorion is totally unaware of this possibility. See Louis-André Dorion, "The Daimonion and the Megalegoria of Socrates in Xenophon's *Apology*," *Apeiron* 38, no. 2 (2011), 129: "Xenophon insists that Socrates would have been accused of lying and imposture if the counsel he had given to his companions, on the faith of his sign, had been shown to be inappropriate." Xenophon, who never once says that Socrates was not lying, did not say the words, which Dorion puts

in his mouth, "on the faith of his sign." Moreover, Dorion fails to consider the fact that Xenophon rests his case, in I.1.5, on more than one interrogative. See note 18 in Chapter 6.

13. See Strauss, *Xenophon's Socrates*, 5.

14. For the view that Palamedes and Daedalus were stand-ins for Socrates at IV.2.33, see Johnson, "*Memorabilia* 4.2," 68; O'Connor, "Enviable Life," 69n24. Neither Johnson nor O'Connor, however, considers the obvious implications for Socrates's "*daimonion*." See also Bandini and Dorion, *Mémorables III*, 100n5.

15. That Socrates knew his death and decline to be imminent is indicated, not least, by the repetition of *mekhri toude tou khronou*, "until now" (IV.8.6–7).

16. Contrast Dorion, "Xenophon's *Apology*," 129: "[Socrates's] condemnation to death is not to be interpreted as confirmation that Socrates was lying when he spoke of his sign . . . because the intervention of the sign before the trial had as its aim to make it known to him that life no longer had anything good to offer him and that the time had come for him to die." By Xenophon's account, however, the sign failed to make this known to Socrates with absolute certainty.

INDEX

Printed in the USA
CPSIA information can be obtained
at www.ICGtesting.com
JSHW081202300824
69030JS00001B/3

9 781512 826845